LOVE LETTERS
FROM THE FRONT

A Lieutenant's Journey to Leadership

A Story of Dedication and Love

I0161054

Bill MacIlvaine

Waterlemon Press
waterlemonpress.com

LOVE LETTERS
FROM THE FRONT
A Lieutenant's Journey to Leadership
A Story of Dedication and Love

Published by:
Waterlemon Press
2517 Georgetown Dr.
Bartlesville, OK 74006 USA
www.waterlemonpress.com

Waterlemon Press
waterlemonpress.com

ISBN 978-0-692-27976-2

Websites:
http://lovelettersfromthefront.com
https://www.facebook.com/LoveLettersfromtheFront

E-book designed and produced in the United States of America in association with PaperClip Press (paperclippress.com).

Paperclip
Press®

For additional copies please contact the electronic distributors. The author is available for speaking engagements. For more information, please contact the publisher at rod.macilvaine@gmail.com.

DEDICATED TO THE MEN
WHO GAVE
THE ULTIMATE SACRIFICE
FOR THEIR COUNTRY
IN KOREA

About the Author

Bill MacIlvaine (B.A. Princeton University; Certified Financial Planner [Ret.]) held various leadership positions in industry on the East Coast and in the Midwest, and ultimately assumed the presidency of a Wisconsin-based manufacturing firm. He completed his career in southern Florida in banking, and in retirement served two terms as a city councilman of Naples, Florida. A strong proponent of active civic engagement, he has served as a Florida Supreme Court Certified Mediator and has led many local boards in southwest Florida. Bill and his wife, Lucy, were married in 1952 and have four children, ten grandchildren, and six great-grandchildren. His avocation is ocean sailing, and he has captained multiple charters in both the Atlantic and Pacific.

His growth as a leader was shaped by his experiences in the U.S. Army in Korea in 1953-1954.

Previous Books

Successful Bareboat Chartering: The Essential Handbook for Captain and Crew (with Rod MacIlvaine)

A note to the reader about my father...

These are actual letters written by a soldier on active duty halfway around the world.

They were penned late at night by candlelight or lantern. They were composed in a tent or on the deck of a troop transport.

Rather than heavily editing his letters, I have tried to keep the raw character of these original wartime documents as is, so that you feel the cadence and tempo of my father's words to my mother.

Moreover, my mother (just 20-years old at the time) continually sent letters back to my dad. Rather than including her letters, we have decided to feature his narrative. We wanted to show how he grew as a soldier and as a husband through the progress of these loving but highly informative correspondences.

Also, please keep in mind that the videos, both in the ebook and on the website, were shot as 8mm analog movies with a Kodak Brownie camera that my mother purchased in 1953 for their first wedding anniversary. The cost was just under $40.

When my dad shipped out, he carried the camera constantly, and it became a perfect way for him to share his experiences with her. Back then, the purchase price of film included prepayment for development. Once the roll was finished, he shipped the exposed film to Hawaii for processing. Then Kodak shipped the finished reels directly to my mother.

Today the sequences may appear dated and a little fuzzy, but hopefully, they give you a feel for what life in Korea was like in 1953.

Rod MacIlvaine

Contents

Foreword

When the histories of wars are written, they're generally written at the macro level. We read about international events shaping policies and troop movements. We imagine armies taking vast territories and then sometimes clawing for just one square mile of ground. Perhaps in the middle of the book, we see maps with arrows and shaded areas indicating DMZ belts.

But behind each macro view there is also the micro view. There are individual GIs, usually very young, with aspirations and dreams for the future. They leave families at home. And sometimes they leave spouses, just months after their wedding day.

And how do they keep their love alive during days of deprivation and conflict in hot zones? Before the days of Facebook and Skype, they wrote letters. And those letters were often wonderfully descriptive, with lots of affection and hopes for the future poured forth on every page.

One December, when I was home from college for the holidays, I discovered that my father had written 171 letters to my mother during his time in Korea. They were stuffed in a beat-up old shoebox in my parents' closet. For some reason, he brought them down to our den to show them to me. As he started reading, I saw a side of my father that was quite compelling. He was roughly my age when he wrote these letters, and he was expressing his commitment and love to his new bride who was just twenty years old at the time (my mother!).

We didn't read through the entire shoebox of letters that morning, but my immediate response was this: "Dad, you must publish these!" I kept that refrain going over the years, especially when I discovered that there were dozens of color pictures (Kodachrome slides) and about half a dozen reels of 8-mm home movies illustrating his year in Korea.

With the advent of electronic publishing, we can now combine the letters, video clips, and pictures into a seamless whole. This ebook (and the companion traditional version) tells the story of a young GI who grew in love with his wife while serving his country at war. But these letters also tell the story of a young warrior who matured from an inexperienced officer into a trusted leader.

Over 33,000 Americans died in the Korean War. By any reckoning, that's a massive number.

My father and I are immensely grateful for all the men and women who gave their lives for their country in this conflict. What follows is the story of one soldier who came back. As you'll see, he came back stronger, and he never forgot the leadership lessons learned on the front.

Rod MacIlvaine
Waterlemon Press
Bartlesville, OK, November 2014

1
Jersey Shore

I was halfway across the Manasquan River bridge in a borrowed Chevy on what I thought was an important errand. Suddenly the music on my car radio was interrupted by a news bulletin briefly reporting an invasion and fighting in some distant and obscure country: Korea. It was late June 1950. I was twenty one and had a great seasonal job. It was promising to be a glorious summer on the Jersey shore.

During the winter, two college friends and I had heard of the possibility of jobs in an ice plant in Seaside Heights. We piled into the Chevy in Princeton and hit the road for the Jersey shore. Upon arrival we were interviewed by the boss, and without further ado, each of us landed a summer job. Terms of employment were one dollar an hour, seven days a week, start at seven in the morning, off at three in the afternoon.

We listened to a summary of our duties. One of the tasks was to "pull cores," part of the process of making 300-pound blocks of ice. This turned out to be somewhat of a chore, but consumed only a short hour or so each day. The greater part of the job, and the most fun, was managing the sales platform: selling cases of cold beer, soft drinks, frozen bait, and 20- or 40-pound cakes of ice while engaging our customers in conversation.

The boss required us to memorize the eight available brands of beer. We repeated them so often over the summer that Rhinegold, Schaefer, Ballantine, Schmidt, Trommer, Piels, Pabst, and Budweiser were engraved in my memory, though most of those brews are long gone. Pabst and Budweiser were the "premium" beers and a bit more expensive. Schmidt was "the Philadelphia Schmidt," not to be confused with another, more costly, beer of the same name. If a customer neglected to mention a brand, we were to bring out Schmidt, since the boss could buy it for less and the regular brands all sold for the same price.

The sales arena over which we presided was a waist-high loading dock overlooking a parking lot behind the ice plant. Back inside the walk-in freezer, we learned how to divide 300-pound blocks of ice along scored lines, making 20- and 40-pound cakes. With a little practice, we could split the big block, making the correct sizes, with a few well-placed jabs of an ice pick.

Each size had its own rack, which we stocked inside the freezer. A trap door opened onto our sales platform, and the act of delivering ice down the chute onto the platform became a feat we relished as the most challenging, dramatic, and perhaps even artistic highlight of our work. When a customer ordered a cake of ice, one of us would give a mighty tug to a handle on the back wall. A low rumble would emanate from deep within the freezer and grow increasingly loud as an ice cake careened, unseen, down the chute. When it reached the bottom, the ice blasted open a hinged rubber door and skidded across the loading platform straight toward our startled customer. We could stop the flying ice instantly by hooking an ice tong into its forward edge.

The challenge was to execute that action as closely as possible to the edge of the platform. Too soon reduced the drama, while too late resulted in an indignant, agitated customer, the ice lost and broken on the ground, and trouble for us if ever our theatrics were observed by the boss. This routine, however, was always an effective method of gaining the attention and admiration of young ladies, of which there were many.

Most Seaside Heights summer rentals in 1950 lacked a refrigerator but were icebox equipped, so repeat business was brisk. The vacationing crowd during those hot summer days regularly needed ice and most had a natural thirst for our chilled brew, which brought them back often.

We made many instant summer friends, most of them college aged and ready for fun. We routinely got three hours of sleep in the wee hours of each night and another three on the beach in late afternoon. I never remember any rainy days clouding that summer. It was wonderful to be young, carefree, and independent.

The combined weekly earnings of the three of us totaled $168. This restricted our rental options to the very bottom rung of the semi-poverty ladder. Together, we could afford thirty dollars a week for a one-room cabin. It barely contained the minimum necessary living essentials. We had a phone booth-size stall for a toilet and no bathroom sink. A single showerhead attached outdoors on the back of the house provided us cold water only. In consideration for our nearby neighbors and for modesty, we restricted our showers to the hours of darkness. We brushed our teeth in the kitchen sink.

Housekeeping was minimal. A broom came with the house, and when enough sand accumulated to crunch underfoot, we swept it out. Once we were given a nice fish, over two feet long, identified to us as an albacore tuna. Since we were equipped with only a single pot and couldn't find the knife, we boiled the thing whole, tail in the air. As I recall, it was very tasty. Another time, I mistakenly bought a head of cabbage believing it was lettuce. We used the leaves in sandwiches for days until someone informed us of our hopeless ignorance and culinary incompetence.

Ready for a job interview.

Ice from the ice plant was always free to us, and we needed it several times a week. One afternoon after work, we put a 40-pound cake in the trunk of the Chevy, but were thoroughly distracted by festivities on the way home. When we remembered and opened the trunk, on the morning after, we discovered a flood of water and a very small ice cube. I suspect rust may have shortened the life of that car's rear end.

Little did I imagine that only a few years later, I would look back and remember the summer of 1950 as an easy time, a life in Spartan but semi-comfortable accommodations. The important errand that held my attention during the first news of Korea is lost from memory today. Perhaps it was a run to Asbury Park to buy an electric shaver blade. It seemed an inconvenience back then that to obtain a basic need I had to drive a dozen miles. I never gave a thought at the time to the luxury of a smooth, paved highway.

Summer ended far too soon. Back at Princeton in my junior year, I joined Tiger Inn club, dug back into studies, and lived the casual college routine. Korea was half a world away and of no concern to most students. Even the looming draft, we all knew, could be deferred by proper planning for graduate school or the right job. Those of us in ROTC (Reserve Officer Training Corps) had a gnawing tinge of uneasiness, however, knowing we had signed up and were destined to receive a lieutenant's commission at graduation. Call to active duty was considered a doubtful possibility, and then only in the unlikely event that an armistice wasn't yet signed. Besides, graduation itself seemed a remote, almost unimaginable event in the far distant future. Meanwhile, college life demanded full attention.

Front row center, in college uniform. Few went to Korea.

Then time began to accelerate. The interval until graduation dwindled. The next summer I drove to North Carolina, where neither the days nor the nights bore any similarity to the Jersey shore. Fort Bragg was our artillery ROTC summer camp, and also home to the 82nd Airborne Division. It was dry, dusty, and sweltering hot. I remember standing outside a mess hall in the breakfast chow line before dawn, already sweating in my fatigues. The radio was reporting through an open window that the two hottest places in the nation the day before were Yuma, Arizona, and Fort Bragg, North Carolina. I planned never to visit Yuma and couldn't wait to get out of Bragg.

Reveille sounded at 4:45 am and taps closed the day at 10:00 pm. The good life had slammed abruptly to a halt. To make life more miserable, but reminiscent of the previous summer's cold outdoor shower, all hot water in our barracks failed. Returning hot, sweating, and dusty from a day of drilling in the piney woods, we took chillingly cold showers. The water heater was never repaired during our time in residence.

We were convinced it was the army's underhanded attempt to toughen up the college boys.

It was a grubby, exhausting, and uncomfortable summer, but there was an upside. The airborne training area was close, and we had an opportunity to experience a taste of preliminary parachute instruction. A primary attraction was the thirty-four-foot jump tower. After strapping on a parachute harness and climbing to the top, we were instructed to stand in the tower door, hands on the doorframe, and stare at the horizon. "Don't look down," we were ordered, and then, "Jump!" This took a most substantial bit of concentration—also trust in the strength of the harness—but everyone made the leap.

Fortunately, the harness risers were slightly shorter than the distance to earth, so our descent jerked to an abrupt halt before we hit the ground. The operation might be compared to bungee jumping with a non-elastic bungee. When my fall reached the end of its tether, the jolt felt like a wallop on the head with a two-by-four. I saw stars as my helmet whacked down, creasing my nose. Blood or no blood, I decided one jump was enough for me to get the hang of it.

The toughest part about summer camp was the announcement that certainly, without doubt, no question, we would all be called to active duty upon graduation. The police action in Korea was in actual fact a war. It had continued for over a year, and apparently no end was near. Six months after the North Koreans initially crossed the 38th parallel the previous summer, the seesaw war was first almost lost, then almost won. As our forces neared the Yalu River that 1950 Thanksgiving, they fully expected to be home for Christmas. Then the Chinese poured hundreds of thousands of foot soldiers across the Yalu, and we again were vastly outnumbered and on the defensive. For two more years, the conflict, termed a stalemate, continued to inflict increasingly heavy casualties. It became very personal when my recently married best friend from junior high school was killed one week after I realized that I, too, would be going to Korea.

Before my senior year started, I met a classmate's younger sister at his wedding. Lucy was a bridesmaid, and I was an usher. It was amazing and overwhelming love at first sight.

Lucy at high school graduation.

I'll never forget seeing her standing with the bridal party during the ceremony and thinking, "What a gorgeous, graceful, charming person!" Our engagement was announced in February, on her nineteenth birthday. I graduated in mid-June, and Lucy pinned on my second lieutenant bars.

We're talking about marriage.

We were married June 28, spent ten days in Bermuda on our honeymoon, and reported to Fort Sill, Oklahoma, in mid-August 1952.

The June Wedding.

Lucy at Cambridge Beaches.

Korea is miles away.

At Fort Sill I caught my first glimmer of the new responsibilities creeping over the horizon and into my life. I hadn't been overly stressed by the anticipation of marriage. After all, we were blindly in love, and I was a college graduate and had a steady job with thirty days' annual paid vacation, free from layoffs. Obviously, thousands of people survived on a lowly second lieutenant's pay. In Oklahoma, we rented and furnished an apartment, shopped together, and tried to plan a budget and modest savings. I finally realized I was entering a unique, very different, uncharted era of life, and this beautiful teenager would be a lifetime responsibility, in addition to being my partner and best friend.

The army reinforced my realization of new responsibilities. Although I was in school again for the next four months in the Field Artillery Battery Officers Course [BOC], it was as an officer. Fort Sill provided red oval stickers for officers' windshields, yellow for enlisted men. Driving through the gate into Fort Sill with a red sticker got me a crisp salute every time. I wondered what I had done, if anything, to merit that salute, and what might possibly be required of me in the future.

William Rodman MacIlvaine

Lieutenant
United States Army

I also got used to looking for the collar insignia of rank, which determines who salutes first and who salutes back. One afternoon, at the Fort Sill PX (Post Exchange, an army store), another officer came quickly out the door as I was approaching. The only visible insignia on his collar was the crossed artillery cannons that we all wore. I smiled and continued in. Immediately behind me, shouting erupted. I turned, amazed, and confronted the angry voice and red face of the officer. Now I could see the twin silver bars on his other collar. This was one very irate captain. I appeared contrite, apologized, and offered the lame explanation that I had been unable to see his rank. I saluted, but he remained angry as he returned my salute, wheeled about, and departed.

In my civilian mind, I asked myself what kind of person would feel the need to raise such a ruckus. What made him demand my acknowledgment that he was so important? My developing military mind's response was: The army alone determines your importance. Your rank is visible, and it counts. Whatever other talent you might possess is unknown and invisible. Your worth is exhibited by symbols and is external, not personal or intrinsic. I was doubtful that I could ever bring myself to conform to this environment. Later I would discover how wrong I was.

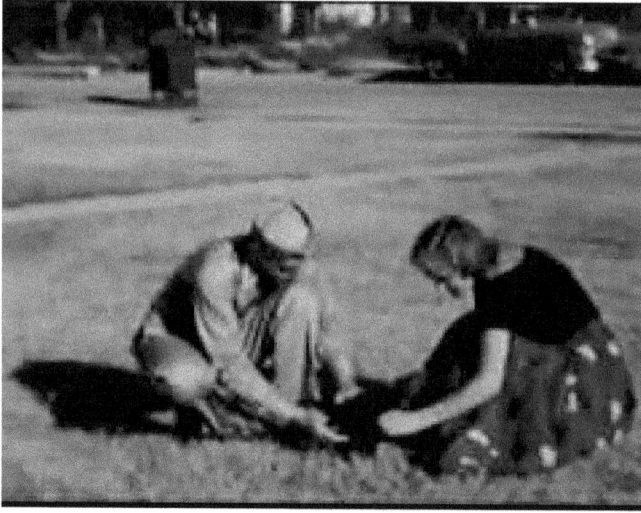

Together we bought little Jag.
Video Link: http://lovelettersfromthefront.com/videos

Four months of school passed quickly, and Lucy and I happily settled into married life. When my class graduated from the Battery Officers Course, almost the entire class received orders, as expected, for permanent change of station to the Far East Command, better known, without affection, as FECOM. There was no illusion that some of us might be retained in Japan; everyone anticipated being shipped out to Korea. Two or three of the class, whom we believed had political pull, were assigned to Germany. However, there was one officer in our group, with assuredly no political pull, who was mysteriously assigned as an instructor in the Field Artillery Basic Training Center at Fort Sill. This was an assignment made without apparent reason or any known probable cause. There must simply have been a mistake made somewhere along the daily processing path of one of the thousands of pieces of paper handled routinely by some overworked clerk in the Pentagon.

I was the blessed and highly elated recipient of that wayward slip of paper! I had orders to remain at Fort Sill in an artillery training role.

The Field Artillery Replacement Training Center, known rather indelicately by its initials, became my first opportunity to show any hint of leadership since being commissioned. Our training battery accepted newly drafted, young civilians and transformed most of them into Korea replacements, with six weeks of infantry basic training, followed by six weeks of artillery basic training. Three officers and a handful of enlisted men were responsible for leading Training Battery "E" during the twelve-week cycle.

The infantry tactics were a mystery to me. Thankfully, during the first six weeks of basic, we were assigned a new infantry second lieutenant. He ran the troops, by squads and platoons, over the Oklahoma hills and taught us specialized infantry doctrines such as "interlocking bands of continuous grazing fire." The first weeks of basic were mostly grunt work. The sergeants led calisthenics and taught close-order drill, rifle, and other basic disciplines. I revived my ROTC experience by marching the battery, teaching artillery gunnery classes, and inspecting the progress of training. The day the captain needed me as instructor for the battery bayonet drill, I deferred to the infantry lieutenant; I'd never even attached a bayonet to an M-1 rifle. I soon discovered that in the army, you often learn it today and teach it tomorrow.

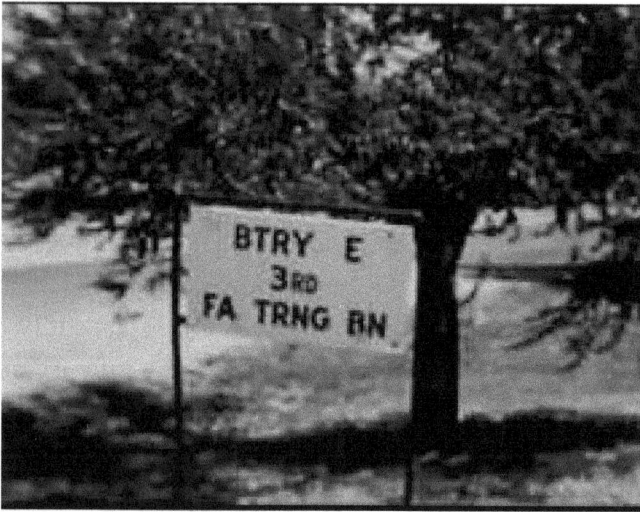

We traveled to the firing range.
Video Link: http://lovelettersfromthefront.com/videos

It was common knowledge that no orders for overseas were cut if you had less than a year of active duty remaining. I kept close count of my remaining active duty days as the war ground on, battles intensified, and casualties mounted.

The letter from the Department of the Army was postmarked 8:30 pm, July 10, 1953, and handed to me by the battery clerk. I stared at it, but the order was impossible for me to read or understand because of my instant, intense anxiety and because all the phrases were in army lingo. However, one word, FECOM, stood out sharply in the alphabet soup. There was no question now. There would be no more training recruits, no more stateside assignment, and no more living at home and commuting to work on the post. FECOM, Far East Command, could only mean Korea—and Korea was deadly hostile to lieutenants.

I told Lucy late that afternoon when we went out for a meal at the Quicki Chicki in nearby Lawton. We had often enjoyed that little mom-and-pop place with its fried chicken and homemade chili. This night, however, was made simply for hand-holding and Lucy's tears. The food sat untouched, the surrounding people unnoticed. We had known this dreaded day could very possibly happen; it had separated so many of our friends. But even with that head knowledge, the heartache of the reality was almost unbearable. The war was continuing unabated, and at the very least, we would be apart for a year. Or it might be much worse.

Home for Christmas 1952.

2
Involuntary Adventure

The Overseas National Airlines DC-4 swung onto the main runway, still idling its four propellers. As the throttles opened and the engines roared to full power, we began our roll forward to takeoff speed and to a new experience, unchosen and unknown. The plane climbed out of Travis Air Force Base, passed over San Francisco Bay, and turned west as I watched the Golden Gate Bridge, far below, creep slowly behind us out of sight. Finally, in the bright late afternoon sun, puffy white clouds began to obscure my last view of California. Soon, even the Pacific Ocean disappeared behind clouds.

Leaving Camp Stoneman.
Video Link: http://lovelettersfromthefront.com/videos

It was Sunday evening, September 6, and world events, now affecting me personally, had taken a dramatic turn since I'd received my orders for the Far East. My orders had been sent from Washington weeks ago on July 10. An uneasy, and perhaps temporary, Korean cease-fire had been called, effective July 27. While this reduced the imminent danger to my life and limb, it did nothing to ease the pain of separation.

Lucy and I, after accepting the unhappy reality that orders are cast in stone, became fully absorbed with the details of departure from Fort Sill. I was allowed a thirty-day leave before my reporting date to Camp Stoneman, California, near San Francisco. Saying goodbye at Fort Sill, packing our few belongings, and driving back to the East Coast was accomplished without delay or much difficulty.

We had decided early on that if I was assigned to go overseas, Lucy would take her sophomore year at college. We made arrangements for her to room with four friends in a small dormitory annex across the street from the college's main gate. Lucy's "room" was actually a second-floor closet with a small bed. Donna was the friend who offered half of her single-size room to accommodate Lucy and her bed. She was a premedical student, engaged to another premed. Puss was married to a West Point lieutenant who was already in Korea. Adrian was engaged, and Tatiana, as I recall, was most serious about her studies. The arrangement seemed to be a viable solution to our looming long existence apart. Lucy would be able to visit her parents, or mine, on vacations or occasional weekends. Neither was more than an hour or two drive from college.

We split our thirty-day leave between visiting Lucy's parents in Scarsdale, New York, and mine in Summit, New Jersey. We flew to Boston to visit a couple in Marblehead that we'd met on our honeymoon at Cambridge Beaches in Bermuda. Lucy and I enjoyed an unforgettable weekend with our new friends. We sailed their nineteen-foot Lightning sailboat from the Corinthian Yacht Club, enjoyed a lobster bake on the beach, and for a brief time, forgot all worldly problems and fully enjoyed life. Another enjoyable event for us was a day-long visit from Donna and her fiancée while we were staying at my parents' house.

A few days later, Lucy and I decided it would be encouraging and fun to spend a day house-hunting, and perhaps projecting a glimpse into our future life. It began as a lark, but this fanciful daydream was discouraging; the attractive houses were expensive and the affordable houses were unattractive. It was a difficult four weeks. We had no real home or the possibility of one anytime soon, so we felt a disheartening loss of independence.

We watched the end of my leave steadily approaching, anticipated a year apart, and knew, after that, my gainful (army) employment would end. However, we were unable to visualize or make any plans for our civilian future. At that point of distress, Lucy remembered something she'd heard from an army wife whose husband was in Korea: "God will give you sufficient strength to meet times like these." We both took these words to heart; it sustained us then, and would in the months to come.

Finally, Lucy drove me to LaGuardia from my parents' home in New Jersey. She would continue on to Scarsdale, to her parents' home, after leaving me at the airport. Years later she told me it was the saddest day of her life. It was mine as well. We promised to write every day, without fail, regardless of where we were, or what our circumstances. Since my commercial flight to California had a refueling stop in Chicago, I even promised a postcard from O'Hare Field and another from San Francisco. Long distance phone calls were prohibitively expensive. We kissed goodbye, held each other tightly, and with moist eyes said one more goodbye. Then I turned and walked to the plane.

My first letter was a postcard from Chicago, as promised.

1 Sept. 53
POSTCARD

Dearest Lucy,

It's been 3½ hours since we took off from LaGuardia. We were out of New Jersey in about 10 minutes. O'Hare is hot, busy, and so crowded that I'm writing standing up. Called your friend, Lorraine, but got no answer. Will call you Wednesday night.
I love you,
Bill

* * *

1 Sept. 53
POSTCARD

Hi Chicki,

Just had dinner at the Golden Pheasant, which is more like a thrifty Child's Restaurant in New York than the fancy Golden Pheasant of Dallas. I'm now having a solitary drink atop the Mark Hopkins, where you can see all of San Francisco for miles around, except for tonight when you can't see two feet because of the fog. There is a convention in town so I am living in a flea trap of a hotel. Such is life in cold and damp San Francisco.

I dedicated my drink to you. I love you dearly and miss you dreadfully.

I'll write about the plane trip.
Love,
Bill

* * *

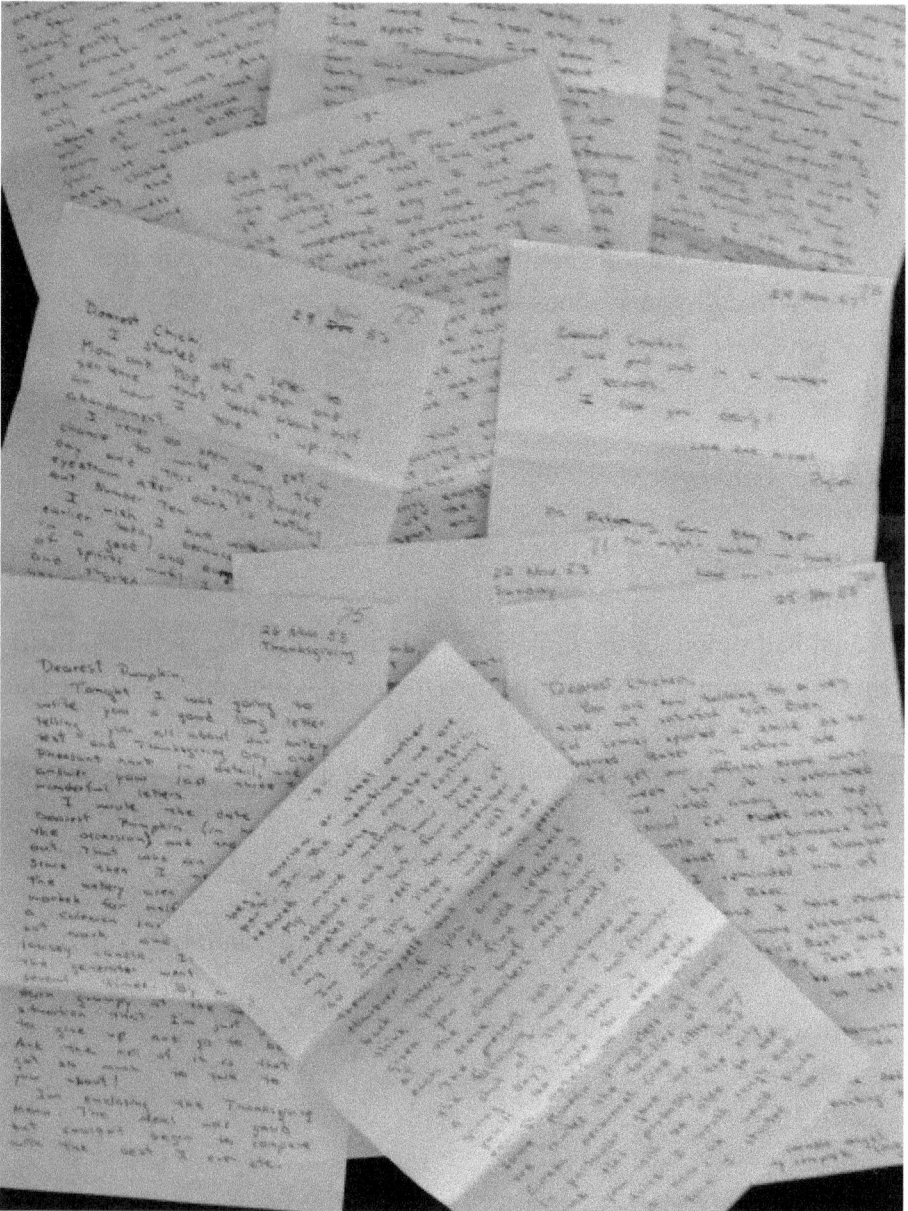

Love Letters.

Dearest Lucy,

I've sent off two postcards, which I trust you have received by now, and here comes a letter.

I guess you must know how much I love you. I felt so sad and lonely at the airport. Now when I think about something sentimental and how much I am going to miss you, I get even sadder. I love you with all my heart and soul, Lucy, and I always will and don't you forget it. I think goodbyes are the saddest time of all. I still feel lonely, but I know I have a job to do in the coming months and I'm going to give it my best to buckle down and do the best I can.

Do you want to hear about the trip? I hope so, Chicki, because I'm going to tell you about it.

I put my face close to the plane window and waved hard when the plane turned at the gate and started away from the boarding ramp. I was on the right side, about halfway back.

We climbed out over New York City and headed over northern New Jersey. It was beautiful country, hilly and wooded like Connecticut.

I remember thinking how soft and insignificant the world looked down there when we were flying high above the melee and humanity below. You and I talked about that once when we were driving home from the plane ride we took at the Westchester County airport.

I also learned something about perspective by watching the clouds. Sometimes a little white fluffy cloud would cast a shadow on the ground way out of proportion to its size. It depends on what angle the sun shines on it. Perhaps this translates into life situations.

Amazingly enough there were no mishaps as in our past flight experiences with stuck landing gear or motionless propellers. The only near mishap was when I took a sip of coffee exactly as the plane entered bumpy air.

We passed over Cleveland and the Lakes and got into Chicago in 3½ hours, as planned. We could leave the plane for a half hour, so I had to hurry to buy my box lunch and 29¢ Scripto ballpoint. I then called

Lorraine without results, wrote you and Aunt Wawee postcards, and off we went again.

Aunt Wawee had given me a letter of encouragement that I was serving God and my Country at a time when they need me. She also enclosed $50.

We ran through lots of clouds, and part of the way between Chicago and San Francisco we had some very bumpy going. I took about twelve feet of film out-bound, but won't promise such good results.

The trip was long and got a little boring and I was glad indeed to finally see the fog that shrouded San Francisco. It was cold and windy when I got off the plane with an elderly California gentleman who had been pointing out local fog marks. I really couldn't identify any of the locations he pointed to. After landing, I called half a dozen hotels before I wound up in this joint, which looks nothing like the picture of the Hotel Spanning on the letterhead. It's the most tumbledown place I've ever lived in, but perhaps once was reasonably stylish.

After checking in, I dumped my baggage and walking around the block twice, found the Golden Pheasant, established 1896. Not too bad, but it looked like a Child's and cost like a Schraft's.

Then I checked on the means of getting to Camp Stoneman. I can take a bus at either 9 AM or noon tomorrow.

I next called Sid Liebes (roommate first-term freshman year Princeton). We had a pleasant chat and I am to call him when I know if I'll have free time. He is taking graduate work in physics at Stanford, not at all worried about the draft.

Then I walked a few blocks and took a cab to the Mark Hopkins, where I had one drink at the Top of the Mark. I silently dedicated the drink "To Lucy and our eternal love." Then I took a cab back here.

It's 11:10 my time and 2:10 AM your time. Yours is the time with which I started the day, so it's late. I'm praying every night for you, darling, and I'm sort of cuddling you by myself. I think of you always and love you with all my heart and soul.

Good night, pumpkin. Love, Bill

* * *

3 Sept. 53

Hi Lucy,

This is just sort of a note, late in the evening, 11:00, to tell you that I love you dearly and I'll write more of an informative letter tomorrow.

I'm not as certain now as I was earlier that I will fly to the Far East, but they say the chances are about ten to one we will. I hope so! Thirty-six hours by plane, including a couple of hours in Hawaii and Wake Island, sound far superior to two monotonous weeks on a crowded troopship.

The last twenty-four hours of processing have been one continuous road march. Every place we must go to check into is at least two miles from the last one.

I've been working hard during the last twenty-four hours to overcome loneliness by doing all the processing I can right away, and by meeting as many men as possible. I learned quite a few interesting things from a lieutenant at the Officers Club last night. He plans to go into his own business as soon as he gets out, and outlined for me his road map for getting started. I also had a long talk with Billy Seal's roommate at Fort Sill. Then I encountered a lieutenant from my Ft. Sill BOC whom I'd never met. He knew half a dozen Princetonians from Ft. Bragg, including Bob Morgan, Tom Knight, and also John Lowry.

I met two interesting guys from Boston and New York, respectively, who had said goodbye to their wives at LaGuardia the same day that I did. We all found that we had felt about the same. I listened mostly, because I knew I couldn't find the words to say what I felt, and I didn't want to tell anyone but you anyway.

I love you desperately, Lucy. I miss you awfully. I've been trying to keep very busy and interested but I have a feeling that a month after I'm assigned to a unit, and the novelty of the trip and the adventure of an Oriental country has worn off, I'll hit my low point of the decade.

I love you with all my heart and soul, I loved talking with you last night, and I'll write you more tomorrow.

I pray for you, Lucy. My thoughts are always with you.
I love you,
Bill

* * *

4 Sept. 53

Hi Pumpkin,

I've already gotten confused with my letter numbering. I can't remember whether I sent two or three postcards. Then there was a letter I wrote from the hotel. Then the letter at 11 o'clock last night, which I forgot to number. It doesn't make much difference while I'm still in the States, so for the record I'll call this number five.

You can use the return address on the envelope, which will probably be good enough until I get my final overseas address. All mail is automatically forwarded to me. Don't forget to number the letters! I'm keeping my records straight from now on.

At last! Our shipment orders and alert came down this afternoon. We are definitely flying. Flying time is 36 hours with an hour stop in Hickam Field, Hawaii, and one at Wake Island. We land at Haneda Airport, near Tokyo in Japan. I've heard we may be in Japan only about 48 hours. Then it's another four hours over to Korea. That's where all of us will surely end up. There is one bit of very encouraging news; my shipment orders showed only a single Military Occupational Specialty for me: MOS 0606! That's not a Forward Observer. Perhaps possibly, I am to be a rear echelon commando after all. What a laugh—not a chance!

Goodbye Golden Gate.
Video Link: http://lovelettersfromthefront.com/videos

Departure date is almost certainly tomorrow, 5 September. We should arrive in Japan 7 September your time, but we cross the International Date Line so it will be 8 September our time. As of 6:45 tomorrow there will be only fourteen officers in line ahead of me. My departure time depends on how many spaces Travis Air Force Base has available.

We are all packed and ready to go. I addressed a package to Summit containing my suit, which needs cleaning, and ties, shirts and some O.D. [olive drab] uniforms.

The nights here are really cold, even with two blankets! Since that first afternoon the daytime high temperature has never gotten much above 70°.

This morning we had a three-hour lecture on how to live in the Orient. Then most everyone sacked out until lunch. After lunch, finally, my individual orders were published. Takeoff is set at four tomorrow afternoon. The rest of today was spent in some last-minute little details like buying movie film, repacking and weighing, and trying to pick up some extra information on our ultimate destination.

Later this afternoon we went over to the Officers Club to jawbone the situation over a few beers and dinner. John S. Johnson from Long Beach, California, whom I met as we left our hotel in San Francisco, bunks next to me. We've hit it off pretty well, and have done most of our processing together. He leaves at 0645 tomorrow. Scheduled on my flight are two Fort Sill officers, Walt Kiley from the 553rd, who was at CBR (Chemical, Biological, Radiological Warfare) School in San Antonio with us, and the Group Communications officer, Bill Goetzman, both of whom are interesting characters.

Tonight as we were leaving the Officers Club a polished, shiny army car drove up and stopped and we heard the civilian-garbed passenger tell the driver to come back for him at nine. The license plates were red with a single, big silver star, so it must have been Post Commander, Brig. Gen. Lewis. We were walking back down the road when the car pulled by us. The driver looked over our way and slowed, so I called out, asking him if he was interested in giving us a ride. He didn't say anything, but he stopped. So the three of us piled into the back seat and were driven back home to our BOQ [Bachelor Officers' Quarters] in the general's private car.

Because the large silver star prominently displayed on the license plates did not match the single gold bar on our collars, we had quite a debate. Our dilemma was: Should we paint over the general's star and replace it with a nice gold second lieutenant's bar, or should we each simply throw away our gold bar and replace it with a solitary silver star? We hadn't yet resolved the question by the time we arrived at our destination. Needless to say, when the general's car pulled up in front of our BOQ lodgings, it caused quite a stir among the small crowd of lieutenants standing around. And then when three young second lieutenants smilingly stepped out, the place went wild with cheering and applause!

I love you so much, Chicki, and I wish I could talk to you and hold your hand right now. You are all I have and ever want. Take good care

of yourself and write. I pray for you, dear heart.
Good night and kisses, Bill

* * *

6 Sept. 53
Sunday afternoon
Travis AFB

Hi Chicki,

It's now 2:30 PM. Takeoff time is set for 4:00. Baggage is checked. We've got our gate passes and we are all set. I bought, as a matter of course, a flight insurance policy which I'm forwarding to you.

Next up is Hawaii. It will take less time from California to Hawaii than from California back to New York. I wouldn't mind too much if I were going back the other way.

It was wonderful to talk with you last night. You're such a darling pumpkin and I love you with all my heart and soul.

I pray for you and think of you always.

All my love for always,

Bill

* * *

6 Sept. 53

Certificate of Insurance:
  Transport Accident Policy
   2/Lieut. William R MacIlvaine
    Casual Personnel Section. APO 619
     Care of postmaster San Francisco California
      $10,000 insurance three-day term
       Premium: two dollars
        Beneficiary: wife

* * *

7 Sept. 53
1:40 AM
Honolulu, HI
POSTCARD

Dear Lucy,

We just landed and have only one hour here. It's a little damp with a cool breeze, much like a Bermuda evening. From what little I've seen, Hawaii is beautiful and green, many wild sport shirts and Hawaiian music.

Twelve hours after we take off, we land at Wake Island after crossing the Dateline. Having a good trip.

My love,
Bill

* * *

9 Sept. 53
Tokyo, Japan
2:35 PM CABLEGRAM

ALL WELL AND SAFE WRITING IN DETAIL MY THOUGHTS AND PRAYERS ARE EVER WITH YOU

WILLIAM

* * *

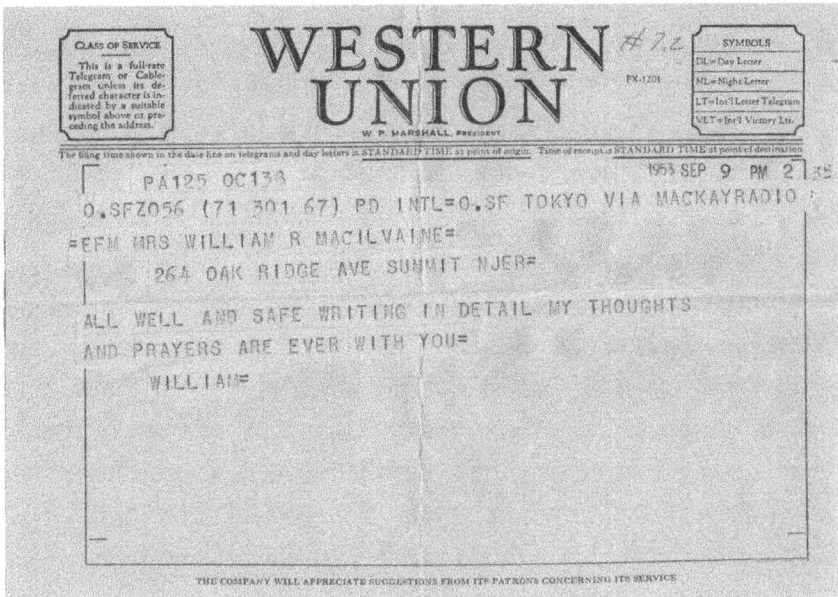

Camp Drake, Tokyo
10 Sept. 53

Dearest Chicki,

We took off Sunday from California at four in the afternoon local time, in the oldest-looking DC-4, the only passenger plane Overseas National Airlines owns. They are a contract carrier for Military Air Transport Service (MATS). We were lucky, however, having regular comfortable seats and good service all the way over. Regardless, it was a long time sitting and I was really happy, about a day and a half later, to finally land at Haneda Airport in Tokyo.

The first leg of our flight was to Hickam Field in Hawaii. After a smooth and relaxing ride we arrived in the dark of four in the morning California time, one in the morning Hawaii time, and seven in the morning New Jersey time.

We had less than an hour on the ground, just enough time to eat a hot breakfast in the mess hall and write a postcard or two. There were palms around the airport building, much green grass and balmy breezy weather. Although I couldn't see any landmarks, I'm told we flew in over Diamond Head and Waikiki Beach. After breakfast and takeoff, we passed over the lights of Pearl Harbor and climbed westward into the darkness. During the entire flight, for every five hours of flying time we set our watches one hour earlier.

After leaving Hawaii, we flew and flew and flew some more. I snoozed the best I could, but thought daylight would never arrive. Finally, about nine the next morning, Hawaii time, about six our time, the sun started to rise behind us. The highlight of the day, which featured very few high (or low) lights, was my chance to sit in the co-pilot's seat for a while and get a flying lesson. That is, I received instructions without, however, touching the controls. Nevertheless, try borrowing the copilot's seat on a commercial New York to Chicago flight! Anyway, it helped pass time and is a good indication of the informal nature of our flight. Every seat on the chartered plane was occupied by a 2nd Lt. on his way to Korea.

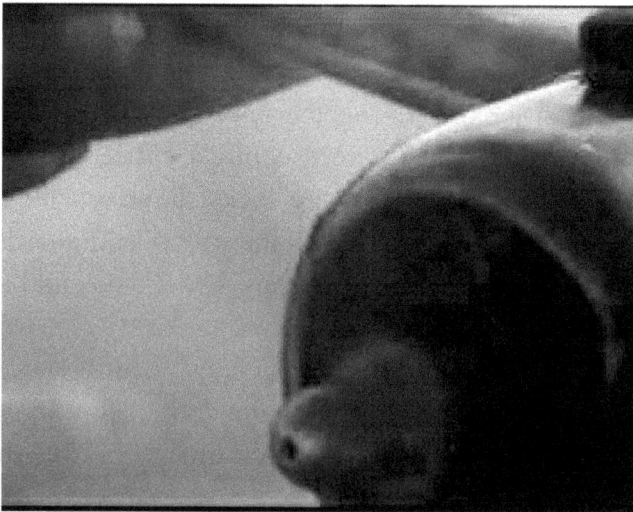

View from the cockpit.
Video Link: http://lovelettersfromthefront.com/videos

Around midday we landed at Wake Island. I got great shots of an old half-sunken Jap troop ship just off the beach as we were landing. I also got some shots of a few rusted tanks all chewed up by U.S. shells. Then there is the shot of me holding up an old battered helmet. Wake is flat, small and all coral, with only scrub brush for vegetation. The ground is white and the sun is blinding. Across the island, I'm told, is the lagoon where Pan Am Clippers landed to refuel on their way to Manila pre-WW II. It must have been exciting and exotic here in those days. Now it is not exotic. It's a HOT and humid, very informal spot. The standard dress for those unlucky enough to be inhabitants, or stationed on Wake is: sport shirt, khaki Bermuda shorts without belt, and Japanese sandals. Walt Kiley took a short sequence of me reboarding the plane.

We land at Wake Island.
Video Link: http://lovelettersfromthefront.com/videos

The first two legs of the trip took about twelve hours each. The last, from Wake to Haneda, was only about ten hours, but about an hour of it was extra rough. Not only did we rise and fall like an elevator, but we jerked and jolted and bounced, and at one time we snapped with a loud crack, which threw me up against my safety belt. I thought for sure we'd lost our tail. No such luck, and after shooting through a few more clouds and finally a rainbow, then more flying, we finally passed over the lights of the east coast of Japan.

Wake Island's rusty relics.
Video Link: http://lovelettersfromthefront.com/videos

Haneda was fairly warm at 8:30 PM Japanese time and abounded with multitudes of scurrying, short Orientals. We exchanged our dollars to military scrip (MPC, Military Payment Certificates), had a glass of iced tea in the PX snack bar, and then waited for our several buses at the front entrance to the airport. What an experience! Little Japanese cars and taxis would pull over and screech to a stop at the curb. The instant one stopped, a chorus of horns would start to beep. The little driver would jump out of the cab, scurry around and pick up baggage and an occasional passenger or two, jump back in, then leap out into traffic at twenty-five miles an hour with not so much as a glance in any direction.

The object of the game is go as fast and as recklessly as you can, and beep your horn every four seconds. Nobody minds being honked at and nobody pays the least bit of attention. Brakes are never used; the cabbies only drive, honk and swerve.

An hour for lunch then off to the Orient.
Video Link: http://lovelettersfromthefront.com/videos

Tokyo is the third-largest city in world population, but it hasn't the feel of a place like New York. I guess it's because its little shops and buildings spread over half the Orient. Finally our bus arrived in the able hands of a little skinny Japanese with big round glasses and buck teeth. We barreled almost twenty miles through the outskirts of Tokyo, northeast to Camp Drake. The road felt like it was a bumpy kind of cobblestone, but was actually asphalt. It was narrow but fairly straight. In the last eighteen miles, we passed only two stop lights and perhaps four stop signs, where we slowed down. The entire route was lined with little open-front shops and people, people, all over the place. Stalls that looked like penny arcades seemed to be the most populated. The countryside and towns are all a hodgepodge of little wooden tumbledown houses and shops. Every tiny open plot is a vegetable garden fertilized, I'm told, with human manure.

The overall impression is that of a small-town slum district. However, in the center of Tokyo we later saw the Imperial Palace grounds, the Diet Building and the Diet Library, which are fine, imposing granite structures. I have yet to see the scenic part of Japan, or even get a glimpse of Mount Fuji.

We arrived, tired and grubby, at Camp Drake late Tuesday evening (our time; I've lost track of your time) and got about forty minutes of orientation. Then a shower, and at last to bed.

The BOQs here are no prize. In ours, there are several hundred officers bunked in double-decker army cots in twenty-five-man dormitories. The BOQ is a long, frame, two-story building with a burning time of five minutes—no one smokes in bed!

The next (Wednesday) morning we had chow which was borderline good—not outstanding, but plentiful; served by a "boysan," which is what waiters, or anybody who might be called boy, is called. The "sahn" means something like mister and makes the name more polite (my spelling is entirely phonetic). A waitress is "girlsan," an old man or woman servant is "Papasan" or "Mamasan." Two other well-used words are "tocksan," meaning many or much, and "scoshee," meaning few.

After breakfast we had another, longer orientation which boiled down simply to the fact that we were going to be assigned to specific different places and were going to get there by specific different means. Sounds fairly logical to me. It took many words and much time to get the message across.

My orders came out this morning assigning me to the 8th Army in Korea. We will take a train south to Sasebo, Japan. We'll process again there, and perhaps then take a small landing ship to Inchon, on the west coast of Korea, near Seoul. From there we will be assigned to a Division; then in turn, to a Battalion, and then to a Battery. I wasn't overly pleased with the final news that Korea was my definite destination, but of course it was no surprise to any of us. Nobody is staying in Japan.

No one here seems to be overly optimistic about the future military situation in the Far East, but at least, few expect the shooting to restart. I hear morale is really low in Korea, with training being conducted in twelve-week cycles, seven days a week, a sort of secondary basic training. To make matters worse, they have dropped my 0606 Military Occupational Specialty and given me back my previous 1189 and 1193. That is Battery Officer or Forward Observer. The duties of my assignment will be just like those at the Field Artillery Replacement Training Center (FARTC) at Ft. Sill, only probably worse.

Thank the Lord that my army career is in its final stage. I will only have ten months in Korea—but think of those officers and men who will have to serve sixteen!

My morale hasn't fallen too low yet because everything is new and sort of an adventure. I am intrigued with the scenes and places. The things that make me saddest are first, that you can't be here to share every experience with me, and second, that it's impossible for me to describe in minute enough detail all those things I've seen, heard and experienced. I'm doing my best efforts to hit the high spots, trying to give you the feeling of the unique sort of adventure this is. I miss you very much, Sweetie, and I love you so much. I'll be so happy to see you again—you'll have to be a good listener because there'll be lots to tell you about. Probably I'll be so overcome with joy when I see you I won't be able to open my mouth.

After breakfast and the orientation yesterday, I sent you the safe-arrival cable and then called your Aunt Mary Dot in Yokohama. In the afternoon Walt Kiley, John Johnson and I went to the Officers Club gift shop and the PX. You will surely get that black-and-white pearl ring! Please send the ring size of the finger you'll wear it on. You can get all grades of cultured pearls. The cheapest run from one dollar up, for average-size pearls.

The better pearls are selected by higher luster, different shade, and age. I'll get your ring with the best pearls I can find. In the meantime I plan to get you a pair of silver and pearl earrings. The pearls are the regular cultured variety, but not of the highest quality available.

I bought Chris a pair of hand-painted silk tiger posters for his room at Princeton, but they will not arrive in time for his birthday.

Tell me what kinds of stuff you'd like. I can get some cocktail glasses of the same lacquered wood the Walkers have. Would you like some? I am also sending you a few pretty, but unimportant gifts that I think you'll like.

Tonight John Johnson and I will go into Tokyo to look around and do a little shopping. We'll have more time and more money to buy gifts later when we go on R&R. That's when I'll get your ring, although I've already seen some I like very much.

When I talked with Mary Dot yesterday afternoon she asked me to come down to Yokohama for a visit. So last night after I got off, I took courage in my own hands and struck out for Yokohama. Having been in this strange and foreign land for less than twenty-four hours, I was a little dubious about ever getting there. I speak no (and that's a fact) Japanese, and most Japanese I've seen speak no English. All their signs are Greek to me, but off I went. I took a taxi to the Tokyo RTO (station), paid the driver his fare in yen. I finally found the right ticket window for the right destination and Yokohama (120 yen, or exactly 33 cents). I tried to find out what time the train left, but all the guard could do was write 13 with his finger on the wall. Finally I showed him my watch and he pointed to about three minutes ahead of where the minute hand was then pointing. He knew I was going to Yokohama, so I assumed the "13" meant track 13. When I got to track 13, there was a train in the station. I asked the conductor, "Yokohama Express?" He nodded and jabbered and grinned and bowed, so I got on, not knowing whether I was getting a bum steer or not. There were two non-Oriental men in the car, so I asked them if I was on the Yokohama Express. They turned out to be neither English nor American, but they answered in halting English that this was indeed the train, and Yokohama was the third stop.

The ride was fast and creaking and rickety. The car was old, with a wooden floor and blue upholstered benches that ran the length of both sides. It was arranged very much like a New York subway car. When I got to Yokohama I elbowed my way through the station amid crowds of milling Japanese, with me the only American in sight. Finally I found a waiting room with several officers in it, and a telephone. I called Mary Dot and then struck up a conversation with a Marine 2/Lt. from Red Bank, New Jersey. Mary Dot, who now sports the gold leaf of a Major, arrived in a borrowed Fiat. She is wonderful! We had the greatest time. We went over to her apartment, which she shares with Lt. Col. Rhodes, W.A.C., and poured a drink.

There, I brought her up on all the latest news from home—Scarsdale, your grandmother, and the two weddings. She told me about you when you were born, the baby with a broken arm, and the time she drove you and Bob and your Mom to Chicago. Later, Lt. Col. Rhodes and Lt. Col. Harris came in and we argued about the greatness of Texas. I'll stick up for EAST Texas only. We had dinner together at the Officers Club: two colonels, a major and me! Your aunt is very interesting and easy to talk to. She's smart and sporty and understanding. When she returns to the States in two months, she may be able to be of help to you. I know you'll enjoy seeing and talking with her. She will be able to give you a first-hand account of Japan and what it's like and what I've seen and done during the last few days.

Tomorrow night, with John Johnson, I'm again going down to see Mary Dot and attend a party for her boss, Gen. Howard.

This has been an all-day letter and it's now chow time, after which John and I are taking our shopping spree into Tokyo.

I love you with all my heart and soul, darling. I miss you and pray for you.

Goodnight, Chicki,

Bill

Camp Drake
11 Sept. 53

Lucy dearest,

I stopped yesterday's letter abruptly. Then in a big hurry, just about made it to the end of the chow line when I remembered it was C-Rations night. It was then decided by John and me that the best idea was to take a taxi into Tokyo right away, eat at the Urocka Hotel, an R&R hotel run by the Army, and then do our shopping and/or window shopping. We got a cab and after a particularly harrowing ride, paid our fare of 1120 yen (360 yen to the dollar).

When we got into the dining room there were no vacant tables. However, one table had only one officer. He said sure, we could join him. So we sat, called the boysan and ordered our New York cut steaks. Were they ever good! Big, thick, juicy for $1.25 MPC. The Officer at the table was a Lt. Commander in the Navy, assigned to the U.S. Army for an operation called Big Switch. He was in Tokyo for R&R., was about fifty, had a young but weather-beaten face and was a well-traveled gentleman.

He said if we thought Japan was crowded and smelly and the people were unpleasant (which we really didn't), Korea would be ten times as bad. He had no use for Korea or Koreans. Syngman Rhee, the president, was a crook, he assured us, and the people will steal anything they can get their hands on.

His jeep was stolen in Seoul one day. When he went to the police, they said they knew the members of the ring of car thieves, and who its leader was. The police said they would bring in the Number One Man and torture him until he produced a jeep, not necessarily the Lt. Cmdr.'s jeep, but a good, serviceable one. The police then said that for $50 they would beat up on the ringleader until he produced the specific stolen jeep of the Lt. Cmdr.

He also told us that children would come up to you waving a paperback book pretending to sell it. Their trick was to slide the book up against your shirt pocket and hook the cover under the clip of your fountain pen while you were telling them you weren't buying. Then they would scamper off taking your pen, unnoticed, clipped to their book.

After dinner we found that the Imperial Hotel Arcade closes to shoppers at seven, so we walked down to the Ginza (shopping district). The Lt. Cmdr. had been around Tokyo and he led us up and down all the side streets while we looked into tea, hardware, food and jewelry shops. The array is colorful, to say the least—people all over the place, great neon signs in Japanese characters, thousands of little open-front shops with white flags with red characters painted on them. The side streets are narrow and lined with the little shops. Ginza Avenue and the main streets are very much like Broadway except that the buildings are not more than a few stories high.

We looked around until a little after nine, when the shops were beginning to close down, and then went over for a drink at Japan's most swish and expensive night club—bourbon and water 350 yen (95 cents). It could be any New York night club except for a large stained glass window which subdued the ultra-modern decoration. The place was filled with Japanese girls called Hostesses but were evidentially the prostitutes you hear so much about. However, they are not at all aggressive. We didn't talk to them or look toward them, so they very discreetly kept to themselves. We had one drink at the bar while the Lt. Cmdr. told us about the Korean thieves, and then we left.

We walked him back to the R&R hotel and said goodnight. John and I then wandered about for a while trying to find a taxi that could be bartered down from 1100 yen to 800. After trying to make ourselves understood to half a dozen drivers, who stopped in the middle of the street and created great commotion from the cars behind, we managed to find one who consented to make the trip for 800 yen.

The trip back was even worse than the ride out and we bounced and careened along in the battered little Japanese car until we thought out teeth would chatter loose, or at very least our upper fillings would fall out.

Our shopping resulted in some results; this afternoon I am sending a fan to Mom and three gifts to you and also the roll of film to be developed by way of Hawaii.

Tonight John and I are traveling to Yokohama to see Mary Dot and attend the reception for Gen. Howard.

I love you, sweetie, with all my heart. I wish I could be with you even for a few minutes. I'd love to put my arm around you and hold your hand and kiss you. The more I think about you, the more tender and loving I feel. You are a wonderful pumpkin and the only sweet darling person in the world for me.

I love you, Lucy,

Bill

P.S. Enclosed is a one-yen bill (1/360 of a dollar).

* * *

Camp Drake
12 Sept. 53

Dear Chicken Pot Pie,

It's been very warm, overcast and humid today and I've been moving very slowly—feeling sort of foggy.

We had a fine time last night at the Golden Dragon—the Yokohama Officers Club—where we met Brig. Gen. Howard. John and I had no trouble navigating our way back to Yokohama or to the Club.

Arriving a little after seven, we found the officers and wives at cocktails in the Green Room (la-dee-da). Mary Dot met us at the door, got us a drink, and then we met the Majors, Colonels and the Big Man himself. Actually, there were some Warrant Officers and a Captain, but no Lieutenants. Major Mary Dot was the life of the party.

* * *

13 September:
En route by train to the replacement depot at Sasebo, Japan.

I was interrupted yesterday after that one page, by chow, packing and our shipment.

We took the bus a couple of miles to a troop train and pulled out of Tokyo about 9:30 PM. The trip to Sasebo is two nights and a day. It's a little after noon now and I imagine we're about halfway. We've passed through Yokohama, Gifu, Osaka and Kobe and should arrive in Hiroshima at seven tonight.

We're on a twelve-car troop train with a kitchen car in the middle. We're carrying about 330 men and 37 officers, mostly captains and warrant officers and a few second lieutenants. To visualize our car, take an old commuter coach from the N.Y. Central, remove all the seats, cut it down to a third its normal length, then line eight bunks along each side. The bunks are Navy type, made of tubular steel with canvas bottoms, and hang from the wall by chains. The bunks are quite comfortable but quarters are crowded and despite three electric fans, the air is close and humid.

It was drizzling last night as we sat on our duffel bags by a deserted siding and waited to board the train. I chuckled when I thought of how you would probably have been cussing the army over the delay. You know it's always been "Hurry up and wait." Actually, we haven't had too bad a time so far. We've had plenty of time to sleep, sightsee, and write letters. The food has been pretty good and when it isn't, there is always a top-notch Officers Club, where the best filet mignon (my spelling is disintegrating) is $1.25. I've been with some pretty good guys so far and enjoyed the sights of the Orient. Of course, through it all I've missed you every second. I love you so much, Lucy, you can't possibly ever imagine how much I love you.

I imagine we'll stay a day or two in Sasebo and then take a ship to Inchon, thence to 8th Army and probably a Division. (This train is bucking and rolling like a West Texas bronco.) I've stopped in each location, so far not quite long enough for my mail to catch up and I don't expect I'll hear from you for a week or more. I talk to God every night and I know He is watching over and taking care of you as He is of me. I also have great confidence in you and your ability to keep your chin up when the going gets tough. Keep smiling and keep occupied and always remember, Lucy, that with God to guide you, and with me behind you loving you with all my heart, you can't help but be the most serene, confident and wonderful person in the world. This time that we're apart is not a time to sit back and feel unhappy or wronged, but a time to build ourselves for our reunion, for our life together and for our future children. I love you until I could burst—you are the most beautiful, wonderful, sweetest wife in the world.

The second roll of film starts, if I remember correctly, on the plane. I didn't get a chance to get any interesting footage of Tokyo, but the sun came out late this morning and I took what I hope are some fairly scenic shots of the rice paddies along the tracks and the countryside. I also got one sequence while our train skirted the ocean and went through many very fishy-smelling fishing villages on the Japanese east coast. Despite what a lot of people say, I think Japan is very pretty. Once you get out of the cities, everything, every square inch of ground, is green. Much of the land is perfectly flat, with heavily wooded, steep mountains rising out of the rice paddies every mile or so. I have never seen so many shades of green, from the pale, almost yellow-green of the rice to the dark, almost black-green of the strange, angular pine-type trees. Numerous rivers, streams and little irrigation ditches cover this part of Japan.

To get back to the party at the Golden Dragon. After the cocktails we all adjourned upstairs to the dining room, complete with dance floor and band. Our party had a long table for about thirty people. Along one side sat, first, Mrs. Howard, then the General on her right, then Mary Dot on his right, then your dear husband Bill, then John. The General seemed young for his rank, was very easy to talk to and was very nice. His wife was gracious, very nice and from Charlottesville. She thinks she knew your Mom, but I couldn't remember her maiden name.

On the troop train from Tokyo southbound.
Video Link: http://lovelettersfromthefront.com/videos

Whenever Mary Dot danced, the General and I leaned across her empty chair and shot the breeze. We hit it off very well, talked about movie cameras, Charlottesville, the Far East, etc. I was interested among other things to hear him say that he sent all the officers assigned to his command to Korea first, for a tour of duty of ten months, and then gave them an intra-command transfer to spend the rest of their tour in Japan. He said the Korean tour is a very important part of an officer's education. Don't blame Mary Dot for never ever trying to influence my assignment.

Even if I had stayed in Japan, I'm not too sure you would have wanted to come over. You would have been with career army people and Japanese, uneasy about going about alone, and living expensively in fairly poor quarters. What it boils down to is that this is an Oriental country which was only recently at war with us, is no longer completely subjugated by the occupation, full of transient soldiers and a long way from home. It would have been really great if by some mistake I had been assigned to the 24th Division, currently here in Japan. In the very near future, rumor has it, some or all of the division will be returned to Hawaii. That would have been the life!

I pray that you are well and happy, I miss you with a great longing and I love you with all my heart and soul.

Your loving husband,

Bill

3
Sojourn in Sasebo

Camp Drake
14 Sept. 53

Lucy m'love,

Here we sit waiting in Sasebo, a town on an island, in the country of Japan. We're twiddling our thumbs. My morale is lower today than it's been since I left LaGuardia. First, we sat in Camp Stoneman and it wasn't too bad because we were excited about going somewhere, had pleasant companions, and facilities were generally quite good. We could even talk long distance.

Then we sat in Camp Drake outside Tokyo and facilities and companionship were still good and we had this strange foreign land to investigate.

Now Sasebo. Instead of going right to our goal, Korea, we're sitting in another ex-Japanese base and being orientated and processed, turning in and drawing out equipment all over again. Now it's your turn to chuckle and mine to grumble about army. I could have taken a ship from San Francisco and probably arrived at Inchon in the same elapsed time as flying to Japan and then going from camp to camp for processing. Think how much money the government would have saved! The only possible excuse I can muster is the U.N. currently isn't allowed to put a man into Korea until the one he replaces leaves.

At any rate, I do not like these Japanese barracks or the way we are stuffed into them. If I think about it a little, however, I realize that the more time we spend idling around in Japan, the more time we're stuck in any transient place, it means less time in Korea. I guess what really has dumped my morale is that this sitting around just puts off the time when I'll start getting your letters. I am lonely, Chicki, and I miss you so much and I love you so completely. I keep saying those same things over and over to you but I mean them with all my heart, so you can just plan to keep on hearing them.

I caught up to Dick Riordan from Princeton, also Fred Schultz, Craig Walton, and of all people, George Steele. They all came over by ship, left the states around the 22nd of August and left Sasebo for Korea today. Dick Riordan said Gough Thompson was wounded, but not seriously, and was shortly returned to his unit. I had quite a chat with Riordan and Walton about nothing in particular—the trip over, what we've been doing, etc. Steele said he'd heard that Dan Pope's orders had been changed, but he wasn't too sure.

John Johnson, who was with me in CBR School, and Walt Kiley came on down on the train to Sasebo along with me. We had a long scenic ride to the south of Japan. Follow our route on a map.

The country in these parts is really quite pretty and wooded and hilly, the hills being very steep and green. Near the town of Sasebo is Japan's greatest naval base of WW II, as well as their Naval Academy. I could imagine the ghosts of nine years ago as we drove through the base this morning. I could almost see those giant, top-heavy battleships and fast-looking, bent-funnel destroyers at the docks, as the little Nippon stevedores swarmed over them loading provisions for the Battle of the Coral Sea or the sortie against the U.S. Fleet and our carriers at Midway.

The great concrete dry docks and feathery girdered steel cranes are still here, and now service the very vessels they were built to defeat. Sasebo is today one of the U.S. Navy's main Japanese bases.

I didn't realize it, but while we were on our pre-Korea leave, the army published Circular 61, which provides for early release for officers and men under certain conditions. Now, don't get excited; I don't happen to fulfill any of the conditions, but it may indicate a possible trend. Some of the conditions were: completion of two years active duty for those officers who had signed for three (à la Bud Patten), or 90 days service during WW II, or active duty to include six months before the Korean war started, etc. If they ever come out with a provision for Reserve time (I've got three years) and, say, 18 months active duty, I'd go wild. There's no indication that they will, but at least it's a happy thought. There I go, being a happy, foolish optimist again. Anyway I'm keeping my eyes and ears open, and if any new regulations are published, I'll be the first to hop on the bandwagon.

Despite all these so-called top-notch PX's I haven't been able to buy any 8 mm film. I doubt I'll be able to get anything in Seoul. Nor have I seen any Sunbeam Electric Model W shavers or parts. I would appreciate very much if you would send me some replacement parts just in case. They are the Cutter or (blade), the Comb (the grille your whiskers go through to be cut) and the Comb Cover, the metal protector for the comb when the shaver is not in use. I am reasonably certain I have the right terminology. They are small, light parts and won't cost much to airmail.

In case you're wondering why I need a Comb Cover, it's not that they wear out. Mine may still be sitting, forgotten, forlorn and lonely, on a shelf, over a sink, in the wash room, near the landing strip, on Wake Island, in the middle of the Pacific Ocean. That sounds pretty remote, doesn't it? I was rushed while shaving cuz I didn't want to miss my plane. Ha ha.

Incidentally, I made out a continuing allotment to you today for $250 per month. It will start with October's pay. It will be a check made out to you, mailed to Summit. Deposit it in the savings account, or have Mom do it, and draw out whatever you need.

Tomorrow it will be two weeks since I left, but it seems like two years. It's been a tremendous experience and a lonely one, and yet I feel so close to you right now that it's almost as if you were sitting beside me looking over my shoulder as I write. I love you with all my heart and soul, Lucy. God, you and I are very close.

Goodnight, Pumpkin,

Bill. P.S. My morale has improved.

15 Sept. 53

Dear Chicki,

Item One is that just after I mailed your letter last night I checked the bulletin board and found myself among a dozen or so who was assigned a work detail for the next day.

We fell out at 7:30 this morning and four of us were sent to the Replacement Company next door. The Battery Commander assigned me to one of the 480-man barracks, told me the Colonel was going to inspect it and I was to take about a hundred men and put it in shape. There never was an inspection and I spent the entire dull day having the sergeants get the men doing things that obviously did not need to be done. The only aim we were trying to accomplish was to keep the men physically busy. Ugh!

Tonight they posted tomorrow's roster. It is identical to today's! What a squawk went up! Repeating a duty roster is one of the army's most unpardonable errors. No one around would take the blame for the action, but one of the orderly room personnel said that he thought the repeat was because the men who were on today were so familiar with the job, Ha! The so-called mud will hit the fan tomorrow when our BOQ Battery Commander comes in. I doubt we will have to repeat the duty tomorrow.

Now that you've heard the most pressing and important problem of the moment, I can go on. About this Early Release—nothing official, but I've heard again from two new sources that there is a new circular out that authorizes release after 19 months, or perhaps 21, after certain conditions have been filled. What these condition are, the rumor hasn't yet decided. However I am still trying to uncover the official regulation. If it doesn't come out in the "Stars and Stripes," I will undoubtedly be able to get the official word after we get to Korea.

I love you, Chicki. I surely wish I could get a letter from you. It's been a long time since I've heard what you're thinking and doing and how you feel and how much you love me. I often picture you going to church with me in the blue dress you made, or sitting in the relaxing chair, or washing the dishes in Lawton, and wearing those white verti-cal-blue-striped shorts, and I think of you wearing Aunt Helen's white peignoir—you always looked so beautiful then. One of the very best times was when you stood next to me in the receiving line wearing a long white wedding dress. I don't think you can ever know how much I adore you, Lucy. I cherish and love you with all my being. I always have and I always will. I look forward to coming home to you, getting a job and a real home and four little kids who look just like you. Then we'll be together and we'll work to understand each other and take care of each other and be the best parents in the world. You're my wife, Lucy, and the most wonderful and darling wife that ever lived.

We're still here in Sasebo and chances are we will be here for sever-al days to come. I'm looking forward to moving out and to the next part of our trip, an ocean voyage to (not so) scenic Inchon.

I saw and had a chat with Russ Forgan today. He doesn't seem to be too happy in the army although he did enjoy the good fortune of assignment to Camp Drum in upstate New York after Ft Sill. He then spent two months at Ft. Jay on Governor's Island—some life! How did he manage that? He told me Kirby was engaged. Also, Tom Knight from Princeton is in Korea. Then we discussed getting out.

I only have about 18 feet of film left, so I'm taking it easy. I'll check the PX again tomorrow. Also tomorrow, if it's at all possible, I'm going to try to call you.

I love you with all my heart and soul, I miss you, darling, and I pray for you.

Goodnight, wife,

Bill

* * *

17 Sept. 53
Thursday
(I read these words on the banner atop a Japanese newspaper today and could probably start each letter this way):
NEWS FROM NIPPON.

Dearest Lamb,

Well, here we are, still in Sasebo, with the latest rumor circulating that the next ship for Inchon won't be until the 24th. Groan! We are nowhere, or about 800 miles south and west of Tokyo, 100 miles from Korea, and over 8,000 miles distant from New York.

Relative times are still a little uncertain; however, to the best of my belief we are fourteen hours ahead of your Eastern Standard time, or thirteen hours ahead of Eastern Daylight time. What I mean is add fourteen hours to your Standard time and have our time.

It was so magnificently wonderful to hear from you yesterday!! I got five of your six letters and a letter from Aunt Wawee in the morning. I didn't open them at once but, like a foraging chipmunk, carried them back to the BOQ and sat on my cot to read them. They were all good news and I read them over and over and almost cried when I read about and pictured you in church in Bronxville, and mentally holding my hand at grace and cuddling me at night. It made me feel awfully proud and happy to know how brave you are acting. You sounded so smart and capable that it makes me feel very happy and warm inside, a sort of "That's my Wife" kind of feeling.

I was overjoyed at the prospect of becoming a father. I wanted it so much for you and for me. I sat here for a long time during the morning trying to picture what it would be like, what it would feel like to come home to you and to a new baby of ours. Never before this morning did I feel anything but joy at the prospect. This morning I felt a little sadness because I could not be with you and watch the baby grow, and be a part of the early growth, and comfort you when you felt uncomfortable. I wanted to be with you when the baby was born, and hold your hand when it hurt and hear the first squawk. I felt badly that I would be away from you during almost your entire pregnancy and birth. It would be as if you had bought a new car when I was gone. I would look at it and admire it but it would take time to feel that it was really mine. Despite all this I was thrilled, and pleased as anything that it was possible we had started our own family.

In the afternoon I again went to the post office. No new mail had come in, but curiously enough, one letter that had come in for me in the morning's mail had been mis-sorted and was finally handed to me with apologies. I brought it back to my bunk and read it. You said the time had not yet arrived for us to start our family. I was crushed. I couldn't believe it, I still can't, really. I hadn't been able to phone you and I couldn't write until I thought about it.

Later, at five in the afternoon, Walt and I went over to the single room which is the Officers Club and started drinking Danish beer. We talked about getting out, going home, and this grubby Japanese Camp Sasebo, and I kept on thinking about you and the baby that wasn't. We had a hamburger and talked about morality. He is Catholic and obviously fairly devout. I excused myself from what had grown to become a small group by seven o'clock, and came back to my bunk.

I wondered why God had built me up so much by delaying that one letter and then letting me down so hard. I think it was to give me a chance to feel what I've said earlier in this letter. Maybe it's more important than we realized. I'm awfully sorry, sweetie, I know how unhappy you must be about the whole thing. It must be for the best. It's what God has planned. When I come home, Lucy, we are going to have so many darn kids so fast it's going to look like a nursery school and kindergarten combined!! Always remember, God makes the decisions and we three are a team. I love you with all my heart and soul. I worship and adore you. I think you are the finest person in the whole wide world. Keep loving me, stay brave and optimistic, and before you know it I'll be flying home again.

Talking about coming home, and the orders that make it possible: another comment was made to me last week that the Artillery Career Management people in D.C. dislike Ivy League ROTC officers. A friend-of-a-friend went to visit the Pentagon, as I thought of doing last November, to try for assignment to flight training. He asked to go to some school which would have resulted in delaying his tour in Korea. Instead, they wrote out FECOM (Far East Command) orders for him on the spot. We'll never know how fortunate we were that I never could get the time to go to Washington, no matter how much I wanted to get into army aviation.

It's more than hot in Sasebo and I've never experienced such humidity. I'm clammy walking, sitting or sleeping. Today it rained all day and everything is mud.

I tried to call you all morning. Connections were made to Summit in about an hour, but evidently you were in Scarsdale, which didn't answer. Your time, it was Wednesday evening the 16th. I'll try again tomorrow. It's $12 for three minutes, no tax. As for the mail, please pay my class dues and the Tiger Inn dues when they ask for them. I'll write the Alumni News when I'm permanently assigned.

I just came back from dinner at the Officers Club followed by a Cointreau. Shades of our honeymoon. I love you so desperately, Lucy. It's funny, some people put value on some things, others on other things. A lot of these guys here, married or not, will take out the local Jap mooses [prostitutes]. To me, that's as foreign as it would be to turn myself inside-out and join the Communists as a party member. It's just a different world, a life completely separated from my own. I love you only, darling, think of you only and, as a matter of fact, you have developed into sort of a human angel (without wings) or perhaps a lovely white wooly lamb to be cherished as one of the few true values of life. You are mine and I am yours and it shall be that way forever. I feel it stronger every day. Besides that you are a beautiful Chicki.

I'll mail this now and hit the sack. Tomorrow I'll call. I love you, Lamb, and pray for us. God is with us always and looking out for us. I am close to you now as always, always longing for you, yearning for you, and most of all loving you.

Bill

* * *

Friday 9:40 PM
18 Sept. 53

Chicki Chicki!!

Wow, was that phone call ever great! It was just like being home to talk with you like that!! Do you know how long we talked? About ten minutes and about fifty dollars worth. It was more than worth every second of it. If we had talked only three minutes, we could have just said hello, a couple of words, then goodbye. This way we could chat and talk and have a wonderful time. I love you so much, and talking to you again was the biggest thrill and excitement and fun I've had since we first looked at houses together in Summit.

I could hear you very clearly and it was just as if we were talking across the breakfast table. Even so, on the telephone you can't begin to say all those wonderful intimate thoughts and feelings that we have for each other. You can never know, sweetest lamb, how much I admire and respect and love you. It is a complete, full love and because of it I miss you terribly.

But Chicki—that phone bill! Ha ha; your father will think somebody has been calling from halfway around the world when he sees the bill. Actually, it's not quite halfway around the world. I think Burma or South Central China is the longest distance from New York. Anyway, you had best pay the bill. If I'd been a little smarter, I'd have called prepaid and there would have been no 25% tax, but I never thought the bill would run so high.

I thought I told you that I had danced with Aunt Mary Dot and the General's wife. It was expected of me and I would have been rude not to. Both are old enough to be my mother. Naturally we didn't dance close, and naturally you were the main topic of conversation. Official

Military Protocol—you understand, don't you, Lamb? I thought you would or I never would have danced. You are a billion times more important than any or all the generals and protocol in the world put together. I love you, Lucy.

I'm glad to have your ring size. I may not be able to get it made right away because we're out in the sticks and never know from day to day how long we'll be here. But Mikimoto has a branch in Sasebo and I'll go into town for the first time today and see what he has.

I also want to see if I can contact Charlie Reach here at the Naval Base. Remember I mentioned that I saw his mother in the travel agency when we were in Summit. He was married in July and took his wife to San Diego. When he arrived he found he was slated for a Far East cruise in a few days, to last about 6 months. That's one good way to get your plans disrupted. He is on a stubby, rolly "Landing Ship, Tank" (LST) with Sasebo as his home port.

The rain has stopped and it is a beautiful sunny day, not really hot, but still about as humid as the ocean floor.

I met an old Tiger Inner today, Phil Summer. He was a year behind me and got tossed out of college after mid-terms his junior year. We had a long talk over coffee at breakfast about politics at Princeton, and some of the old parties, and clubmates. Phil will have to return to Princeton to finish. In his former college days he was as wild as any, but when he returned to House Party weekend last spring he sensed something had changed during the past two years. He just couldn't raise hell and sling beer around anymore; it seemed stupid and immature.

I know what he means, because even while I was still in school, my senior year, I got embarrassed over some of the parties. I guess you and I are turning into the family type—but just you wait until I return. We two are going to have the time of our lives. I can't wait to see you, Lucy. Maybe it will be a quiet blast, but at least it will be a good and glorious time. I won't want to see anyone for a while except just you, and we can be alone together.

It's funny when I write to you now. The letters always come along easily and fast. I've got so much to say, even when I do absolutely nothing, that I never seem to be able to stop.

I love writing you and I love hearing from you. As a matter of fact, I love you!

Now I've got to take a shower, polish the brass for the first time in three or four days, and get ready for chow. See you later, wife. I love you tremendously and I'm so thrilled and contented after our phone call. I'll be seeing you before too long.

All my love,
Bill

* * *

19 Sept. 53
Saturday Night

Dear Pooh Bear,

Saturday night isn't as lonely as it could be, because we experience it at different times, fourteen hours apart. Therefore the heightened sadness that I would feel if we were both unhappy at the same time is cut down considerably, if you know what I mean. You are just getting up Saturday morning two days before school starts and are probably very busy.

After supper, three of us decided to hit the flicks, but when we got in the theater we found it so crowded and hot, and smelling like the Monkey House at the Bronx Zoo, that we got our money back and left. Then to avoid returning to the BOQ, we hit the library and browsed around until eight or so, when we returned to the BOQ dayroom for a Coke. I came up here a little before nine to write and then sack out.

Doesn't sound too exciting, does it? There have been a couple of interesting items, however. First, after not receiving any more mail for two days I was sure there would be a tall stack waiting for me when I checked at the post office. Getting to the window, we found it closed. Tacked to the window was a notice with these words; "No Mail Today.

Train Twelve Hours Late." This was so disappointing that it instantly struck us as a remarkably cruel joke. Shades of the Old West, Wells Fargo, a stage coach and a shipment of gold nuggets. Can you imagine the train being attacked with bow and arrow by hostile Indians, or perhaps a band of Japanese Robin Hoods decided it was fair game? Actually, our troop train down here from Camp Drake, carrying the mail, rolled along with split-second timing.

The second event of today was a fairly reliable confirmation of this nineteen or twenty-one-month Early Release. Of course I haven't yet personally seen the regulation and won't until I'm permanently assigned, but an officer just off the Korean Ferry from Pusan said there definitely was such a program. He didn't know anything about the conditions of release. I shall try to quit mentioning it, but as you can see this thing is uppermost in thought and conversation at present. I wish we'd hurry up and get to Korea. Never thought I'd want to go to Korea, did you?!

I haven't seen Mr. Mikimoto's establishment, but I have been inquiring about pearls and what makes them good. Black pearls are scarcest and therefore relatively more costly. Then come the pink, the silver and the blue pearls. After color, each pearl is then judged by size, shape, flaws and luster. Many pearl rings or any type of mounted pearl sell for less than they seem to be worth because the pearl, otherwise perfect, has a flaw or nick on that portion of it set into the mounting. I've looked at so many necklaces and rings and broaches and loose pearls recently that I'm beginning to know just a little bit about what I want. I know, a little knowledge is dangerous, but I'm sure when I finally get it, you'll love it.

I think about you all the time, sweetie, and I pray God will continue to take care of us both, you especially. I pray that he will give us the courage and the willpower to be brave and conquer all the problems and unhappiness that we face. I pray that he will take care of us and give us the strength to take care of ourselves and I pray that he will give us a sense of humor and mellowness that are always essential to real happiness. I love you so much, Chicki, and I admire and respect you so much.

You are a wonderful person and I even feel a little smart myself, having the sense to marry you.

I am nearing the end of the second roll of film. After the sequence from the train you will see shots of Camp Sasebo, with me walking around on a little toe of land that juts out into the East China Sea. I took a short shot of a helicopter and slow pan of Sasebo and then Walt took a short sequence of me walking around, and a few close-ups.

Goodnight, precious Lamb, I love you dearly and I'm constantly close to you.

Bill

* * *

20 Sept. 53
Sunday at Sasebo

Hello Chicki,

Started with a sore throat; seems to be coming along much better today. It's localized and I'm feeling more lively. Continuing medication and rest.

In Sasebo awaiting my ship.
Video Link: http://lovelettersfromthefront.com/videos

The mail did quite a bit better today also. I now have your letters 1 thru 9 and 11. The letter of the tenth of September evidently was overtaken by the following day's letter.

The Protestant Service was at 0900 this morning and the chapel was jam-packed to overflowing. E.M. sat in all three aisles and even inside the rail around the altar. The minister was sincere, with a simple but effective message. There was time for silent prayer and the hymns were the old roof-raising kind that we both love so much. During every hymn the ceiling rose three inches and vibrated there until the final Amen. Enclosed is the program.

MORNING WORSHIP
CAMP SASEBO, ~~8028d AU, APO 27~~

Chapel 1, Headquarters Compound, 1100 hours
Chapel 2, Replacement Center, 0900 hours

Colonel Austin C. Matheny, Commanding
Chaplain (Major) Edwin W. Armstrong, Camp Chaplain
Pvt. Frank J. Kreider, Chaplain's Assistant

SUNDAY	0900 - 1100 HOURS	September 20 1953

ORDER FOR WORSHIP

ORGAN PRELUDE	Organist
CHORAL INVITATORY	People

(Please follow the Order for Worship from the
Army and Navy Hymnal as printed on the card.)

HYMN NO. 159 "Holy, Holy, Holy, Lord God Almighty"		People
CALL TO WORSHIP	Chaplain and	People
DOXOLOGY	Chaplain and	People
CALL TO PENITENCE	Chaplain and	People
GENERAL CONFESSION	Chaplain and	People
ASSURANCE OF PARDON		Chaplain
PASTORAL PRAYER		Chaplain
THE LORD'S PRAYER	Chaplain and	People
ORISON		People
HYMN NO. 402 "Saviour, Like a Shepherd"		People
THE CREED	Chaplain and	People
RESPONSIVE READING Selection 64	Chaplain and	People
GLORIA PATRI		People
SCRIPTURE LESSON 1 Colossians 3:10-23		Chaplain
OFFERTORY ANTHEM OR SOLO		Choir or Soloist
PRAYER FOR PURITY OF THOUGHT		Chaplain
SERMON: "Yours, Christ's God's"		Chaplain
HYMN NO. 413 "Take My Life, and Let It Be"		People
BENEDICTION		Chaplain
CLOSING ORISON		People
SILENT MEDITATION		People
POSTLUDE		Organist

*The hand-printed address (my Dad's writing on the next page)
was added much later.*

AT CHAPEL NO. 1

Sunday Evening Bible Class at 1900 hours in the Servicemen's Center, Major Euless B. Moore, Jr, leader.

"Youth for Christ" next Saturday at 1930 hours, Ens. Norman Bell, sponsor.

The Offertory Anthem is under the direction of Cpl. Val Chalk, with Mrs. Fielden H. Wright, organist. Choir rehearsal is every Thursday at 1900 hours. Those who like to sing the great music of the church are cordially invited.

AT CHAPEL NO. 2

Offertory Solo by Sgt. Charles Potts; Miss Mary Lou Hiott, organist.

0830 hours, Sunday Holy Communion
0900 hours, Sunday Morning Worship
1900 hours, Sunday Vespers
1900 hours, Tuesday and Thursday Devotions

In addition to the regular hours of worship this chapel is open until 2400 hours each day for private meditations and devotions. You are cordially invited to visit the Chapel.

☆   ☆   ☆   ☆

The Chapel Offerings today will be donated to the National Christian Council of Japan, Christian Center Building, 2 Ginza 4 Chrome, Tokyo, Japan. This organization is comparable to our National Council of Churches in America, and is affiliated with the World Council of Churches, to which all major denominations belong.

The Chaplain has often conducted memorial services on behalf of the bereaved when they have not been able to attend the funeral service for a member of the family who has died. Such a service is usually a part of the regular Chapel service. The Chaplain makes a brief announcement of the bereavement, reads an appropriate scripture selection, and asks the congregation to stand with the bereaved in memory of the deceased member of his family, offering a brief prayer. Anyone desiring such a service in the event of death within his family is asked to notify the Chaplain.

The Morning Prayer

We give thanks unto Thee, Heavenly Father, through Jesus Christ Thy dear Son, that Thou hast protected us through the night from all danger and harm; and we beseech Thee to preserve and Keep us, this day also, from all sin and evil; that in all our thoughts, words and deeds, we may serve and please Thee. Into Thy hands we commend our bodies and souls, and all that is ours. Let Thy holy angel have charge concerning us, that the wicked one have no power over us. Amen.

My greatest joy in life these days are your letters. You bet I read them all word for word. Your progress with the scrap book really is great. I've been meaning to mount those pictures every year since I first started collecting and cataloging them. When I get home it will be fun to go through them together and label them.

As for the homemaking and sewing, I am very pleased, especially with the sewing. It sounds like you are doing a good job of it, and always I'm very proud of my very smart and darling wife. Now, if you would only drop in here and help with these shoulder patches.

The reason my Tokyo cable was ended "WILLIAM" instead of something less formal like Lamb or Pumpkin, or perhaps even Bill, is that it was sent under a packaged arrangement for service people and the package did not allow for a signature. Apparently as sender, my name was transmitted with the message and the operator in the States inserted my full first name for the signature.

Incidentally, I haven't had a headache or sinus trouble since I visited that foolish doctor in Newark. There was no hay fever in California, nor here in the Far East.

You mentioned in a letter that Tokyo sounded so far away. It sounds that way, but really it doesn't seem very far at all. We all very matter of factly climbed on a plane in California. Then we talked and read and snoozed for the amount of time it would take to drive from Summit to Pittsburgh. When we got off the plane to stretch our legs at Hawaii, the sights were a little different but were still the same people and we still talked and read in the same way and when we got back aboard the plane we still snoozed. It was the same sensation arriving in Wake and Tokyo. The sights were different, and when you repeat the names of the places they sound far away, but because the time was short, the distance also seems short. At the moment I am roughly four 10-hour hops from Newark Airport. It's a far quicker and easier trip than any of our drives out to Oklahoma.

I love you, Pumpkin, I love you so much and admire you so much and feel so close and warm and with you. Don't you dare ever get a sinking feeling that I might forget Us. Sweetie, the only loneliness I have in the world is that same loneliness that you and I are sharing. I am always, without shadow of doubt, forever yours (no candy bar puns intended). I love you, Lucy, very completely and very exclusively for always.

You know that I must yearn and long to be very close to you, to taste your lips and touch you and feel you warm and soft and responsive, but tomorrow is another day and it is not so far off. Until that day when I can hold you in my arms and cuddle you, you are an ever present symbol of all that is good, and beautiful, and pure, and I shall never forget it.

As for the tone of your letters, Chicki, that's very hard for me to answer. Most of all I like to hear what you've been doing, and how, and what you've been thinking about and seeing. What it boils down to is your natural self, lonely, but trying hard and acting brave. That's how I think of you, you old horse's muffin, tell me if I'm wrong.

My O.D.'s were shipped home because the army supplies practically everything you could need in the way of equipment. We heard they weren't wearing O.D.'s in FECOM anyway but rather the new (O.G.) olive green field uniform.

Please tell Mom that I hope the fan didn't come too long after her birthday and also that I'm sorry I didn't get a chance to put a card in the package. To avoid future embarrassment, could you please send me everybody's birthday and anniversary date?

It's not that I've forgotten them, it's just that I've never really memorized them.

I got Marty's birthday present off (for Charlie IV and Rita), and for Chris are the field jacket and tiger prints, which should arrive very late.

I've almost finished "The White Tower" now. It's getting better now that they're actually on the mountain, climbing.

Always remember how much I love you, darling, and how little real difference the hours or miles make when we and God are so close.
Goodnight, dearest Pooh,
Bill

* * *

21 Sept. 53
Monday

Dearest Lou,

Tonight in an old Japanese barrack, at a former Japanese naval base, on the southernmost island of Japan, the Princeton Cannon song burst resoundingly through the second-floor shower room. I bathed again.

The cold is abating gradually but still is a pain in the (front of the) neck. We were assigned that detail of inspecting barracks in that Replacement Company again today, so I took the opportunity to go on sick call and got some nose drops and cough medicine for the sore throat. The cough medicine is of the exact color, smell, consistency and taste of Cointreau. It even burns going down. However, I feel very boorish not to have a cordial glass. I have to slug it straight from the bottle.

I managed, as I look back on it, to do absolutely nothing today except go to the... (fooled you) post office twice.

On the second trip, I was delighted to get your very wonderful letter, #10.

It was a morale builder. I read it over and over. You know, you are to be classified as a first-rate interesting writer. Your trip out to Dingman's Falls must have been good fun. When I read about it I felt that I had been there too. Now as a matter of fact I remember a family outing many years ago. It was a fall day and we drove to somewhere near the Delaware Water Gap, it might even have been Dingman's Falls. I remember it being heavily wooded, with narrow twisting roads, pines and little country stores. Like Maine, that is beautiful country, and I agree whole heartedly that after my return we'll have to go up there. Maybe we can even find that cottage on the private lake.

Hey, do you know what! Just as I mentioned Maine on the last page, I heard two officers a bunk away talking about a scenic spot. I asked one if he were from Maine and he said he was from Stroudsburg, Pennsylvania. I asked him if he'd ever heard of Dingman's Falls and he said "Hell yes!" and it turned out to be only an hour or so from his home.

We've just now been talking about it. He says the most beautiful place around there is Shoe-String Falls. Cliché or no, it's a very tiny world, isn't it, Lamb?

I surely do love you and miss you, Chicki, and I hope and pray that I'll be able to get out after 21 months. My tour in Korea would be cut by nearly half! It sounds good, sweetie; I just can't wait to see you again. What a day it will be! How can one person love another as much as I love you?

Good night, dear sweet wife. I love you with all my heart and soul, I think of you and pray for us always.

My love,
Bill

* * *

22 Sept. 53

Hi Lamb,

There was much excitement here this afternoon when our orders were finally published. Next stop: Inchon. We've drawn our field equipment, i.e., blankets, mess gear, poncho, and the like. There is only one catch. Our ship still hasn't arrived yet. The latest poop is that we'll take the USNS Walker, which (ha-ha) left the Port of San Francisco four days after I left by plane. Its Far East first stop will be Yokohama. Then we expect it to come into Sasebo and give us a ride.

They say the shipboard chow is first rate—steaks and ice cream. Personally, I have decided the time is high to lose weight. I've been trying to eat only meat, vegetables and fruit and go easy on starch, sugars and grease. Have noticed no results yet; maybe I'll do better when I start to exercise (or when I quit drinking Pepsi).

The sore throat is gone, but I'm still resting and reading. I talk as if there is an alternative. I'm now reading "The Legacy" by Nevil Shute. He also wrote "Pied Piper" and "Pastoral." I read "Pastoral" at Lawrenceville and I recall it being very good.

I would like very much to have you send me "The Bible and You." I know Dr. Erdman, or at least have met him on several occasions through Wawee, and your report of his book sounds very interesting. When I look back on the night we propped ourselves up in bed and read most of the book of Revelation, I get a very warm, happy, close feeling. You are such a sweet, darling, considerate angel. I love you so terribly much. It's very sad that we are both so lonely. It's awfully hard to be apart. I pray that God will see fit to bring to realization a shortened tour of duty here, and bring us together again in half the time we originally planned on. You are such a darling Pumpkin. I love you so completely, Lucy. I can't even put it into words. I just keep repeating it to you over and over again. I mean it, sweetie, with all my heart and soul!

I am constantly trying to condition myself so that I will never be critical of you again. I don't know if I'm making any progress, but I am working on it and asking God's help. The same goes for grumpiness. I really want so much to be the sort of person you will always love, admire and respect.

One thing I know. During our first two years of marriage we have, and will have gone through, so many problems and trials together that we will be so rock-bound as husband and wife that we could survive any test. Our love, Lucy, is with God, the strongest and most powerful thing that has ever happened in my life. It is also the most wonderful.

The announcement just came over the loud speaker. We will ship Thursday, Sept. 24th, at long last! The shipboard transit time is about 36 hours, as was the plane trip to Japan, and as was the train ride from Tokyo.

Then, when we arrive in Korea, we will go into another Replacement Depot, I hope for a shorter length of time!

Incidentally, I just talked to that M.P. lieutenant from Ft. Sill who was with us at C.B.R. School. We saw again him when we had our car inspected by the Post M.P.'s this spring. He's on his way to Korea now after having spent six weeks at Camp Zama, Yokohama, where John and

I visited Mary Dot. I can't remember his name, but I'll think of it later. He wasn't too sure he knew Mary Dot.

I wrote her yesterday thanking her for showing me such a good time in Yokohama. I also wrote Mom & Pop about her birthday and the present I had sent. I still should write Chris and Aunt Wawee.

Goodnight, Pooh. I pray that God will always watch over and guide us. I love you very dearly.

Sweet dreams and cuddles,

Bill

* * *

23 Sept. 53
Wednesday

Dearest Chicki,

We are still here at Sasebo, existing and nothing more. We are scheduled to leave tomorrow at 12:45 PM, but it looks now as if we won't board the ship until Friday. It means just another day of sitting around with nothing to do except think about how much I miss you and worry about you every now and then. It gets very depressing after a while, and as you can see I am feeling very low tonight. The worst part about it is that surroundings and life in general will probably get worse before they get better. I so hope and pray that I'll be able to get out after 21 months. That's the bright spot on the horizon, along with your love and God's.

Last night we took a Japanese bus into Sasebo and went to the Allied Officers Club for dinner, which was very good. The band wasn't too bad; they had a good jam session. But the singer was so thoroughly Japanese in appearance and pronunciation that for my money, she ruined every song she sang. It reminded me of the little "Made in Japan" toys we used to get in the States before the war, sort of cheaply made, shoddy imitations.

Four of us took that bus together at great risk to life and limb. Hartman Axley, the M.P. Lt. from C.B.R. School, Walt Kiley, and a big R.A. (Regular Army) 1st Lt. from Shreveport who is not too bad a sort.

There's no need anymore to cuss out the Army. Everybody just takes for granted a sort of continual disgust for the immediate job and this place. That's true here. I can't speak yet for Korea.

The bus ride in and the taxi ride back last night, wow! The road is under construction, very winding and hilly, about as narrow as our driveway. The right-of-way had no fence or wall, and on many occasions I could look out the window straight down into deep water or a steep ravine. The driver thought he was on the Pike's Peak Labor Day Hill Climb. We hurdled around blind corners on the wrong side of the road and rumbled across rickety wooden bridges without railings. I imagine the little Nipponese driver figured he and his bus could demolish any other traffic, but I wonder if he thought the bus would float. Typically, he leaned on the horn the entire trip.

Latest poop: We load on the ship at noon Friday and sail at midnight—should arrive at Inchon noon Sunday.

During the course of this letter my morale has lifted considerably. That is, from rock bottom to medium low!

Walt just came in and wants me to join him and the R.A. 1/Lt. at the Officers Club. It may help the morale to have a few beers and throw a little bull.

I love you, darling Chicki. I love you with all my heart and soul, passionately, tenderly, and in a friendly companionable sort of way. You are all I have and desire, you are the symbol of a happy wonderful life. You are my beloved wife. I miss you terribly, I love you completely.

Goodnight, darling.

Bill

* * *

24 Sept. 53

Lucy dearest,

"Subject, of course, to change," it stated in the notice, but we are now officially slated to depart this station at five-thirty tomorrow afternoon. I think this time we will finally be on our way again. Our records have been air-carried to Korea, so perhaps the delay won't be as long there as we were expecting.

My morale is better today, although I did absolutely nothing but sit around and read and eat C Rations and see a fairly crummy flick this afternoon. I got a cheerful letter from you today and that makes all the difference. It was written the Sunday a week before you started college. I love to hear about beautiful, crisp, sunny fall days, and Sunday dinner with turkey, and TV in the evenings. We've had clouds continually for the past week and rain every other day. It's been muggy, hot mostly, until today, when it gradually turned cooler with some wind. We may be in for a little outside edge of the typhoon that's south of Okinawa.

The biggest excitement of recent days occurred when a local chimney caught fire, and in charged two big red, wailing fire engines and an ambulance. It was short-lived, however, because one of the Japanese cooks put out the fire in a stove, and that stopped the fire in the chimney. The engines never got a chance to squirt an ounce. Too bad; it could have been quite a show!

I forgot to mention this because it has become so commonplace, but we sleep under mosquito bars every night. I didn't use them the first night we were here since I hadn't seen any mosquitoes, and the bar cuts off the last of the breeze. However, after our stern lecture on Oriental diseases, and malaria particularly, I rigged it. Still haven't seen a mosquito or heard any buzzing, although many here have reported encounters.

You know, talking about being critical, especially if one (who, me?) had those tendencies, I believe that a general unhappiness in one's job and frustrations tend to make it more of a potential pattern. I'm not belittling or excusing past behavior in myself in the least. I have just been thinking hard and trying to work myself into the reverse pattern. I'm going to change that pattern, sweetie. I so fully want to.

I love you, Chicki. I hope and pray everything is going well with you! Now that you're into your first week at school, I hope you're enjoying it and happy and everything is working out. You are so wonderful, Lucy; your welfare and happiness are of the utmost importance to me. You're my wife, a very valuable, precious, darling half of me, whom I love very much and miss. May God watch over and carefully guide us both until that glorious day when we come running to meet each other with arms outstretched.

I love Lucy,
Bill

* * *

25 Sept. 53
1300

Hi Lucy,

About four hours from now, we'll be loading on the buses for the ride to the naval base. The Far East Radio Network weather report just announced that the rain will stop just about the time we load, and the temperature for the next 24 hours will range from 63 to 75 degrees. We'll have a windy and overcast ocean voyage, but the temperature is right. Am I ever glad to leave! It's been announced that we are to turn in our sheets and blankets, so departure looks certain.

It was also announced that no mail came in today, so I didn't venture out in the rain to the Post Office.

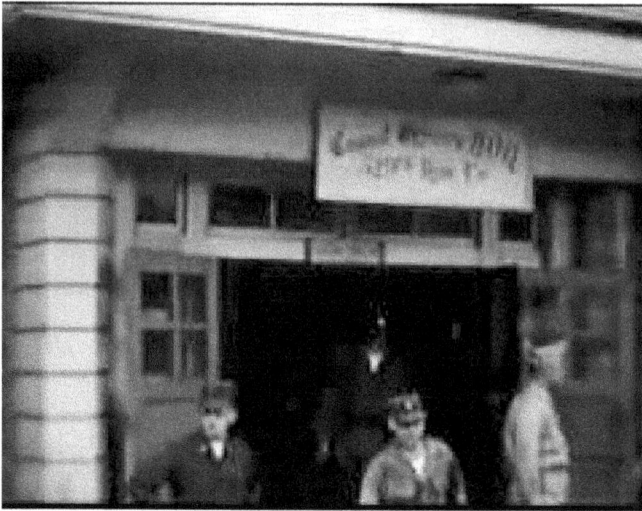

In uniform for Korea.
Video Link: http://lovelettersfromthefront.com/videos

I slept all morning after having gotten up for 0700 breakfast, got up again and shaved before lunch. As soon as I end this letter, I'll turn in the linen and repack my duffel bag for the hundredth time so my issue blankets will be on top, right under my field jacket and raincoat. Then I'll take a shower, pack all last-minute details, check the PX for movie film and the Post Office for a letter, and I'll be all set.

I'll be so glad to be doing something again, so I can get the staleness of Sasebo out of my system. It will be great to find out about the potential Early Release and start my last, and I hope shortest, tour of army duty.

I love you with all my being, my love. May God watch over us.
Love always,
Bill

* * *

4
From the Yellow Sea to the 49th

26 Sept. 53

Hi cutie,

If you measure happiness in terms of chow, we're really living! I'll tell you about it in a second.

We boarded the USNS Gen. Nelson M. Walker about six yesterday afternoon while she was tied at the pier in Sasebo harbor. Nine of us were assigned a compartment about half the size of our bedroom over the garage in Summit. I don't mind the cramped spaces too much anymore except that all our gear is piled in one corner and it requires moving eight 50-pound bags to get to yours. The compartment is arranged with six bunks on one side in three tiers and three bunks on the other side, one atop another. I arrived in the cabin first and quickly chose the top bunk on the three-bunk side. This way, nobody has to climb over you, stepping on your face, after you are in the sack.

After we got situated, we went on deck and watched as the E.M. filed aboard with their duffel bags over one shoulder. We stood and watched the sun go down over the high green hills, and the lights of Sasebo and the harbor came twinkling on one by one. Finally a full yellow moon glided out from behind a high bank of clouds, bathing the harbor and ship in a pale yellow glow. I thought of you the entire evening. At eleven we cast off the lines and were pulled away from the pier. Slowly we started moving down the long harbor, passing many American and British naval vessels. We could see them dimly in the moonlight as well as by the lights on their decks and in the portholes. They were all at anchor. We first passed several British Light Cruisers, then an American

Destroyer Tender with her little Destroyers tied along side. We passed a hospital ship lit up like a Christmas Tree, with a red cross in lights on her funnel. Finally, down at the entrance of the harbor we steamed past the mighty, sleek battleship New Jersey. It was a wonderful sight. I surely stumbled into the wrong ROTC program at Princeton. The navy's got it made!

Cruising the Yellow Sea.
Video Link: http://lovelettersfromthefront.com/videos

I stayed on deck until midnight and then retired to our 8' x 15' compartment complete with eight roommates. Not having a porthole to reveal the morning sun, and not being situated on a main passageway, meant that nothing woke us until I looked at my watch at nine this morning. Wonderful sleep. I've got a great sack, right under the fresh-air vent. The vibration and gentle rocking of the ship puts you right to sleep.

When I stepped onto the floor I realized it was a little more than just gentle rocking. It was a few minutes before I could stand without being toppled over against one or another of the bunks. When I got on deck,

I found it wasn't especially rough but we were going broadside to the waves and rolling with every swell. There was a strong breeze, with whitecaps, and the flying fish were making the most of it. They'd shoot to the surface, wriggling from stem to stern, then spread their fins and glide along the crests of the waves, finally diving into one when gravity took over.

Well, I've seen Korea and am now ready to take the first available transportation back the other way.

We passed the southwestern tip of Korea this morning and saw some of the offshore islands in the distance. We then left the East China Sea and are presently steaming up the west coast of Korea out of sight of land, in the Yellow Sea. It's supposed to be yellow because all the Orientals from China, Manchuria, and Korea dump their garbage into it. Out here it looks as blue as any sea I've ever seen. It could even be the ocean off Mantoloking or Norwalk. Despite being miles away from home and you, I don't feel very far at all. You are very close to me, darling; you're right here, everywhere I go.

After watching the water and the fish and land, I headed for chow. It was the first free meal on the government, free! And it was the best one they've yet served me. The floor of the dining room was green linoleum squares, the walls were light green. The chairs were an aluminum variety with cushioned seats and backs in faux leather. The tables were a long banquet type with white cloths and set with two forks and knife and two spoons, a coffee cup and a glass drinking glass. From one end to the other, the center of the table was loaded with dishes of fresh fruit, olives, celery, cookies, real butter, bread, crackers, scallions, etc. Then there were all sorts of condiments, real cream instead of evaporated milk for the coffee, and your individual salad. We gave the mess boy our orders, and for the rest of the meal he hovered at our elbows, doing his best to supply our every need. The dessert was hot apricot pie (which I usually won't touch) and the best coffee you ever tasted. It's a lovely cruise!

★ UNITED STATES NAVY ★

U.S.N.S. GENERAL

O.H. FRIZ
MASTER

MILITARY SEA TRANSPORTATION SERVICE

SATURDAY   MENU   26 SEPTEMBER 1953
                L U N C H E O N

GREEN ONIONS   PICKLES   OLIVES

SLICED CUCUMBER AND TOMATO SALAD WITH DRESSING

ENGLISH BEEF BROTH WITH BARLEY

VEAL FRICASSEE WITH BUTTERED NOODLES

ROAST LOIN PORK WITH APPLESAUCE

ASSORTED COLD CUTS WITH POTATO SALAD

BUTTERED FRESH PEAS

CAULIFLOWER AU GRATIN

BOILED POTATOES

STEAMED RICE

APRICOT PIE

PRESERVED FRUIT AND ASSORTED COOKIES

CHEESE: BLEU CHEDDAR AM. PROC. SWISS

FRESH FRUIT IN SEASON

COFFEE   HOT TEA   COCOA   ICED TEA

The Navy fed us well.

Incidentally, I finished off my Japan roll of film with our preparations for the ocean voyage, and mailed it from Sasebo. It isn't a very comprehensive picture of Japan, but there are plenty of shots of your husband looking foolish. In the rush of posting the film I forgot to enclose air mail postage for the return of the film after it had been developed in Hawaii. I'm very sorry, but it may be several weeks in arriving. The same goes for the first film I mailed.

After lunch I took a few shots of the ship and then got Walt Kiley to take some of me. The day we left Sasebo the PX got a new shipment of film in and I bought five rolls at $3.00 a roll. Cigarettes on shipboard go for $0.85 per carton, the very best $9.00 Scotch sells for $1.60 a fifth!

A few fill-in details: The Gen. Walker is a large, 611-foot, twin-stack, civilian-style steamer. She was built in 1945 to carry 4,000 troops and a crew of 300. We have 4,100 troops aboard, so the extra 100 have been assigned to the brig. To prevent them—all 100—from becoming hardened, habitual convicts like so many jailbirds, a chaplain has been appointed as their compartment commander!

You know, sweetie, what a Chicki you are and how much I love you. I love getting your letters every day, because that's the most tangible contact I have with you. I know that some days you are busier than others and that some days not many obviously reportable things happen. You many not realize it, Chicki, but anything you do, see, hear or feel is fascinating to me and I love you so much that anything and everything you do I'd love hearing about. Tell me that you love me and that I'm a bit of a chicki too, just as if we were talking on the telephone together.

I love you, Lucy. I love everything about you. I love being with you and talking to you and touching you. You are a very wonderful person and wife. I don't know how I could have been so fortunate as to have married you. I love you, Lamb, very completely. I pray that God will take care of us and give us the strength to do His will.

Goodnight, wonderful wife.

Bill

Dearest Lucy,

The Lieutenant has landed and the situation is well in hand. We hit the beach at Inchon as the noon whistle blew, shouldered our barracks bags, which for some odd reason seem to increase in weight every day, and walked about half a mile to the trucks. I got some good shots of the harbor. With loaded bag and baggage, we started off through the battered city of Inchon, out through a green valley, and 12 miles along a route marked U.S. 2 to Yong Dong Po. That's where we are spending tonight, in a compound known as the 34th Replacement Company, not very many miles from Seoul.

I have been assigned to the 7th Infantry Division for further assignment to an artillery battalion supporting a regiment of that division. The division patch is a red circle with a black hour glass inside. It's also known as the crushed beer can. The only person I know of with the 7th is James Clark, so maybe I'll get to see him. I'm not sure yet (actually, somewhat doubt) whether the 7th was the division I'd have asked for, if I'd had a choice, but I guess I'd better begin liking it now.

Amazing as it might seem, stepping into Korea is not like stepping into another world. Very decidedly, living conditions have deteriorated from California and Camp Stoneman as we have traveled westward. If I were plopped straight from Stoneman to the 34th Repl. Co. it would have been a rude shock, but Camp Drake and Sasebo have provided us a gentle letdown. The native populations from California westbound have also greatly deteriorated in affluence, paralleling our living conditions. If we thought Japan after WW II was primitive and slum-like, Korea is much worse.

Inchon harbor activity.
Video Link: http://lovelettersfromthefront.com/videos

I hardly know where to start. My movies should give you a much more complete idea than I could write in a thousand words. What movies don't reveal is the smell.

Next day: It has now become the 28th of September. They turned out the lights on me while I was writing last night. As I said before, our compound is set right in the residential district of town, best described as one of the worst slums you ever saw, complete with broken-down shacks made of any available material and complete lack of what we call sanitation.

The troops land and head inland.
Video Link: http://lovelettersfromthefront.com/videos

Our BOQ is a Quonset hut complete with double-deck canvas army cots on wooden frames. We have rubber mattresses that you blow up like a surf mattress. They are comfortable but only partially protect you from the biggest fault of canvas cots: cold air coming through the canvas beneath you. The BOQ is right on the edge of a barbwire-enclosed compound, five yards from our outhouse-type latrine, and ten yards from the nearest row of shacks. The populace saves their excrement for fertilizer but will urinate anyplace, anytime. The combined smell pervades the atmosphere.

Our wash-house is a unique affair. Down one side of the room is a counter equipped with a long row of uncovered, evenly spaced holes, like an elongated outhouse. In each hole a steel helmet is located, upside down. You walk in, pick up a helmet, fill it from either a lukewarm or cold water tap, carry it back to the stand, and wash. A very good arrangement when plumbing is in short supply.

It's all true, what we were warned about the town kids being experienced pickpockets. Yesterday six of us walked down to the Yong Dong Po PX through the crowded, dusty, dirty streets, amid the beggars, past the endless sidewalk markets. On the return trip a crowd of eight-to-ten-year-olds began following us, shouting out, trying to sell us handkerchiefs and paperback books. I tightened the grip on my essential movie camera. However, the next thing Kiley knew, his breast pocket pen and pencil, with the quick flick of a wrist, had been hooked onto the cover of a paperback and were being carried away on the run. He reflectively lunged out, grabbed the youngster, rescued his pen and pencil, and threw the paperback over a nearby roof. The kids hurriedly vanished. Kiley's pen and pencil had been in his breast pocket with the flap closed and buttoned!

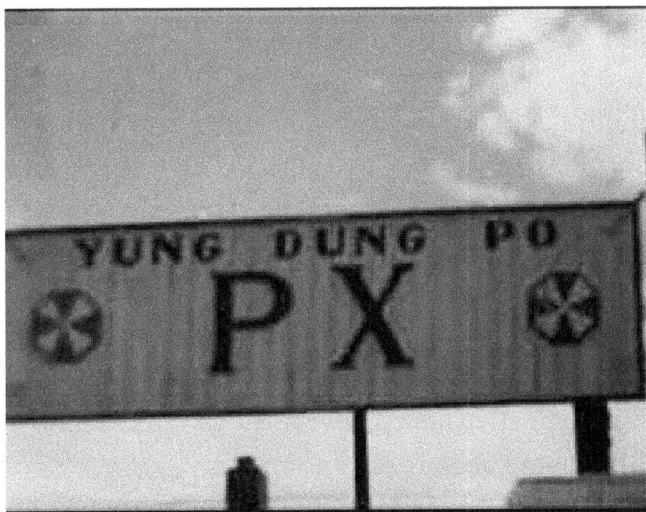

Our lodgings, neighbors, and the broken city of Seoul.
Video Link: http://lovelettersfromthefront.com/videos

This afternoon the kids were around at the back of our compound, calling through the chain link fence, offering to sell us Parker 51 pens or similar articles at a dollar a throw. They certainly are hustlers. Later we had a good laugh about the ironic pun of this operation which is literally "fencing" stolen articles.

We leave at noon for the 7th Division. I should be able to give you my new address either this evening or tomorrow.

I know you'll enjoy the movies when they arrive. I can't wait to get home and see them.

I love you, Lucy, with all my heart and soul. You are a wonderful, darling, perfect Lamb. I'll write again tonight if I can possibly find a chance.

See you later, Chicki.

Your loving, faithful husband,

Bill

* * *

29 Sept. 53

Dearest Cutie,

It's a beautiful, sunny, warm day, for the present at least. We are in scenic country. The 7th Repl. Co. of the 7th Division is located off the main valley road among beautiful rugged green hills. As soon as the sun went down last night, it began to rain and got quite chilly. Not having any heat or lights in this temporary tent, we all climbed into our arctic-type sleeping bags before seven last night and slept snug and comfortable until after six this morning. Our living conditions are much as if we were camping out in Maine; however, a few of the more pleasurable comforts of home are added, such as an outlet for my electric shaver! Although our washroom consists of a five-gallon water can, a steel helmet, and water that is icy cold, it certainly does serve as an eye opener and waker upper if you need one after eleven hours of sound sleep.

Enroute to the 7th Div. The countryside and F-86 jets.
Video Link: http://loveslettersfromthefront.com/videos

At noon yesterday we took a truck from our grubby old compound at Yong Dong Po, where the food, incidentally, was the world's worst, to the Seoul railway station. I stopped long enough in front of the station to get some good shots of the gutted, roofless buildings as well as an old bearded man in his Korea garb, a swarm of children running around, and some enterprising want-a-be shoeshine boys.

We got on the most ancient, rundown train you have ever seen, at one in the afternoon, and crept slowly north through the drizzle, making many stops and poor time.

At four, we reached the 7th Div. railhead and were met by a lieutenant and escorted to a couple of waiting trucks. We then drove south and east for a while, over recently oiled dirt roads, past the 7th Div. headquarters encampment, to this replacement company. Here the lieutenant gave us a short, embarrassed speech of welcome and we signed in on the register and handed over our remaining records to the personnel sergeant for processing. We then drew our arctic sleeping bags, were assigned to two newly erected squad tents, and took off for the officers' mess.

The mess turned out to be a squad tent with a wooden floor, rolled-up walls and two long tables. Dinner was served by a Korean boy on enameled metal plates and was quite tasty. We wolfed down cheeseburgers, creamed corn, mashed potatoes and lemonade, with chocolate pie, coffee and vitamin pills for dessert. By the time we set up our sleeping bags and canvas cots (without an air mattress), it had gotten dark and we discovered that, unlike most of the other tents, we had no electricity. A couple of brave souls ventured over to the supply tent and returned with a half-dozen candles, but these proved to be of little use in creating any degree of heat, or even much light, so we all decided to turn in.

To refresh your memory, a squad tent, 20' x 40', is exactly the same as my old Easy Battery Hq. tent at the FARTC in Ft. Sill. They normally sleep 6 officers or 11 E.M. to a tent. Twenty-three of us are here awaiting assignments in the 7th Div., five in one tent, eighteen in another, so you can see that with all our gear, it's more than a little crowded.

This morning after washing with ice water, in the dark and cool before dawn, we hiked over to mess for a breakfast of fried eggs and bacon. After a good cup of coffee, back to our tent, we repacked our gear and drew our steel helmets and liners. By this time the sun had risen over the hills and the new daylight had cut the chill from the air.

A half hour or so later we formed up and marched the half mile down to Division Headquarters to the briefing and orientation building.

Our first speaker was Maj. Gen. Trudeau, 7th Division Commander. He seemed like a no-nonsense, good man, tough and smart. He gave an interesting talk, saying he realized that none of us wanted to be here and many of us were civilians at heart. He presented quite a good pep talk on character and ended up saying that the experience we get here working with men, he believes, will be more valuable later in civilian life than if we were actually at home working in a civilian job. Maybe so, or maybe no. It is, however, an interesting thought. Additionally, it is very encouraging to think that this time is not a total loss, that we are working, building and developing leadership skills toward a better future. Something positive to keep thinking about.

After the General's talk we all filed by and shook his hand. Then various members of the staff gave us briefings on the enemy-and-friendly situation and on supply and allied problems. Most of the information was classified secret; still, I can give you a basic idea of where the 7th is and what is near us. Our present location on a map is halfway between Seoul and the 38th parallel. We are in "I" Corps in the western part of Korea. After the shooting stopped, the 7th Div. was pulled off the line and placed in corps reserve. This is what is known as a damn good deal if you're in the 7th!

The main job of the 7th now is to build a secondary line of resistance to be used if the shooting starts again and if the main line (the truce line) were broken through. Because artillery is never placed in reserve, the 7th Division Artillery is now situated just behind the 1st Marine Division to give them additional firepower on the line. I can't think of any more reliable ground troops than the Marines that I'd rather support. Naturally there are extensive operations and preparations under way in case of renewed hostilities, and we are receiving premium combat pay, but your knowledge of the chances for a permanent truce are as good as, if not better than, mine.

After all the orientations we strolled back here for chow and then drew more equipment, pup tents, etc. Now we are waiting for transportation to those units to which we will momentarily be assigned.

By tomorrow I should be able to give you my new address and also the possibilities of the 19 or 21 month Early Release program.

I love you, Lucy, more than I can ever say. You are very precious to me, Pooh, I think of you constantly.

Your devoted husband,

Bill

30 Sept. 53
Arrived an hour ago.

Dearest Chicki,

Just a couple of words to give you my new address and to tell you that I love you with a tremendous, everlasting devotion.

It's late now and past time to hit the sack. I'm with Baker Battery of the 49th Field Artillery Battalion of the 7th Infantry Division. The 49th Bn. normally supports the 17th Infantry Regiment of the 7th Division, but since our division is in reserve (and artillery never goes into reserve), the 7th Division Artillery temporarily is in "general reinforcing support" of the 1st Marine Division. Our 49th Bn. is currently supporting the 1st Korean Regiment of the 1st Marine Division. That's a mighty mouthful, but explains exactly what we're doing.

I had dinner with Lt. Col. Moore, the Battalion Commander, and Maj. Lathrop, the Battalion Executive Officer. Both are widely known to be first-rate officers and outstanding leaders. I am more than pleased with my assignment. The surrounding countryside is beautiful. The Baker Battery Commander, Capt. Sosa, and officers here are the very best I've met.

I'll write more details tomorrow. I love you tenderly, with all my heart and soul. I think of you constantly, and pray for us every day.

Goodnight, Lamb.

My Love,

Bill

* * *

1 Oct. 53

Lucy m'love,

Well, I finally have arrived after four vagabond weeks of vacationing and sightseeing. We are located in a very pleasant area with low but steep scrub-pine-covered hills. Scattered among the hills are many abandoned rice paddies, and along some of the hard-packed dirt roads grow tall, slender poplar trees. We are at the extreme west end of the truce line, about two miles southwest of what I believe is the junction of the Han and Imjin Rivers and not far from Freedom Village where the truce negotiators are located.

Since the 7th Division is now in corps reserve, we are currently supporting the First Korean Regiment of the First Marine Division. The sector we are in now was called the R&R sector due to the fact that the river in front of us is bordered by quicksand on either side, which makes crossing by the enemy virtually impossible.

I have been assigned as Motor Officer of Baker Battery of the 49th Field Artillery Battalion; however, tomorrow I'm going up on the hill to the Battalion OP (observation post), which is a few hundred yards from Charlie Battery, for a week of simulated Forward Observing. I should have lots of time then to write you some more complete details on what I've been doing since I left the 7th Repl. Company.

I've been really busy during the last two days getting orientated and organized. It's a curious thing that everything I do and see and hear is infused with thoughts of telling you about it and trying to imagine what you'd think about it. You are constantly in my thoughts, Chicki, and I love you very, very dearly.

John Hurbert is in this Battery, and there are several other Princeton lads in other Battalions of 7th Division Artillery. Roger McLean is the one you probably know best, but I'll tell you about the rest when I have more time.

The officers here say time goes very fast. I hope so for you, as well as for me. I can't wait until the time when I will take you in my arms and hold you tight and tell you in person how strong and everlasting my love for you is.

Goodnight, angel,

Bill

P.S. Tomorrow will be the real beginning of my Korea experience of living outdoors in the hills and rice paddies of a combat zone during this "cease-fire" period. Tomorrow I will finally be looking across the river, face-to-face at the still potent enemy in his front yard. I can't imagine what it will be like, and I can't wait to find out.

5
The Hilltop Bunker

2 & 3 Oct. 53
8:30 PM

Dearest Chicken Pot Pie,

I'm writing both yesterday's and today's letter today. I promise to try to keep current. Yesterday was my amazing first day on the hill. I'll try to explain what it's like.

Climbing up, up, up to our hilltop bunker.
Video Link: http://lovelettersfromthefront.com/videos

The song on my mind is Home on the Range, but should instead be translated: Home on the Hill. I am sitting at a home-made table which is strewn with plastic-covered maps, on a stool which is made of one solid chunk of 12" x 12" lumber about 2 feet high. The light in this room consists of one candle set in a battered tin can. I feel like old Honest Abe studying his law books by the flickering fire. Or perhaps Sergeant York in a WW I trench, awaiting dawn and orders to scramble over the top and attack the Huns.

I just called this place a room. Actually the entire underground bunker is about the size of a modest twin bedroom. The floor and three sides of the room have been carved out of solid rock, in some places up to fifteen feet thick. The entrance is a narrow passage chipped through one of those fifteen-foot sections of solid rock. Back home, most houses have a roof built on 2" x 6" or 2" x 8" beams. Our roof is supported, in addition to solid rock, by 12" x 12" beams which run lengthwise along the ceiling. Crosswise above these beams are steel railroad rails. Above the rails are heavy wooden planks running lengthwise again, and above that is three feet of tightly packed earth and stone with weeds and vegetation growing on it. Around all the openings are piled tightly packed sandbags.

This must be the most heavily constructed forward observation post (OP) in Korea. Built by South Koreans two years ago, it consists of four small rooms and a narrow hallway. It isn't very pretty but is reasonably comfortable, and I marvel at the terrific labor and effort that the building required. Each one of these beams must weigh close to a thousand pounds and was carried up a hill so steep that it's a struggle to haul yourself up carrying nothing. More about the hill later.

Of the four "rooms", I am now in the observation room. The main item of equipment—besides the two homemade desks (a loose definition), a radio transmitter and receiver, two field telephones, water cans, sundry equipment, and one elusive rat that I can hear when dirt trickles from overhead, but have been unable to locate—is the Battery Commander's Telescope (BC scope). The BC scope is a binocular periscope (still with me?) mounted on a stand, with lenses that protrude from a small opening in the wall just below the roof. Sitting down inside the observation room, and completely concealed, I have a perfect view of the river in front of me and the hills across the river.

My "bedroom" is about 6' by 7', carved from solid rock, containing two wooden bunks built into the wall, one above the other. With an air mattress and arctic sleeping bag, comfort is unexcelled. My bedroom

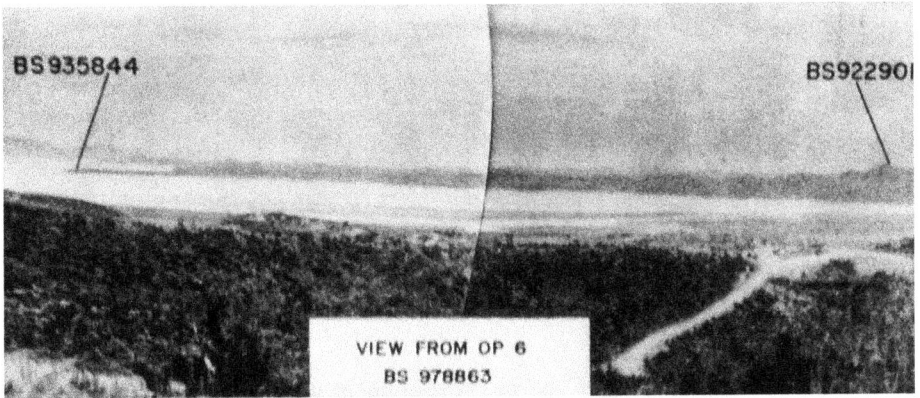

View of the Imjin River from our hilltop bunker.

connects to the rock hallway, which connects the other two cramped bedrooms to the observation room. It's a very neat arrangement, cool during the day and warm at night.

Our hill rises about 400 feet above the rice paddies and towers above all the neighboring hills on this side of the river. Like the others, this hill is covered with scrub pine and underbrush. The view from the top is wonderful, and peacefully scenic, although through the BC scope I can see North Korean/Chinese activity (more of that later). At the base of our hill and a little behind us, but almost straight down, is Charlie Battery. Baker is just the other side of Headquarters battery, about a mile up the road. Then comes Able and, a little farther, Service Battery.

A view of the Other Side.
Video Link: http://lovelettersfromthefront.com/videos

Baker Battery is just about four miles northeast of the junction of the Han and Imjin Rivers. The Imjin is the river out in front of us, and right here it runs north and south. We are facing west. The truce line runs along the two-mile wide river. Directly to the north, where the river bends, we can see the twinkling lights of the U.N. Indian base camp where (I think) the anti-communist POW's are being held pending repatriation.

There are three of us up here for the week; my reconnaissance sergeant, wireman, and me. We take turns going down to Charlie Battery for chow so that one of us, at least, is always up on the OP. The procedure for chow is to climb almost vertically halfway down the hill, where we meet the jeep in low-low gear and four-wheel drive which then bounces and jolts us down to the bottom.

The chow isn't bad. Usually we have juice, cold cereal, eggs (powdered, often) and French toast for breakfast. We get plenty of meat, canned vegetables, cheese, jam and occasionally hot rolls! No real butter, but what I miss most of all is fresh, sweet, bottled milk. All of our milk is either powdered or canned. It's barely passable in coffee, and for me, that's the extent of its use.

Most of all my thoughts, Chicki, I miss you. I love you so terribly much, Lucy; you are everything in the world to me. You are a wonderful, sweet, darling, precious, beautiful, loving wife. Always keep in mind that you are, for me, the most wonderful and valuable thing on earth.

Now to bring you up on a little recent history. I believe it was Wednesday morning when ten of us piled in a truck and were driven away from the 7th Replacement Co. First stop was Division Artillery Headquarters, then to one or another of the four artillery battalions of the division. At Div. Arty. Hq. I met Don Oberdorfer, an interesting classmate from Princeton, and another officer from William and Mary who knows Griffin and Dick Lewis. We had another orientation and then I was assigned to the 49th Field Artillery Battalion. A little while later a jeep from the 49th picked me up and, bag and baggage, we hit the road again.

Once arrived at 49th Bn. Hq., I met Lt. Col. Moore, the (West Point) Bn. CO, and the Bn. Exec., Maj. Lathrop. We walked over to the mess tent, quaffed a 3.2% beer, and ate dinner. After dinner a little army ditty, "Here's to Mac," etc., was sung in my honor by those Hq. Btry. officers present, and I was escorted back to the jeep and off to Baker. In the BOQ (squad tent) at Baker I found John Hurbert, several other officers, and Btry. CO Capt. Raphael Sosa, who seems a quiet, capable, likable gentleman of Hispanic descent. I believe he hails from Puerto Rico. I remained in the Btry. only one day and can't give you much of a report on it yet. The next day it became Baker Battery's week to man the Battalion Forward Observation Post (Bn. OP). I was the logical choice for a week on the hill; all the other officers had previously had a turn at the job. So here I am.

So far, so good. I like the people. I like where I am (if it must be Korea). Up here, it's comfortable, interesting, you get an idea of surrounding terrain, and except for routine observation report and instructional requirements, I'm my own boss. It is also a considerable responsibility. I am the sole eyes of the Bn. for the week, observing and reporting intelligence activity, if any, which can be detected on the other side of the river.

Who do you suppose is in Charlie Battery? Ray B. Jones. He came over with Griffin, whom he reported is in the 40th Div. Artillery. I haven't seen anybody who knows Bill Bliss or James Clark. Clark is probably in the 1st F.A. Observation Bn., which is now in the 25th Div. sector and probably 100 miles away. I suspect that having been in the army over two years, he is eligible for immediate release under Circular 61. I'll be able to give you more poop on people we know when I get back into circulation with the battery again.

As for my Early Release, I don't know too much more than I did a couple of weeks ago. At present writing, it is possible for a Category IV (that's me) to apply at the end of 18 months for release at the end of 19 or 21 months. It's up to the division commander. He makes his decision based on the availability of officers. If my 19 months were up now and I applied for release today, I'm sure it would be turned down. However, the officer situation is improving and there is a possibility that by February 11th, when my 18 months are up and I apply for release, it might be approved. However, I wouldn't plan on it.

I love you so very much, Lamb, and miss you so. My every thought is of you, and my only desire is to return home to you and be the person whom you love and cherish close at hand as well as spiritually.

Goodnight, darling wife. May God watch over, guide and protect both of us and grant that the time be short before we are reunited and life is complete for us again.

I love you with all my heart and soul,
Bill

* * *

4 Oct. 53

Hi Lamb,

It's been a very peaceful and beautiful Sunday. It got quite hot this afternoon and we received a few unofficial visitors. I felt somewhat like a Forest Ranger on his lookout tower pointing out local points of interest to the Sunday afternoon hikers perhaps somewhere in the area of Dingman's Falls. A Lieutenant from Service Battery brought up a group of men who had never been on an OP before and I showed them our maps and BC scope, and how I reported all movement of military importance on the other side of the river to Fire Direction Center (FDC), who plots it and then reports to the intelligence section, which collects all information for evaluation. The Lieutenant, who had previously told me that he was a veteran of the infamous Pork Chop Hill battle, where he was a Forward Observer (FO), then began observing through the BC scope. After a few minutes he gets all excited and says he sees a Chink truck going north on a road about three miles away, across the river. That would be reportable information, but before I reported it I needed to see it myself, fix its position on the map, and report the coordinates back to Fire Direction Center (FDC).

So I took a look through the BC scope myself. The object was a little hazy and quite distant. But there was no mistaking it. I had seen them many times before; it was a farmer carrying a heavily loaded "A" frame on his back piled high with rice stalks. Next to him was walking a big, also heavily burdened, ox loaded down with rice stalks. I chuckled, told the Lieutenant what I saw and gave him another look. Sure enough, the grizzled, heavily experienced combat forward observer and artillery spotter agreed that perhaps he was actually looking at a farmer and his ox.

I had a good time while the Sunday hikers were visiting us. After they left, three Korean Marines stopped by our hilltop to return a shovel we had loaned them. Despite a little language difficulty, they stayed for quite a chat, pointing out the major positions that they hold in front of us. One of them told me he lived only two hours away from here and he hadn't been home in 18 months. They are sturdy little characters and their discipline is really tough.

After the sightseers left, I got out my Bible and conducted my own Sunday service. It's 8:15 in the evening now and I expect in another five hours you'll be in church. I wonder if you will be in the Scarsdale church where we married, or in Orange, or even in Bronxville. You have finished two weeks of school now. I hope the weather is still nice and that it's a glorious, crisp autumn morning. I love you so very much, Lucy. One thing this backward, poverty-stricken land teaches us is how lucky we are to live in such a wonderful country. With all of its faults and shortcomings, the United States is a magnificent land.

Another thing I learned by being away is how overwhelmingly important you are to me. I guess a person appreciates most the things he has when their removal exposes their prior matter-of-fact importance. I mean you, sweetie. I appreciate and cherish you now more than ever because having to live away from you like this makes me realize more than ever how very important you are to me and how very much I love you—you are such a darling pumpkin.

The last letter I've gotten from you was #15, written on 15 September, almost three weeks ago. I'm hoping, now that I have a permanent address, my mail will soon catch up to me. How long does it take my letters to get to you? It should be about six days. I can't wait to hear how the movies are turning out. I can't help but wonder and worry a little about how things in general are working out for you.

They issued us some of our winter clothing a few days ago, including heavy liners that button into the field jacket, field trousers of the same material, and O.G.'s. That is something new—Olive Greens. They are heavy wool flannel of a brownish dark green. They are very warm, and quite sporty when worn open-necked with the artillery's bright red silk scarf tucked at the throat inside the shirt.

I read in the Stars and Stripes that Princeton just squeaked by in its first game of the season, 20-14. They played a reportedly weak Columbia yesterday. Tomorrow I'll be able to see that score, but there won't be much of a write-up. Do you suppose you could send me the Sunday sports section each week until football season is over?

We listened to the rebroadcast of the second game of the World Series a few days ago. It was the Dodgers' second loss in as many games of the series. Hope you are pulling for them. They've won many National League Pennants, but never a World Series.

You know, it's funny how various expressions become popular. Remember the old "Whattsa matter, ya got rocks in yer head"? Well, around here there are two very popular and widespread expressions in addition to extensively used Japanese words for "many" and "few." One is "This place (or that person) doesn't show me anything." More often than not, the expression is modified to: "This place doesn't show me manure" (or words to that effect). The other common expression, a little more polite than the first but equally as widespread, is used when someone does something favorable or when some event turns out well: "There you go." It is spoken with a high inflection on the first word and a lowered inflection on the second two words. A little out of context, this expression was used by the mess steward back at Division Artillery Hq. I asked for "cream" for my coffee and he said, "There you go" and hustled off to the kitchen to get it. It's a very handy expression. It doesn't mean anything, but is handy, since it can be used at any time and for any occasion.

Well, sweetie, it's about time for me to wake my relief and then hit the sack.

Remember, Lucy, I think of you constantly, love you always and pray for us every day. Goodnight, precious Lamb.

I love Lucy,

Bill

5 Oct. 53

Dearest Lamb,

Well, here I am again, back at the same rat-infested bunker, at the same old map "desk" with the same old tin can in front of me, but with a new candle burning in it.

There has been little excitement since I wrote you last night, except tonight I took the ten until two AM shift, partly because I managed a two-hour nap this afternoon and partly I wanted to see the movie down in Charlie Battery.

I had dinner in their mess as usual and after dinner went up to their BOQ and talked to Jones about the old days in Ft. Sill BOC school and where all the crowd is now. We had a drink in celebration of his and Maxine's first wedding anniversary, which was yesterday. He seemed a little forlorn at times, but then who isn't.

The movie was a rather second-rate old affair, a musical in Technicolor, but it was enjoyable. The hero's name was Bill and when the girl started telling him how much she loved him, I closed my eyes and it sounded just like you. For a couple of seconds I almost thought it was you. It was wonderful, Lucy; it made me feel all warm and close to you. I can't help but wonder that maybe you were thinking about me at the time. I love you so, Chicki.

It was a warm, sunny day and I got some shots at the hill and the OP, and tomorrow if the sun is right, I'll have my Recon. Sgt. get some shots of me shaving or something, and then try to take a sequence through the BC scope. If it turns out, it should really be interesting. Someday we can show our movies, like that African explorer we once met! We'll call it "A Glimpse Behind the Iron Curtain" and charge fabulous prices for each showing. I'll try to get some action on film, but all you'll probably see through the 'scope is an ant-sized little Korean farmer struggling under a heavy "A" frame, leading a similarly loaded ox.

Even up here on the OP without electricity, the electric shaver has them all beat! I "procured" a 90-volt radio battery from the communications section, inserted wire into the battery terminals, connected the other end to my shaver plug, and away it hums. It is much superior to the safety razor because there is no hot water up here. Our washing equipment consists of a five-gallon water can, hand carried up the hill, and a steel helmet. While I am on the subject, we have an open-air outhouse affair that is just about as private as Grand Central Station at rush hour. It really struck me as humorous. It is situated on the almost sheer backside of our hill about 25 yards from the top. You can, from that location, see the panorama of the landscape beneath you for miles and miles around, and I imagine vice versa. It is a wonderful spot, seemingly picked for its scenic beauty.

My poor Dodgers, they lost yesterday. The score in games is Yankees three, Dodgers two. The fist team to win four wins all. I bet you already knew that.

I wrote Mom and Pop tonight and also found Griffin's address and dropped him a line. If you send Grandmother's full name and address and Bob & Julie's and the Haywards' new address, I'll scribble them a line also.

I love you very, very dearly, my Pooh Bear. You are a wonderful, darling, perfect wife. Goodnight, Lucy. I'm always proud of you and adore you always.

Bill

* * *

6 Oct. 53

My darling Chicki,

At long last we, in this hilltop OP, have outgrown the flickering candlelight! We are now the proud operators of a gasoline lantern! Reading has been greatly facilitated and I have just finished "Uncle Pogo So-So Stories," cartoons by Walt Kelly. They are great. The animal pictures are inspired and the dialog is priceless. Another comfort improvement is a folded blanket between my sleeping bag and the air mattress on the flat wooden perch I call a bunk.

Like last night, I went down and saw another flick and am now on the ten-to-two AM watch. Tonight it was a Western, old, a bit funny in places, but too much of the singing-cowboy routine.

It was overcast most of today so I didn't get a chance to continue with the motion picture filming. However, I've had plenty of time to think up sequences. Besides the shot through the BC scope and your husband shaving, plugged into his radio battery, I'm going to try to get one of the Korean Marine Lieutenants up here for a typical "brotherhood week" or United Nations shot.

One of the Korean Marine Corps sergeants climbed up our hill today, a nice-looking, very polite, shy, young, diminutive character. However, the second I saw him laboring up the steep slope, I wrongly suspected that without doubt he intended to make off with our $2,000 BC scope, or at least our binoculars, or possibly our new pride and joy, the gasoline lantern. When he reached the top, huffing and puffing, I stood waiting for him. He had a big smile, and in very broken English said a pleasant "Good afternoon, sir." He seemed quite embarrassed, and after a long pause he slowly began pointing out on the hills below where various elements of his unit were located. After about five minutes, another pause. Then slowly he pulls out a flashlight and says, "Good flashlight, no batteries." I say, "Oh?" And he says, "You got batteries, maybe?" Well, as you know the U.S. Army, we have about twenty half-used batteries on one shelf in this OP, along with an almost empty 35-pound can of coffee, an old telephone-wire reel, an out-of date artillery field manual, a can of gummed linseed oil, and even two mail boxes! They are articles that could conceivably be of some value, but never seem to be just the thing you're looking for. I gladly gave the lad two of the batteries. He thanked me very graciously when I returned with the now workable flashlight.

I asked him about kimchi, the famous Korean dish, and he told me haltingly how it was made. Briefly, it is a mixture of cabbage, red peppers, garlic and salt. These are combined and aged for a week until they are well fermented. Then comes cooking, and we're ready to eat. It smells something awful, and anybody who has eaten it within the past day or so is plainly distinguishable by the aroma. Luckily, this young man's most recent meal had been rice and red peppers. He said that was his diet three times a day, with an occasional dried fish thrown in for supper. He also said he had never gotten a chance to go home, sixteen miles away, in the year and a half that he has been in the Korean Marines.

A little later he pulled out a fountain pen and wondered if we could fill it for him. Naturally, we happened to have a half a bottle of mostly dried-up ink on hand, and he was very happy. Finally, a little later he wanted to know if he came back tomorrow we could get him a loaf of bread from the mess hall. He volunteered to bring us some "rice chop" in return, which I politely declined. By this time it seemed quite possible that his safari to our OP might become a daily occurrence, so while trying to be polite and not let him lose face, I said that we could provide several slices of bread and a can of C Rations, that's been lying around here for a while, with an agreement that he come up here (only) one time each week.

This he accepted as a very satisfactory arrangement, and as we have several more cans of C Rations on our "miscellaneous junk" supply shelf, overall 8th Army efficiency will not be seriously crippled, nor will 7th Division operations be impaired. He left smiling, in a very appreciative mood. I think it will pay to keep on the right side of these good troops stationed on line in front of us, but I doubt we'll get chummy.

No letters from you yet! All the camps and post offices that I've recently traveled through are informed of my new address, so I am hoping to receive mail before too many more days go by.

I surely do miss you, Lamb; you are constantly in my thoughts in everything I do and experience. When I shave, I remember how you used to watch me. It was two years ago this fall. And when I heard about the red peppers I thought of that happy time with you at Tiko Molino, that carry-out restaurant across the street from the Japanese Gardens in San Antonio. I think of all the wonderful things we've seen and done together, since the first time I kissed you goodnight on the steps at 12 Ridgecrest West to the day we kissed goodbye at LaGuardia.

The thought of you makes me feel very sad in a way, but more than that, it makes me feel so close and loving and happy to know that such a wonderful person is mine and loves me and is waiting for me. And in the course of a few months, one glorious day I'll come home to you again, a civilian, and we can start a wonderful family and continue to build a wonderful life.

I love you, Lucy, with all my being. I pray that God watch over and guide us in the right path. Goodnight, perfect wife.

Your loving,

Bill

* * *

7 Oct. 53

Dearest Lamb,

I have come to the conclusion that my thrice-daily hill climb is doing me immense good. After chow, the first thing that I do is re-climb my hill; by the time I get to the top I'm hungry again and winded for about five minutes. After that I really feel great. Remember that first set of fatigues I bought that were always one size too tight at the waist? Now I've got to wear a belt to keep them on.

Backyard electric shaving on the hill.
Video Link: http://loveslettersfromthefront.com/videos

When I heard "Breaking the Sound Barrier" was tonight's flick, I had to see it again, so tonight I took the ten-to-two watch once more. Remember when we saw it at the drive-in? I wish I could take you to the movies tomorrow night. We'll go to the drive-in on Route 22 out past Howard Johnson's and put a couple of cold cans in the cooler. I sure do love you, chicki! Remember when we saw "Lili"? I have such wonderful times with you. You hummed the first sixteen notes of the song "Lili" as we were getting dressed to go out to the airport that last day home, and somehow they stuck in my head all the way from New York to California. Flying over Pennsylvania, I remembered the words that go with those notes. I starts out "The song of love is a sad song." It struck me as very comforting, knowing that other people have recognized that love can be sad at times. Sad that two people who love each other so completely have to be apart for a while, and then in a bigger sense, not all sad because a love so great as ours can only mature and grow stronger during that sad time the song "Lili" symbolizes for me.

Maybe I haven't explained it too well, but I feel that the sadness in the song is a promise for tomorrow and that tomorrow is with you, Lucy, and the happiest, most glorious thing I can think of. I love you so very much, precious wife, that I think I'm going to explode!

Don't worry if you haven't gotten your check for September. I didn't get to the Battery until after payday and I haven't had a chance since then to see Finance. I have a feeling my monthly expenses here are going to run less than half of what we previously figured, so I'll be saving up for your ring and a camera. Not only am I getting the combat pay bonus, part of my pay is tax-free. However, I doubt very much if I'll get to Japan between now and November 15, the Christmas package deadline. So I'm afraid your ring will have to wait and be a birthday present.

You are my most precious pumpkin and I love you very dearly. Goodnight, most adorable wife, I think of you every moment and pray for our guidance and welfare every night.

Lovingly, Passionately, Tenderly,
Your Bill

* * *

8 Oct. 53

Lucy m'love,

Today goes on record as the most eventful of the week on the OP and I'm very glad it's the last night I'll be sitting around on a four-hour watch. Tonight it's a six-hour watch, but I'll get to that later.

I got to bed this morning at 2:30 and was totally and happily conked out, relaxing on my air mattress, sound asleep, when sharply at seven, Phillips, my wireman, wakes me to tell me I've been paged on the telephone. Half-awake and half-dressed, I stumble to the phone and find out that today the combat situation has been designated "tactical" for the entire battalion and that my Liaison Officer, a FO's immediate boss, will be up in ten minutes to proclaim the straight poop on what's happening. A tactical situation is simulated combat with steel helmets, all troops carrying weapons, etc. About a half hour later, I am dressed and in a little more receptive mood and the straight-poop man arrives. I got a list of enemy activities which I am supposed to report and to direct fire missions on for the entire battalion, approximately every thirty minutes from now until 3:00 PM.

Then the fun begins and I start jumping from BC scope to map, figuring enemy locations, azimuths and back azimuths, coordinates, coding and decoding messages, and jabbering over radio and telephone. It being a simulated situation, naturally I put the battalion's 18 guns perfectly on target each time after about only three adjusting rounds. (I was also observing where the simulated rounds were landing.) Even so, I was doing the work normally performed by nine FO's, so you can guess I was doing some fast moving.

Observing the enemy.
Video Link: http://lovelettersfromthefront.com/videos

Around three o'clock they put the lid back on the problem and I mistakenly assumed the rest of the afternoon would be sack time. So I decided to wash up and shave but then decided it was a good day to work on my OP movies.

First I have a shot of your tired but devoted husband pouring water into his steel helmet and washing his grimy face. Then he shaves, first at a distance of fifteen feet and then a close-up. To achieve relief from this spectacle, there is then a shot of the valley down behind the OP and then a shot across the Imjin River into communist territory. Incidentally, I was somewhat in error when I previously gave you the height of this hill. It is actually 430 feet high. Then I took a shot through the right eyepiece of the BC scope, which has a grid on it with a little circle in the center. In the center of the circle you should be able to see two farmers walking across a field. Then I took another shot of a low hill through the clear eyepiece. There is reportedly an enemy OP on this particular hill. Then, to give you the feeling of its true distance, I next went outside and took the same shot without magnification. Then hamming it up again, I got out all my personal equipment and you'll see me sitting on the roof of the OP getting ready to fire a mission. In the next scene the mission has been shot, the war is all over, we won, and it's a close-up of me puffing on a Pall Mall again (because the PX doesn't sell any good cigarettes).

I suppose the enemy, across the river, is watching us as we watch them. Perhaps they took a few quick pictures of our (ill-advised) above-ground activities atop the OP and submitted them for publication to Pravda or some Chinese news magazine. Who knows, maybe before you know it, our OP will be identified and we will become famous personalities behind the Iron (or Bamboo) Curtain!

Naturally, by the time I put the camera away, I was being paged again. This time it was a lieutenant from Charlie Battery who warned me that he had just seen a major who seemed to be on his way to the OP. Immediately I got very busy teaching a class in Observed Fire Technique to my cohort of two.

When the Major arrived, he turned out to be the new Battalion Exec. (and I can't resist the temptation of saying it), freshly arrived from the States. He probably knows a lot more of what's going on around here than I do, and might be a fairly decent sort of character, but he surely had his troubles trying to work the BC scope. There are several knobs on the right of the scope, one of which adjusts the interpupillary (between the eyes) distance, and another rotates the head of the scope so that you can look from side-to-side.

I was looking out of the porthole while he adjusted the scope. Finally he informed me that the scope needed repairing because the knob was stuck and wouldn't move anything. When I came over to investigate, I saw that the knob he was straining with was the one that moves only half an inch for the eye adjustment. You can't very well tell your Bn. Exec. that he doesn't know how to operate a BC scope—not this one, anyway, from what I have heard—so I said yes, I thought the interpupillary-distance knob did need some oil. He grumbled a sort of a cough, fumbled around a few seconds with the other knob and came up with the winning combination, as the head of the scope swung from horizon to horizon.

Actually I'm not being very fair to the major, because it is quite dark in here when the lantern isn't lighted and it's possible that he was just trying to adjust the eyepiece knob, which actually does stick considerably.

As you can probably sense by the way this incoherent letter is written, I'm so tired I know that I've gotten punchy.

To complicate matters, Phillips gave himself a pretty bad burn on the arm early this evening and I had him escorted down to the medic, where they bandaged him up and gave him a shot of morphine. They also prescribed a full night's sleep, so instead of three of us doing a four-hour watch, there are two of us, each on a six-hour watch. A few more minutes and then my time will be up.

Tomorrow afternoon my party goes off the hill and the relief party arrives. I stay an extra day with the new party but I don't stand watch, so tomorrow night I'm looking forward to a full twelve-hour sleep.

Goodnight, precious, adorable wife. You are the most wonderful person in the world and I love you very tenderly.

Devotedly,

Your Lt.

* * *

10 Oct. 53

Dearest Lamb,

My letter writing has slowed down temporarily, but not through de-sign. It's because instead of being relieved from duty on the OP yester-day as planned, our entire battalion has packed up and moved out to a new position. Instead of last night's 12 hours of sleep, I took catnaps throughout the night whenever I got a chance and finally finished turn-ing over the OP at ten this morning.

Then, following a terrain map, we headed into the unknown, hoping that dirt roads leading north into hostile territory were marked, barricad-ed and closed off. We drove our jeep over rutted trails, past abandoned rice paddies, over scrub-covered hills and finally found this new battery area, arriving around noon. I'll give you all the details on what we've been doing in tomorrow's letter; it's a pretty interesting tale.

Our new location is just two miles southeast of Freedom Bridge, or roughly eight and three quarter miles southeast of Panmunjon. It's a good area, already lived in, and improved by the Korean Marine Artil-lery Battery who left here at the same time we moved in.

I'm OD tonight, in charge of the interior guard. I need to get out at midnight and inspect the guard, so I think I'd better get two hours of sleep before then.

Everything is going well, I'm back in the battery again, and I'll write you a real letter tomorrow.

I love you, chicki with all my heart and soul. You are a precious, darling, wonderful wife. Goodnight, pumpkin.

With all my love,
Bill

6
Finding Baker

11 Oct. 53

Dearest Lamb,

There are eight officers assigned to Baker Battery at present. Due to transfers, regular release, early release and accumulated points, I will be the only one left at the end of two months. Today I was assigned the assistant executive officer job and there is a possibility I could become the Exec. eventually. That is a harder job, for my money, than being Btry. Cmdr. What it boils down to is running the battery for the Cmdr. in addition to being in complete charge of firing and all that is involved in it, such as gunnery, ammunition, 80 men, etc. The Exec. brings the battery into position, receives the FO's request for fire, figures out the data for the six howitzers, and fires them. The Exec. does <u>not</u> spend time as an FO. Good? Maybe. What I'd like best is to get the hell out of here. Actually, Exec. is the job I would like best in a firing battery, but if you don't particularly like army life [so far], chances are you might be happier in civilian life. That's me!

Remember I told you a new FO from the Battalion was coming up to relieve my party at noon on Friday? Well, at 12:30 PM on Friday, Bn. Hq. called me and said that the Battalion had just been put on movement alert and we wouldn't be relieved on the hill until further notice. Around six we got a call and found out the Battalion was moving out that night and a Korean Marine Artillery Bn. would move in the same night. We were to stay on the OP and orient the new FO. It was expected that the Korean FO party would arrive during the night, we would orient them first thing in the morning, and drive over to a new battery area in time for breakfast.

At that point our 49th Bn. took out our phone lines and a little later pulled out. And there we sat, with a few Korean Marines out in front and no one behind! You can bet we kept a good watch that night. I cut down the watches to 3 hours each, taking from six to nine and from three to six the following morning. The new Korean Bn. came in during the night and occupied our old positions. However, by seven in the morning nobody had showed up on the OP.

I decided finally that I'd better go see what their trouble was. I took my driver and started off through the Korean artillery positions in the jeep. We found their battalion headquarters in the same area where ours had been, and after locating an interpreter, we sought out the Korean Battalion Commander, a Lt. Colonel. You would have really enjoyed the scene. The Col. seemed like a very intelligent man, but his interpreter spoke very little English. We struggled linguistically in the center of a large, silent gathering of solemn Oriental faces.

After about ten minutes or so I assumed that we at least partially understood each other, because the Col. indicated he'd have the FO party ready in half an hour for me to lead back to the OP. Evidently, they didn't know where it was. It was our Liaison Officer who had fouled up the works. Afterward I found out that there were several U.S. Marine advisory officers with the Korean Bn. I talked to one of them later and verified my previous suspicions. I also managed to procure half a dozen cans of beans for my FO party's breakfast.

The reason behind the battalions switching positions is that 8th Army wants to make sure President Rhee doesn't interfere with the prisoners again and their scheduled transfer, and thus trash the cease-fire. Consequently, all ROK [Republic of Korea] units near the prison camp, and between Seoul and the prison camp, have been replaced with U.S. units. We are still supporting the 1st Marine Division.

Here we sit, in a barren new battery area. The departed Koreans came back today with somebody's permission and removed all their permanent installations, so we have to start from scratch to build a comfortable, livable area. Our tent floor is dirt, all my equipment sits on the ground, and the dust blows through here worse than it ever did in good old Oklahoma. One redeeming feature is that there is a stream in the area and eventually a shower unit could be set up over near Charlie Battery. We are now in the process of putting together an oil heating stove, which I think we'll need tonight. The forecast is for 39 degrees. That's cold in a non-winterized tent, especially when you get up in the dark of the early morning.

We've got a radio in here, but I haven't yet heard the score of yesterday's Princeton game. Falling out of the Top Ten quickly dulls the attention of the papers.

You are constantly in my thoughts, wonderful chicken pot. I miss you very much. I love you so very much, Lucy. I don't think you realize how wonderful a person you are and how important you are to me. I wish I could fly home and see you. It would take only about 72 hours to travel from Baker Battery to LaGuardia. Doesn't that sound good? One of these days I'll do it!

Goodnight, perfect wife.

I love Lucy,

Bill

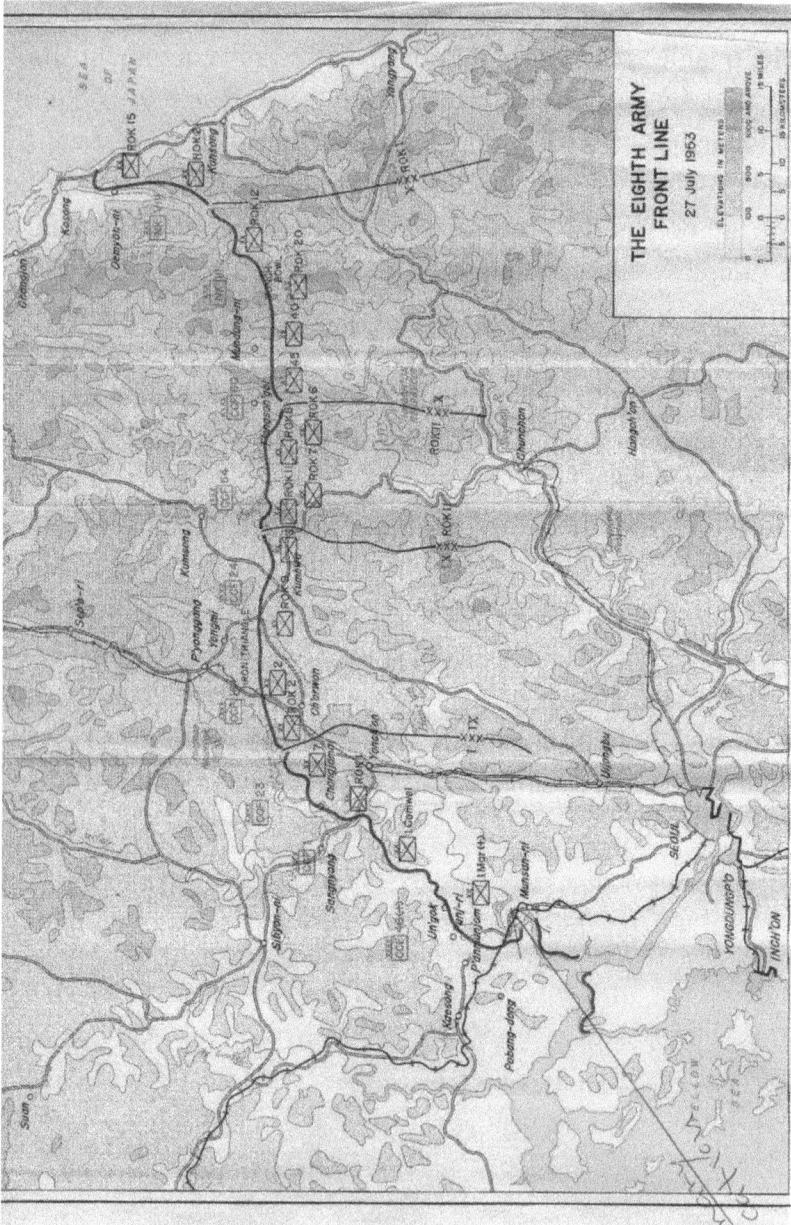

Front lines after the ceasefire. The arrow shows our location ten weeks later.

* * *

My dearest wife,

The PX is temporarily out of writing supplies, so for a few days I'm reduced to a pencil and borrowed writing paper.

First, I received your letters #29 and 30; #16 through 28 will probably arrive in a packet after a few days. I can't help but feel tremendously proud of myself for marrying such a magnificently wonderful person! While I was reading your letter #30 in the BOQ earlier this morning, I unconsciously said out loud, "My wife is the probably one of the smartest people in this entire world." At that, everyone in here looked up at me rather startled, and I just chuckled and went on reading. I want to talk more about that a little later.

I'm really in the doghouse with myself for not mailing a letter to you yesterday. I thought so much about you, as usual, all day and had a million unconnected thoughts and things to tell you about. At one point during the morning I had to go over and check our ammo dump. Climbing up the little hill, I remembered how we had climbed up that snowy hill at the Williams Winter Carnival holding hands and having the best fun in the world. When I get home, we are going to have to take lots of walks out in the country and over the hills and maybe even some camping and canoe trips if you'd like.

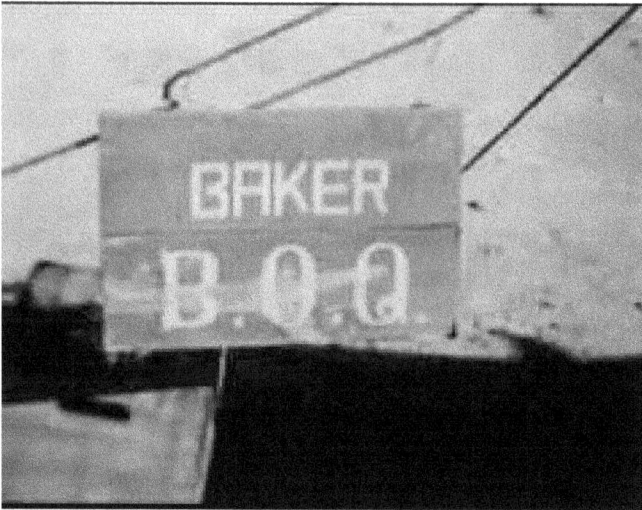

The trouble with me is that as long as I can't be with you during these months, I wish like anything you could be with me. As long as that is impossible too, what I do is share everything I do with you. Because it takes much longer to write about an experience, I feel as if I should spend about two-thirds of the day writing about what happened and what I thought all day and tell you about it. What actually happens is very different. I have to find moments here and there during the day to write a few paragraphs, and I don't seem to get into the swing of really sharing with you on paper before I'm interrupted.

In the evenings we have a movie if the salvaged generator happens to be working and while our makeshift, spliced wiring stays intact. I like to see them whenever I can, but last night, not having a chance to write during the day, I vowed not to go. Then I found out "The Four Poster" was the flick. Remember when we saw it? I had to see it again. It was just like being with you for an hour or so. When I got back from the flick the generator ran out of gas, thus no light. Our stove wasn't working right, so no heat, and the end result was no letter.

These last two nights have really been cold. We are now getting into long-john weather. Yesterday the Btry. Cmdr., Exec. and I drove over to the U.N. base camp for a hot shower and I brought my long johns for the annual change over. When we arrived, we found the hot water had been turned off, so we turned around and drove back again, postponing the trip until today. We'll try again later this afternoon.

The Christmas tree ornaments sound like a tremendous idea! We'll surely have a tree, and the ornaments will make it seem very much as if you're here. Please don't make them too fancy or spend too much time on them, because for some reason it makes me very sad to think of you many miles away doing something extra special for me on Christmas. The reason, I think, is that I'd want too much to thank you in person. You are such a wonderful, perfect Lamb.

* * *

I've just come back from my shower. It feels wonderfully great to be clean again, in fresh long-johns and fatigues. What a difficult shower I had! The hot and cold water had been turned off again, and all the water we could get was from a wash basin. The hot water trickled out and the cold sort of drooled. About half way through, the hot trickle quit entirely and as soon as I had gotten the soap off, the cold also gave up. I barely made it. (pun on "barely" intended). Tomorrow our Bn. shower will go into operation and I understand it will be fairly plush—with genuine hot water, that is.

As for your coming over here, sweetie, even if you could manage to swing it, the situation at best would be terrible. By now you've gotten my letters describing this little gem of a country.

Korea must be the classic example of a war-torn country. The cities are all banged up, the people live in terrible slums. They'll steal anything. Civilian transportation is practically non-existent. As far as the military is concerned, if you're a general you've got it made and fly around in a helicopter. Otherwise, transportation for any good distance is less than untrustworthy. You couldn't get a job anywhere near to where I am now, and if there were any jobs, there's no telling when we'd move again. Most of all, I would worry about you wherever you were in Korea. Even more than Japan, it is still just not a suitable place for an American woman unless her husband is constantly with her. I do hope you understand, Lucy. I love you more than anything in the world and I want more than anything to see you, but Korea is not the place. Someday, my love, before too long, we'll be together and what a wonderful, glorious day it will be!!

It has turned out that Btry. Cmdr. Capt. Sosa and the Exec., Lt. McAllister, are both architects in civilian life. Sosa is the funniest guy I have ever known, telling us about people who came to him with completely impractical ideas on houses they wanted built. We've been having a great discussion on whether or not people know what's best for them in a custom designed home. What these architects say is that a couple should describe their methods and patterns of living, say how much they want to pay and what style house they want, and let the architect go to work. They say, at 7% of the total building cost, the architect usually saves the client more than he charges. Also they say a properly designed house can be a royal palace for $35,000. I'm going to keep the subject going and see if I can get some practical ideas to give to our architect if and when we ever decide to build.

Capt. Sosa is one top-notch battery commander, a wonderful person to work for. He is a great role model for leadership. Although he's now just waiting to get out and go home, he's not bitter. He just makes jokes about it in his Spanish accent, which keeps you laughing constantly. I'll be sorry to see him leave next month. McAllister leaves day after tomorrow and possibly I'll act as the Exec. At least for a while.

Remember the major who visited me on the OP? He turns out to be the son of a well-known four-star general. Incidentally, I picked up a panoramic photo, which the marines took about a year ago, of the view across the river from the OP. It shows the same terrain I took in the movies and scanned with my BC scope. I'll send it to you along with a shoulder pin with the battalion crest as soon as I can get my hands on an extra crest.

One of the things that makes me think you are such a smart pumpkin is what you said in your letter #30 of 1 October. You said it perfectly and you were one hundred percent correct. Aside from my tendency to criticism, which I have vowed to cease, I think that almost every spat we ever had started over something very minor. Then as we started talking about it, both of us feeling our pride had been compromised, our discussion would become less and less rational and more and more emotional and pointless.

You were right, too, about this forced separation being a very powerful object lesson in how important our love and mutual happiness are. You are the most vital thing in the world to me, Lucy, and anything I can do to make you happier and to make me worthy of you is worth it many times over. It seems to get very complicated to talk about, but what I mean is that I love you very completely, darling, with all my being. I'm sure no one could ever have loved with the feeling that I have for you. With our determination to make each other happy to lead us, and with God to guide us, I look forward to the next hundred years with you as the best hundred years of my life.

Goodnight, precious wife.

I love Lucy,

Bill

* * *

14 Oct. 53

Hi Chicki,

What a frustrating time we have had with our heating stove! It never has worked right and smoke would bellow from the chimney as if it were the Queen Mary trying for the Blue Ribbon record crossing. So today around two, we decided that the most important business of the hour was a final reckoning with that stove. Under the watchful eye of our not too fluent houseboy (boysan), we disassembled the entire contraption, had it washed in solvent, and assembled it once again. It took takusan (much) time and no sukoshi (little) thought.

As a result, most of the afternoon was invested in this undertaking. We even sent boysan crawling up to the top of the tent to check the spark arrester at the tip top of the chimney. He resembled a monkey climbing a curling palm tree as the tent sagged under his weight. Any second I expected to see the whole works collapse and we BOQ members spending a night under the stars. It worked! After another half hour of tinkering and cogitating, we cautiously struck a match and instead of a loud boom and blackened faces we got a rosy flame. Very shortly later our cherished unit roared into full operation, and now except for the dirt floor, etc., we live in high style and comfort. We now even have a china reflector for our single light bulb!

I found this pen, broken and discarded, and with an old Band-Aid and a piece of fine wire I am now back in the writing business. I also moved my belongings and cot out of the far corner, over nearer the stove, to one of the recently vacated spots. I'm living in newfound comfort, high on the hog—that is, if you don't mind a drafty tent with a dirt floor.

Tonight the flick was "Desert Song." Again it's a show we had seen together. I think it was two years ago this fall, at the Paper Mill Playhouse in Millburn with Peggy and Charlie. It wasn't too bad a show, even though it was mighty chilly tonight sitting outside after dark, even wearing long johns. McAllister and I had good fun deriding the military actions of the French Foreign Legion. I'll be sorry to see him leave in a couple of days to become an advisor to a newly organized Korean battalion.

I got your letter #31 today and a couple of sports sections from Wawee about the World Series and the Princeton-Columbia game. The poor old Dodgers, they just couldn't make it. As for Princeton, the games must certainly be exciting, but the polish and experience that marked the recent winning years are gone.

I continue to be immensely proud of my wonderful wife and her long, interesting letters. I love you so much Lucy, and admire and adore you so tremendously that I'm about to burst! You are a wonderful comfort to me when I feel dejected, and it's wonderful to know that you are loving and waiting for me and we are preparing for a wonderful future together.

As long as I don't think too hard about getting out, time goes relatively swiftly. There is always something to do, either keeping the battery going or your own personal equipment in order. We haven't started doing any formal training as yet, since we are still building the new battery area. It's been very interesting locating the positions for all our installations, especially our six 105 mm howitzers. Higher headquarters is not harassing us much and most of the decisions are on our own, within the bounds of Bn. and Div. Arty. SOP (standard operating procedures). This is a culmination of everything learned in the ROTC and BOC and FARTC training. The atmosphere in the battery is upbeat. The Capt. is easy going and doesn't fight the problems. Things are going quite smoothly, with minimum strain getting best results, for the present anyway. Morale is generally good, though naturally everyone is just waiting to get the hell out of here and head for the Golden Gate. "California, Here I Come" and "Bye, Bye, Blackbird" (which includes the phrase "leave on the light, I'll be home late tonight") have become very popular songs.

Well, Chicki, I'm Btry. OD tomorrow, and between taking the report at reveille tomorrow before dawn and checking the guards late tomorrow night, it will be a long day.

I love you very tenderly, my wonderful wife. I desire and long for your physical closeness but I am wonderfully happy with our spiritual closeness. God is always with us and we have much to be thankful for.

Goodnight, darling pumpkin.

I love you always, Bill

P.S. I forgot to tell you I wrote your parents last week.

7
Learning the Ropes

PM
15 Oct. 53
Just before the last guard check.

Dearest Lamb,

Big news! - New job, - One notch up! Today I got the nod of approval from above, and was elevated to the position of Baker Battery Executive Officer! It's going to be considerably more work, and a new leadership role. It is more responsibility, interesting, challenging, and will provide a personal test for me. I've been cleared for Secret, so I get to know what's going on (at least on these lowly local levels).

Each night this week I've watched the moon change from a silver sliver to a half circle of gold. A week ago the moon set at dusk and now it disappears behind the hills around eleven. It is a beautiful sight. Our nights have been clear and frosty, with millions of stars, but inside our tent the steady rumble of our oil heater keeps us warm and comfortable.

A portable radio is one of the greatest inventions, after the heater, that we enjoy in this tent. The Far East Network, Korea, operates a local station called Radio Vagabond. Music all day and night, with occasional hourly news reports. Reception is generally pretty good and never, ever a commercial. I never realized what a tremendous difference it makes not to have station breaks every fifteen minutes, Ma Perkins stories, or Duz jingles. Most of the music is really great, with lighter music thrown in also. A few days ago at Hq., during a class for all lieutenants in the Bn., I heard very faintly from a radio somewhere the strains of "Dancing Cheek to Cheek." For just a second or two, you were there.

It's funny how you can be far away from a person you love and still feel so very close. I adore you, dearest wife, I love you with all my heart and being.

Goodnight, pumpkin.

Love and kisses,

Bill

* * *

16 Oct. 53

Dearest Lamb,

This is just a note to tell you that I love you with the greatest and strongest love in the whole world!

Right after the Retreat Parade this afternoon there was a party in the Officers' Mess tent (Bn. Hq.). We had beer before chow. Then a buffet of fried chicken, potato salad, and little sandwiches. When I was full, they brought out a steaming platter of meatloaf and baked ham and I had to start eating again.

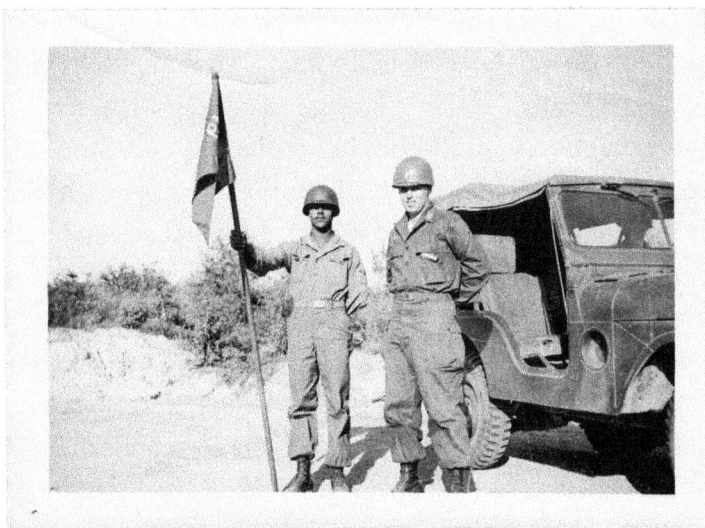

Showing the Battery Flag.

We had a couple of colonels in our midst but didn't let that bother us a bit. It really turned out to be a cheerful party. We sang about ten verses of "They're cutting the orders for staff school," the song I was always singing in the shower. I also got some words to another song, which I'll send along tomorrow.

McAllister is still here and took about fifteen feet of film on the parade this afternoon, including this Lieutenant marching, the band, and the ceremony. It may be a very good show. I love you completely, Lucy, and I'll write a long letter tomorrow. Good night, Chicki,

All my love,

The Lt.

* * *

17 Oct. 53

To my one and only dear Pooh Bear.

Wow! Eighteen letters today, including one from brother Chris, three from Aunt Wawee, and the rest from my favorite wife. Nothing is more wonderful here in this far-away, forgotten and forsaken end of the earth than hearing from you. You are so wonderful, so darling, so perfect, and I love you so very much. To date I've gotten letters 1 through 33, also 35 and 37.

Without exception I am thoroughly proud of you. Although at times you may get that lost and discouraged feeling, it's only natural and completely understandable. What's most important is that you have a strong faith and trust in God and you also have confidence in me. With that foundation you are a very strong person. Add to that yourself with all your wonderful capabilities, and I know that you have the inner peace and strength to come out above all the hardships you may be experiencing. I thank God for guiding me to a person so wonderful. I love you very completely, Lucy, in every way, and I'm behind you in everything you do.

I won't try to comment on and answer all your letters tonight. I'll go through them tomorrow, Sunday, when I have more time and check off those things that I should write you about. However, there are a few things I want to touch on tonight.

Most important, you old horse's muffin, take good care of yourself! I was very sorry to hear you had gotten the bug and had to go to bed. I hope you are all over it now and are in good health. Please don't get tired and run down, and remember that money is the last thing in the world to worry about. Don't sacrifice your health by working long hours to make a lot of extra money. Remember, your happiness is the most important thing to me. If you want to work, fine, but please don't over-do it. I'm spending very little here, primarily from lack of opportunity. Incidentally, let me know when you receive your $250 allotment checks so I'll know how much I should expect on pay day.

Actually, I probably sound like a mother hen, telling you to take care of yourself, and I'm very pleased with your working when you want to, but don't do it because of supposed indebtedness to me or a feeling that you have to. You come first, and way after that come material things.

I am also sorry about our four-footed "Jag." Although I am far in miles, I am very, very close to you in spirit, so remember and be comforted. When I get home we'll get another cocker spaniel that we can raise and train together, and when he's mature enough to appreciate it, we might even take him for a drive in our first new Mark VIII Jaguar!

Again, don't worry about me over here. Even during the roughest fighting, Baker didn't lose an FO, or a man. At present I am the Exec., whose duty is required back in the battery area with the FDC [Fire Direction Center] and the guns. At present we are supporting U.S. Marines of the 1st Marine Division, and even in the doubtful possibility that Joe Chink started the fighting again you would have no need to worry. You and I and God know that I have important work ahead of me furthering His Kingdom.

The party last night was good fun even though we left around 9:30 because I'm OD today and had to take reveille. It will be after midnight in a few minutes and I'll go out and check the guards, but tomorrow I can sleep late, wonderful day! Church is not until 2:30 in the afternoon.

Duty calls, so goodnight, darling wife. I love you with fiery passion and great tenderness.

Devotedly,

Bill

* * *

18 Oct. 53

Hi, Lamb.

As of today, I am complete through your letter #37, which is the first you addressed to Baker Battery. I got another letter from Aunt Wawee, and from Mom an announcement that I'll receive Life Magazine each week and two Sunday sports sections.

Today being Sunday, a bright, hot, cloudless Sunday, I slept until 8:30. Then I leisurely arose and read my mail. After that I slowly (and you know how slow I can sometimes be) washed, shaved and dressed. Those last four words take a good deal more time to accomplish here, where you have to haul out your "surplus" radio battery, wire it up to your shaver, and adjust the mirror hanging on the tent pole before you can start shaving. Then to wash, you pour water from the five-gallon can and heat it over a tiny but very efficient little gasoline burner. It's not as simple as inserting a plug in a socket or turning on the hot faucet. However, by necessity, you get used to it quickly.

After lunch I went over to the Protestant Church service at Bn. Hq. It was far from an elaborate service, being conducted in a squad tent with a little altar up front, by a rather unenergized little chaplain. But it didn't make much difference, because he was earnest and we sang and heard the Scripture, and prayed. I really can't decide why, but for some reason today was a particularly inspiring experience for me. Maybe it's because you seem extra close to me in church.

How do you like the enclosed picture of me? That's what I'm going to do when I get home: relax in front of the fireplace. Care to join me?

Talking about the fire, that good-for-nothing oil stove of ours is at it again! It bellows out black, greasy soot and won't give off any heat.

We finally had to shut it off. On top of that, our battery's generator quit tonight and they never could get it going again. I finally managed to locate a Coleman Lantern, some unleaded gasoline, and a very scarce mantle to get it lighted, so at least I'm not writing by candlelight again. However, it's chilly enough to see my breath and everyone else in here hit the sack about 8:30.

After church I managed to hear a few plays of a rebroadcast of what seemed to be a rather disheartening slaughter in Palmer Stadium. The Naval Academy was going to town at Princeton's expense.

I was called away because all battery commanders (BCs) and Execs. were to go on a reconnaissance with the Bn. CO to pick alternate battery positions. It was a routine procedure which didn't take long.

When we returned, Capt. Sosa and I went down to inspect the battalion shower. It was the first and only real, hot shower I've had the pleasure of experiencing since leaving that not-so-wonderful little town of Sasebo, Japan.

The shower was a memorably enjoyable event, completed by the donning of clean long johns. As yet, I still haven't relapsed back into my former old grubby self.

Driving back from the shower in the back seat of the jeep, I was casually glancing around at the hills and rice paddies and the sukoshi trees and the rocks and the road and the dirt, which now all seem very familiar, when suddenly the thought came to me that I, Bill MacIlvaine of Summit, New Jersey, was bouncing along a back road in the Orient in that awful, distant, much-spoken-of "Land of the Morning Calm," Korea. And strangely enough, it didn't seem so awful, or so distant. It was just me driving down a dirt road, and ignoring a few major scenic differences, it could have been in rural New Jersey, New York or Pennsylvania. It doesn't seem so far away now and it doesn't seem so remote. The most paramount difficulty is that I'm not with you. Have I ever told you how much I love you? I think it possible you may know.

I bought a Parker 51 pen and pencil set yesterday for $9. The pen sells for $12.75 and the pencil for $5.75. I'm not sure quite what to do with it. I could use it here, but rather than have it stolen, I think I'll send it to you. I sort of toyed with the idea of giving it to Dad for Christmas, or maybe Bob. What do you think, honeybun?

As you have probably guessed by now, I didn't get a chance to re-read your letters today to answer them, and I trust you will give me another few days of grace.

Doggone it, I just can't seem to tell you how much I love you and admire and adore you. I can tell you over and over again, but it never seems to carry the strength or the fervor with which I mean it. You must know what I mean because you mentioned the same thing in one of your letters.

I love you, Lucy, spiritually, passionately with a longing, and tenderly with all my heart and soul.

God bless you.

Your affectionate, devoted, loving,

Bill

* * *

19 Oct. 53

Dearest Lamb,

It's late now and I'm taking reveille tomorrow, so just a few words to tell you that I love you very dearly.

I'm now in the process of reading through your letters chronologically, and reading them makes me feel very close to you and warm and tender.

Midway through the evening, however, I got sidetracked by the very interesting conversation going on around me. Nothing very important or lasting was said, but I felt the need to put on my steel helmet while humorous war stories were being tossed around. We enjoy the wise cracking and the personalities we have around here.

The young new lieutenant is a character. He told us cheerfully, among his other tales, that at eighteen he was a railroad conductor in Ashtabula, Ohio, making over $400 a month, and in one week managed to crash and wreck over $15,000 worth of railroad equipment! He plans on going to Ohio State when he gets out.

Got a kick out of relating my experiences on the union job at Ciba Pharmaceutical and at the Seaside Heights ice plant, and what Princeton was like. The captain, comical as ever, gave us a discourse on Puerto Rico and on how, any minute now, a phone call might bring his immediate release, which we and he all know won't come for several months.

Only one thing was missing. I miss my wonderful, darling, beautiful wife. I've said it a thousand times and I'll say it a million times again, and each time it means more than words can possibly express.

I love you, Lucy, always, with all my being. You are my cherished ideal, my wife.

Yours
Bill

* * *

20 Oct. 53

Dear Chicki,

Well, here it is, late again, and I haven't had the chance to write you a good long letter.

After early getting all the details and the program organized for the day, I left the battery area with two of our mechanics and set up a roadblock for all 49th Bn. vehicles on the primary dirt road west of our position. During the course of the day we inspected and wrote reports on 33 assorted rolling machines, including the Colonel's jeep.

We managed to hold him up a particularly good length of time and gave him a very thorough going-over. We managed to find three deficiencies on his jeep, not an exceptional number, but he at least had to notice the zeal with which we were performing our duty on a chilly, drizzling, muddy day. Despite the grubby weather, I didn't mind the job. We were so busy during the morning that the first time I glanced at my watch it was only a half hour until noon.

During the afternoon, business was a little slower and we built a little warming fire down off one side of the road. The drizzle stopped, and we were still muddy and soaked, but reasonably comfortable.

I am now involved in great preparations and studying for a three-day bivouac and service practice on the 26th, 27th and 28th of this month. We will move over to a firing range about 40 miles away, occupy, and I'll lay the battery after dark under absolute tactical blackout conditions and shoot some very tricky problems that night and the next day. As Exec., the whole exercise falls into my hands. I've got to coordinate the survey, figure all data for various types of firing registrations, and take into account effects of weather, worn gun tubes, powder temperature, and multiple other variables. It is without exaggeration ten times more complicated than any shoot in which I've ever participated, and I'm in charge of it! Groan. To top it off, most of the men we now have on the guns and in Fire Direction Center are more inexperienced than I. The only way we can possibly do a decent, smooth job is by working the problems over and over, day and night.

I just came back from Bn., where we had a meeting of Btry. Execs. I was staggered at the enormity of the task. I'm glad that Able Battery will fire the day before we do; I'll be able to observe them and that should be a big help. We're only allowed 150 rounds, so we won't be rushed, and that will also be a help.

I'm OD again tonight. With only three officers in the battery besides the Battery Commander, the duty comes up every third day.

I'm hale and healthy and working hard and wish like anything I were working on <u>selling</u> steel rather than <u>shooting</u> steel. But more important, I wish I were with you.

We dismantled our stove again and after cleaning, kicking, and cussing it, now it works like a charm. Even our solitary hanging light bulb is back in operation. It wasn't the generator after all, but one of the spliced lines into the BOQ which grounded out everyone's power.

I love you, Lucy, so tenderly and so completely. You are always cherished in my thoughts and heart, and I feel very close to you.

Goodnight, perfect wife.

I adore Lucy,

Bill

* * *

Best Chicken,

Late last night we were informed of a pending "unannounced" Command Inspection, to be performed by the 7th Inf. Division Commander, Maj. Gen. Lionel McGarr, along with the Division Artillery Commander, Col. Lester. We worked like R.A.'s (Regular Army) all day long today to whip the battery area into shape. Then, around four in the afternoon, word came down that our battery would not be among those inspected. Actually, I wish we had been, because I think we'd have done well. At any rate, the entire battery area looks a hundred percent better than it did this time yesterday.

Tonight at Bn. Hq. there was another party for the Div. Arty. Commander and a captain who is going home. Actually, I enjoyed myself very much. At a typical, fairly conservative stag affair with free drinks and a steak, I managed to consume three large, juicy sirloins!

Before we left Baker for the gathering, Capt. Sosa suggested we wear our O.G.'s (Olive Greens) with the red "silk" neck scarf. After he was dressed, Sosa informed me that he was probably the sharpest-looking captain in the entire Far East. I told him that I was glad he hadn't said sharpest-looking company-grade officer (2nd Lt. or 1st Lt. or Capt.) and he assured me that the two of us were, without doubt, the sharpest-looking of any two officers, including all the lieutenants and captains in the Far East and all other world-wide locations.

After the first couple rounds of drinks at the party, speech time rolled around. To our great glee the captain who was leaving informed the party that despite the harassment from higher headquarters which had recently begun, he loved the 7th Div. Arty. The Div. Arty. Commander (who originated the harassment) took it all in but seemed more than slightly shaken.

The Marine Division Artillery CO, a full Colonel, was also present, and after his long and rather dull talk he was sung into the Battalion. Using his first name, he was referred to during the song many times as (politely translated) a horse's muffin. Unfortunately he did not seem too shaken.

Even though it was fun, I would have given any and every party I've ever attended to be with you for five seconds.

I love you, darling wife, more than you can ever know, and miss you so awfully.

Goodnight, precious lamb. God bless you.

All my love forever,

Bill

* * *

22 Oct. 53

Dearest Pooh Bear,

Today featured the big event of moving our BOQ tent about 30 yards to the wooden floor that we had built. Our feet are no longer on the ground! It was a major job to get the place rewired for the telephone and our single electric light bulb and reassembling our heating stove, but this is really magnificent, luxury living. The next step is to build a 3' x 3' front stoop on which to knock the eventual snow and current mud off our boots then to build two wooden doors to replace the canvas drapes with which we are now blessed.

I got a couple of brilliant ideas today and the battery really went to work. First I had a nearby deserted bunker torn down and with the lumber thus salvaged we built a bridge across a little stream between the orderly room, BOQ and the mess hall. Then I had wooden steps put in, leading up the high, steep bank which parallels the stream. If it were wider, the bridge would support a 2½-ton truck. The supports are constructed of 8" x 8" beams and the walkway itself is paved with solid

4" x 8" planks. The affair is fastened together with 6" spikes. The ends of the bridge have been dug into each bank and graded with packed dirt. It is a foot bridge designed for people weighing up to 50,000 pounds; however, it was the only material we had available.

I also managed to salvage about 70 steel canisters in which our howitzer ammunition is shipped. When we can get some paint, we will stripe them like barber's poles and stick them in the ground along the steps to our FDC bunker and along the road. It's amazing how much can be done to beautify the local community area when you have lots of manpower and a few basic materials.

However, our biggest problem of the moment is preparation for our Shoot of the 27th. I am a little locked up about it because I can see how little prepared we are at present for the exercise. The Division Artillery Commander will be on hand with his staff, watching how we do. All details and foreseeable problems must be worked out, with nothing left to chance. Groan.

Well, hell, who cares about one lousy old Div. Arty. CO? We'll do our best and see what happens.

Tomorrow I take reveille. Then tomorrow night after taking Guard Mount (formally posting the guards), we will have our first after-dark practice sessions with the Firing Battery: Baker's six howitzer (gun) sections and FDC. The next night we'll pull the guns out on the road and practice occupying a position after dark, getting the battery laid parallel, and getting our communications wire in, with everything ready to fire. I'll report to you day by day how we are progressing.

Always remember, precious wife, that every day I think of you, and yearn for you, and love you with all that is within me. You are an angel!

Good night, Lucy, and God bless you.

Devotedly,

Bill

* * *

Hi Lamb,

I think today was probably the busiest day I have ever spent in my life. I really enjoyed it. I had about six projects going all day and each required my attention and supervision as I went from one to another keeping things going. None of the jobs sound very earth shaking in the telling, but they were jobs that were vital in one way or another and had to be done. One was getting 1,500 odd rounds of howitzer ammunition sorted and stacked by Lot Number. Each manufacturer's Lot gives the shell slightly different characteristics in flight, and as far as possible we should only shoot one Lot at a time. What a jumble our ammo dump was in!

Some of the other jobs included close supervision of a detailed schematic plan for the defense of our battery area, including barbed wire, for Battalion approval, writing up a Battery Guard SOP, trying to procure special items for our Shoot on the 27th, proceeding with arrangement of details for the Shoot, and making sure the gun sections will be so well practiced that the affair on the 27th will run like clockwork.

I had a conference with my six Chiefs of Section right after lunch today, and went through the details of how night bore sighting and laying of the battery should be done. I had the evening movie postponed so that we could have a practice session right after dark and the men would still have a chance to see the show. Able and Charlie Batteries have both been experiencing a lot of difficulty in getting these night problems running smoothly without confusion and errors.

When we ran through the problem tonight, it could not have come out more perfectly! There was not a sound except for the necessary commands and answers and not a light was showing except briefly, when it was necessary to take a sight on a gun to take a reading. There was no confusion, no mistakes and the whole process was performed in record time! I was really pleased with the results and let the men know what we'd accomplished.

A long day. I started at six this morning and worked until eight tonight, not counting the checking of the guard, which I'll do right after I mail this letter. The army may be a wonderful place for some people to become lazy and incompetent, but if you have the right job it can surely be valuable training for civilian life.

For the first time since I entered active duty, I've actually enjoyed the army and the work. The Colonel is a top-notch man who doesn't harass the batteries. The Captain is a hell of a nice guy who is a pleasure to work for. You are given lots of leeway; you can do things the way you decide to do them, as long as they get done.

I almost decided not to send this letter I've started, because I seem to be blowing off steam. At Ft. Sill, I was frustrated with the army and seemed to be batting my head against the wall, but here it's just the opposite. When the problem tonight came out well, I had a great feeling of accomplishment that I had organized something difficult and worthwhile on my own and had it come out a success. The reason I almost tore up this letter is that because I have such a feeling of accomplishment, I have undoubtedly exaggerated what I've done and you don't get a truly objective picture.

Maybe it would be more accurate to say that I did a job today that most people with my training should probably do equally as well. What makes me feel pleased is that I found out it was I who was doing the job well.

I feel much more confident about my future civilian job now because I think if I can find a job I like, and work at it, I will make a great success of it.

I don't think you realize what a tremendous influence and help you are to me. Even though physically you're not standing next to me, loving and honest, with a great faith in God, you are the most wonderful inspiration a person could have. I thank God that He could have allowed me to marry a person as great as you are. I love you, Lucy, if possible, more than ever. You make my life complete.

Goodnight, wonderful pumpkin. I'll write more of a newsy letter when I have more time tomorrow.

My love forever,

Bill

* * *

24 Oct. 53

Dearest Lamb,

Today, Saturday, was a quieter day than yesterday, although I never did get much time to sack out and read Life. The last Life I've read was in Summit before I left. After arriving in Japan, that same issue hit the PX newsstands as the latest issue. Time and Newsweek, printed in Tokyo, are fairly up to date. Life seems to be running up to a month late. I sent my new address to Life's subscription department.

When you ask me about Christmas and what I'd like to have, that's really a tough question. Anything big or breakable would probably be expensive or difficult to transport if we have to move the battery again in the near future. Also you can never tell when your stuff might be lugged away by some light-fingered Korean boysan who might feel he needs it more than I. We lead a very modest life and our needs and are simple. My simple need is to come home to the most wonderful person in the world, my wife. If you really feel you must get me something, why not get something for both of us and you can use it or save it until I get home.

As for your present, I'm pretty sure I won't get to Japan for R&R before Christmas. The selection of suitable gift items is less than meager here and I hope you will explain that to the families. However, I should be able to find something halfway decent at least for you.

I do hope you'll visit Summit as often as you want to. Mom and Pop both write that they enjoy very much having you. Do know that they love you very much too!

Five dollars ought to keep Lawrenceville's fund drive contented. I believe that's what I've been sending them.

Groan, what a terrible final score that was last Saturday with Navy! In a few hours the following week's Princeton game will start. Time is certainly going by fast for me, and I hope now that you've gotten into the swing of school, for you too.

Doggone it, again tonight it's late and I haven't gotten a chance to tell you so many things that I want to. I feel so close to you, Lucy, that I always want to tell you what we've been sharing here during the day together.

Goodnight, delightful and perfect angel. I pray that God will continue to watch over and guide us.

I love Lucy, Bill

* * *

25 Oct. 53

Dearest Wife,

Sunday; a beautiful, sunny, cool-in-the-shade, quiet day. There is no reveille on Sunday, so I slept comfortably and unawakened until 8:30. Then Weiss handed me your letters numbered 44, 45 and 46, mailed Oct. 16th & 17th. I read them in bed. It was a pleasant "Good Morning."

I'm pleased with all the friends you have at Sarah Lawrence. I want you to have just as good a time as possible. Also, glad to hear the Olds is prepared for winter. I'm not completely sold on plastic covers for cars. From what I've seen, they last a few weeks, then start to tear. I have a feeling the snow and cold of the north will do the finish less harm than it got from the sun and dust (then the hailstorm) of the Oklahoma plains.

Again, I'm sorry about Jag, but don't feel too badly, Chicki, we'll get another cocker spaniel. He'll be young enough so that when our four little ones start annoying and beating on him, he won't get grumpy.

Now, cutie, don't you worry about me acting smart and getting hurt. You know I always talked smarter than I acted and besides I have a very healthy respect for safety.

I enjoyed reading your correspondence. You sound very impressive in your job of official receptionist for the college. After reading your delightful letters, I got dressed and shaved and had a leisurely lunch in our newly finished Quonset hut mess hall. Later this afternoon the agenda calls for church at 2:30 and then a shower.

Now it's evening. The church service was very inspiring. Even though the chaplain is young and not very educated, he is a very fervent Christian. While he is a rather poor speaker, his faith and burning evangelism make him a powerful person. I brought Weiss along to church with me. At first I guessed from his name he might be Jewish and wouldn't come. Although he didn't have much to say about the service, he did take communion and seemed to get something out of the hour.

After church we took our Saturday-night-shower (on Sunday) and arrived back at the BOQ all decked out in clean clothes. It was then that I heard the score of the Cornell game. Obviously this is a "building year," as the losing coach's expression goes. Next year, we two will be seeing many victorious (or lost, no matter) ball games and that's an invitation, cutie! This year I hope at least we clobber Yale and stuffy, starched Harvard.

I know what you mean, saying, "You know it's funny how God works things out for us at times when we can't see past our own noses, and think momentarily that maybe He's forgotten about us." This has been specially true for me recently. Here's why:

There are five battalions in the 7th Division Artillery: one anti-aircraft battalion, one 155 mm howitzer Bn. and three 105 mm howitzer Bn's. I knew when I first arrived at the 7th Division I wouldn't go to the anti-aircraft Bn. I hoped to go to the 155 mm Bn., which uses only one or two FO's, while the 105 mm battalions use nine apiece. At my first look at a map of this sector, knowing nothing about the situation, I decided the 49th Bn. was my last choice because it seemed so far away on the west flank. In the event of a sudden renewal of hostilities we could quickly get cut off. In addition, we were supporting a Korean Marine outfit.

I was assigned the 49th and wondered how God was really watching over me. Once the decision on my assignment was final, I forgot about what could have been and started making the best of where I was, and what I had to do.

Today I thought about it again. My two previous objections to the 49th have been cancelled out. Since the move we are now much closer to usable roads, both north and south, we're in closer proximity to the other battalions, and we are now supporting U.S. Marines. Not only that, but after talking to the officers of the other battalions, I discover that we are the best managed (Col. Moore, Capt. Sosa), least harassed, most comfortable, and probably the all around best battalion (Code named "Bell") in 7th Division Artillery. In my ignorance I thought God was allowing me to go to the worst; now I can see that actually He placed me with the very best.

I can't help but feel there is a lesson to be learned from this experience. When we think things are going badly and when we get upset and unhappy and when we pray for a thing that doesn't happen, we must remember always that God is in command. He can see and understand those things that we cannot. As long as we trust and have faith in Him, He will watch over us and guide us through times and situations that seem unduly hard, and finally, unerringly, bring us out to the point where we can understand His wisdom, see His will, and appreciate His infinite greatness and care for us. We are very close, you and God and I, and we can thank God for giving us the opportunity to appreciate fully that closeness. Sorry, I've been a little wordy, I know. But it's important that we take time to share our thoughts, especially when there are so many miles between us.

I love you, Lucy, more than could ever seem humanly possible. You are such an admirable, fine person and such a wonderful, loving, perfect wife.

We saw a pleasant movie tonight, and afterward when we came back to the BOQ, I opened a beer and sat down in front of the stove and thought of you. How wonderful it would have been to have just left the flick at Bronxville and to be sitting at the Greasy Spoon looking at your beautiful face and holding hands. We could be talking about things tremendously important, or about nothing, and still the companionship and warmth of your presence would make me the richest man in the world.

When we meet again and have so much to say, let's not try to do it all at once. Let's just relax and enjoy each other's company and bask in the warmth of our renewed togetherness.

I love you, Lucy, with all the love that is within me.

Goodnight, Lamb.

Devotedly,

Your husband,

Bill

8
Executive Officer

26 Oct. 53

Hi Chicki,

We practiced again tonight for the big move-out and Shoot, which comes the day after tomorrow.

After dark, headlights out, we brought out the 2½-ton trucks, hooked up the guns and equipment and prepared to move out. My plan was to move out down the road a few miles, turn around and reoccupy the position. Everything moved like clockwork as the long, dark, silent convoy of guns and equipment slowly rumbled out onto the dirt road. I rode in the last vehicle, the FDC ¾-ton truck carrying all the maps and plotting equipment.

All vehicles were using blackout "cat eyes" instead of headlights. There was, however, one thing I hadn't prepared for. After dark, our driver couldn't see past the end of his nose! I would say we traveled abut 40 yards on the road when gently and smoothly my world tilted, rolled and turned on end, and our truck lay comfortably in the slime of a recently harvested rice paddy. Although we were almost on our side, the wheels barely left the ground. We merely drove over the rounded shoulder and were dumped into the mud as the driver fell over on me.

I managed to open the door, now directly overhead, and climbed up out of the hatch as if I were departing a submarine, just surfaced. No one was bruised and no damage was done, but the driver was very upset. From behind his thick steel-rimmed glasses he kept saying again and again, "Gee, sir, I was only trying to follow the road." Behind him on its side, wheels still slowly turning, resting in the mud and water, lay

Love Letters from the Front ~ 137

the mute evidence, the measure of the success of his attempt. It was all I could do to keep from bursting out laughing.

Needless to say, we have a new driver now who can see past his nose and I hope at least as far as the front bumper, even in the dark.

The practice occupation was only slightly hampered by our vehicle-rolling and progressed very well once we rescued our plotting equipment.

After the movie tonight, our baker served freshly made sugar cookies and steaming cocoa. Our new cook is #1.

I am returning the map overlay you sent me, with our old and new positions marked, and also the truce line, which may not be completely accurate. If you'll notice, over here in the west, the line runs south of the 38th parallel. Further west of the junction of the Han and Imjin Rivers the line is non-official. We hold all the territory south of the river over there, but it is so wide and difficult that it cannot be crossed in force.

Tonight for a change I'm going to try to get a full night's sleep. Remember, sweetie, how tremendously I love you. You are such a lovable, cuddly chicken. I wish I could kiss you and hold you. I miss you, Lucy, and adore you with all my heart.

Goodnight, precious wife. God bless you.

Your loving, devoted,

Bill

* * *

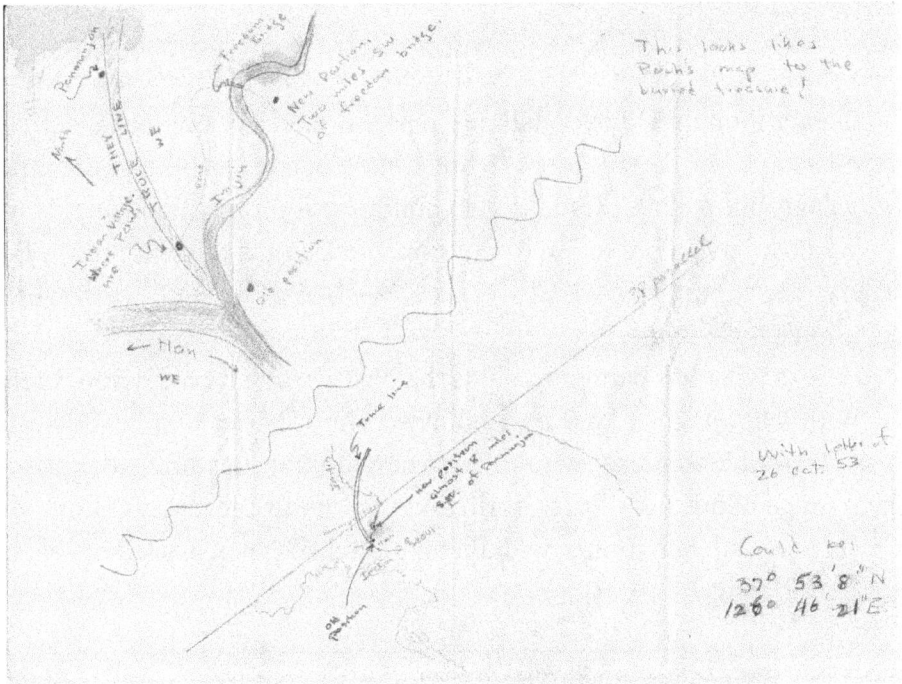

A rough sketch to show where we spent many months.

* * *

27 Oct. 53

Hi Lamb,

Just a note to tell you how much I love you. Our battery doesn't move out for the big Shoot until tomorrow, but I'm going out early to watch Able Battery, who fires tonight and tomorrow. I'll also stay to watch Charlie Battery, so I'll be camping out at the Bull's Eye Range near Yeoncheon for three days. It should prove to be a mighty interesting time.

I love you very dearly, my favorite wife. You're a pumpkin.

Devotedly, Bill

Dearest Love,

I never thought I'd ever call any place in Korea home, but it's great to be back in our battery area. It was a very active, tiring and eventful three days, but from a personal viewpoint it was a tremendous success.

We now have a big red-and-white-painted sign at the entrance to the battery area reading "BAKER—BELL'S—BEST." ("Bell" is the 49th Battalion's code name.)

Here is what has happened since that last scribbled note before I left.

With map, jeep and driver, I bounced out of Baker and headed east to contact Able Battery, who was in convoy and heading toward the firing range about forty miles north and east of our present position. We met on the road, had dinner with them around six, then started off again toward the range.

Baker tested the Best among Bell's three batteries.
Video Link: http://lovelettersfromthefront.com/videos

140 ~ Love Letters from the Front

It was a beautiful, cool, clear night, but there was little time to ponder the stars. Able moved in, set up, and began firing their registration and illuminating shells. My only task was as an observer, and I really took it to heart, because the following day I was to conduct the same operations with Baker. Everything was not perfect, but it seemed to go quite smoothly. Firing was completed at eleven and would be resumed the following morning. I went to bed tired and with suspicions of a cold coming on, and no small bit locked up over how we would do the next evening.

Able's Exec. is about to rotate on accumulated points, having been in Korea for a full year and is about as experienced as you can get. The next morning's firing also seemed to go smoothly, but was slow. By the time they had expended all their ammo, it was four in the afternoon and it had been raining steadily for over an hour. Able left the firing point a sea of churned mud.

Shortly thereafter, Capt. Sosa arrived with the Baker advance party and we picked out locations for our guns and installations. He and the party then returned to the convoy and just after dark pulled up to the firing area. At that point, his job was over and mine had begun. By this time the mud was as slippery as ice and ankle deep and I was soaked to the skin. My boots had filled with water! Strangely enough, my cold seemed to have disappeared. With greatest difficulty and after what seemed like hours, we got the battery in, laid, and ready to fire. Remember this all took place under the strictest noise and light requirements in a downpour which made everyone miserable and fogged all our optical equipment, in deep mud which bogged down vehicles and made even walking a chore.

Soon after I reported battery laid and ready to fire, the Range Officer suspended firing for the evening. In a way I was glad, but it just put off my debut until the next day. I had a cup of coffee, wrung out my socks, and started going over again all the unexpected problems that might arise the next day.

When I got up at 0500 I put my feet into cold, wet boots. My socks were once again as wet as the night before. The cold that I was catching was still not completely gone!

Constant mud meant wet socks and cold feet.

We started firing at dawn. I was pretty lucky. I made several very small errors in Fire Direction, but nothing big went radically wrong. I never got snowed under or panicked. All the time the big brass were nosing around, I acted as if I knew what I was doing.

The sun came out around nine, and we expended all of our ammo a little after noon.

After lunch, Capt. Sosa led the convoy back to our permanent position, and I stayed on to act as safety officer for Charlie Battery.

Charlie's Exec. is a graduate of Virginia Military Institute. They arrived that evening, fired rather slowly, and after a slow start the next morning (this morning) did reasonably well.

I thought Baker had done better than Charlie, but that Able had taken the cake, so I was very surprised when the Bn. Exec. (Maj. Gruenther) came to me after lunch today and told me that Baker had out-performed both other batteries and was best in Battalion! It looks as if I won't be going up on the "hill" doing any more forward observing for a while! I now have landed the permanent job of Battery Executive, unless perhaps some First Lieutenant comes along to outrank me.

Loading a howitzer and life in the open field.
Video Link: http://lovelettersfromthefront.com/videos

I got some movies of the firing, a shot of me standing with the Charlie Battery Commander and his Exec., and a shot of Weiss and me standing by a 38th Parallel road marker which we passed going South on the return trip to our area The firing range is in the rear area of the 25th Division sector, and on the return we passed first through the rear areas of the 1st Commonwealth (British) Division. Those British are a sporty crew! They salute with the thumb extended and the palm facing you, and drive the weirdest vehicles you ever saw. The road took us past the Royal Australian Regiment, the Essex Regiment, and the Royal Scots Regiment. Each had a different uniform, bright cap badges, and fancy while puttees (leggings). We even passed a rugby game in progress, which astonished my lanky Tennessee jeep driver.

Shooting finished.
Video Link: http://lovelettersfromthefront.com/videos

Its good to be back and it was wonderful to have three letters await-ing my arrival. The New York excursion with the Ellises sounded like fun, but I'm sure seeing Cammie will be the greatest. I hope you have a good time. I love you so much, Chicki!

I was thinking of you while I was off at the Shoot, as I do while I'm around here. I hope you got my letter saying what I'd been doing in time to be thinking about me and plugging for me. Even so, I know you would be plugging for me anyway and maybe that's why Baker came out on top.

You are a wonderful, darling, perfect pumpkin and I love you with all my heart. You are the world's best wife.

Goodnight, Lucy, God bless you.

Bill

* * *

Saturday, 31 Oct. 53

Hi Chicki,

Capt. Sosa's morale has been very low this afternoon. First they postponed his long-awaited R&R, which kept him available for our recent artillery Occupy-and-Shoot practice, and now again, because we have a Command Inspection by Maj. Gen. McGarr, the new Division Commander, coming up on November 10th.

Each day, he says, is the final day before his Early Release comes through. And every day I tell him how much fun we'll have at a delightful Merry Christmas celebration together a couple of months from now, right here in our spacious, gracious tent home in the Baker BOQ. We've had a good time this afternoon around the BOQ deploring our miserable existence and location. I think I've gotten a little punchy ever since eating those steamed franks we had for lunch.

Sosa says he's inventoried all the battery property and is recommending to the Battalion Commander that I be given command. Each time he tells me it's time for me to start signing the inventory form and taking over the battery equipment, I tell him where he can go with his BAKER—BELL'S—BEST. The dialogue has been keeping Weiss thoroughly entertained all afternoon.

We are invited this evening to a Halloween party to be given by the officers and men of Service (often pronounced circus) Battery. Refreshments will probably consist of military (3.2%) beer and pretzels. We'll also probably have entertainment in the form of a talent show, which might be passable. Anyway, McAllister called this afternoon from his new battalion and we talked him into coming over. It won't be anything like our old New Year's Eve parties hosted by the Bachelors' Club, but it could be a fairly enjoyable evening.

I love you with a great, enduring, an everlasting devotion. You're always with me and in my thoughts.

Goodnight, most perfect wife.

I love Lucy. Bill

1 Nov. 53

Dearest wife,

Somehow Sunday always seems to be the most beautiful day of the week. Today is quiet, bright and cool with a gusty breeze occasionally rustling the tall dried grass and the tired, twisted scrub trees.

We arrived back from celebrating Halloween at Service Battery about 10:30 and I slept till 8:30 this morning. The party was very well organized and I actually had a good time. Like Joan Oven's wedding reception in Oklahoma, there were flashlights to guide our jeep driver to the parking area. When we got inside the nightclub (Service Battery's Quonset mess hall), the hat check girl (an enlisted man) took my great-coat and homburg (field jacket and cap) and we shook hands with the proprietor (Service Battery Commander).

The Quonset hut was decorated with cardboard skeletons, black cats and witches, and one large table was laden with ham and cheese and crackers and spread and peanuts and all the rest. The beer was carried around and served from mess trays.

Unlike some of the battalion parties at Fort Sill, there were quite a few people at the party with whom you can have an interesting conser-vation. McAllister was there when we arrived and told me that discus-sions were not so upbeat over at the 31st F.A. Battalion. He lives with the 31st and works nearby with the new Korean 633rd F.A. Bn. He had some interesting accounts of his experiences as an advisor. It seems that the Koreans are very eager to learn. More on that later.

Back in the 49th Bn.: Also at the party was Lt. Collis, whom I've seen in church every Sunday. He is Able Battery commander. Also at-tending was Charlie Battery commander, Lieut. Eison, who was at Fort Bragg and is good friends with many Tiger Inners from Princeton '51.

Lt. Col. Moore, the 49th Battalion CO, had two Cokes and, with the Bn. Exec., left quite early. When he went over to John Herbert to thank him for the party, Herbert thought the Col. wanted a beer and promptly placed one in the Colonel's extended paw. Great merriment was enjoyed by all, including the Colonel.

Incidentally, your $250 allotment for October will arrive late in November. November's check will arrive around the 10th of December, and thereafter you should get the check regularly on the 10th of the following month.

I also have around $350 due me which I haven't bothered to draw yet. I'll pull it out in a few days and send it to you via money order so we can start accumulating some interest from the bank.

Just heard over Radio Vagabond that Princeton beat Brown and Dartmouth overwhelmed Yale. We should be able to take Harvard this weekend. Then the test with Yale, and finally Dartmouth. Next year we'll be there to cheer the Tigers on to victory!

Although I have an idea of what you mean, still it makes me sad to hear you say sometimes you really wonder if you are really married. I know it must be hard for you because we have never yet had a permanent home of our own, or children, and you are now back in school. Our separation now is hard on both of us, but Lucy, the time is passing and I will be home with you again soon. I love you, Lamb, with all my heart and feeling and faithfulness, and we together will soon start building a home with four children and the future and a life with the closest of all loves. You'll be very happy and secure and will know always how very married and intimate and close we are.

It's time for church now. We'll be together there, at least in my heart. I'll write more later.

Hello. I'm back, Lamb, and I love you and miss you so much. I've gotten bored and sad and lonely tonight and the only possible thing that could change it is seeing you and being cuddled. When I think back on all the wonderful things we've seen and done together and all the happy times, I can't help but think and pray for our future to come quickly so that we may be together to live and love for always.

As you said, sometimes if you think very hard about the person you love so much, it is difficult to clearly picture the person or to hear their voice. I think this is because we know each other through thousands of different moods and expressions and tones and feelings and it is very difficult to roll them all into one composite mental photograph that includes all we know of each other. Today's picture in the mind's eye doesn't make much difference when we have the eternity of the person locked tight in our heart.

I think of you and love you always. You are with me always, giving me encouragement, and God is with us both, guiding and guarding.

Good night, best wife.

With all my love and prayers,

Your faithful husband,

Bill

9
Acting Battery Commander

1 Nov. - plus, 1953

Hi Chicki,

I've just sealed up today's letter but more news has landed like a bombshell, so here goes!

It seems if you do a good job in one instance, you get another job. You're now talking to the new Commanding Officer of Baker Battery of the 49th Field Artillery Battalion! Thank goodness it's only temporary, but I'll tell you in a second about the challenge I'm going to have.

It so happens that Capt. Sosa convinced Col. Moore, and is going, day after tomorrow, on a two-week R&R, which now puts me in command. By itself that's not so much of a problem, but to complicate matters the division commanding general has decided to make a command inspection of one of the batteries of the 49th F.A. Battalion on 10 November. Capt. Sosa told me tonight that the Col. is very impressed with my work and even though Capt. Sosa will not be here, the Colonel told the Maj. General that Baker Battery was his best battery and as a result your husband and Baker Battery have been chosen as the showpiece for the 7th Division on November 10th.

If you think I was locked up over that lousy little Occupy-and-Shoot exercise, you should see me now! Not only do I have to whip the entire battery into perfect shape in nine days, but I've got to snow a tough old regular Army General. What I have to do is demonstrate to the General such confident leadership and show him around so energetically and thoroughly that he hasn't a chance to dig into any of our faults, or ask any questions that I can't answer. This seems to me like a tremendous undertaking. The Capt.'s and the Col.'s dependence on me, as well as the reputation and honor of the Battery and Battalion, is at stake.

I know you're behind me, Lucy, and that would help tremendously. Don't do anything on November 10th except plug for me, with perhaps a prayer or two. I'm going to need it. Groan.

Good night again, wonderful wife. I love you completely.

With all the emotion,

Bill

* * *

2 November 53

Dearest wife,

Tomorrow evening Capt. Sosa leaves for R&R and the responsibility for the battery becomes mine. If this were a civilian job, I'd be getting my first big raise now and begin thinking about my progression to eventual Chairman of the Board, or at very least President, and I would probably become mighty gung ho. In the Army you just get the added role and responsibilities that come your way. I can't even get promoted until I do 18 months in present grade.

I miss the opportunities that business offers, the freedom of civilian life, the beautiful countryside of the East Coast, eating a good home-cooked meal in my own dining room, going to a real party, driving an Oldsmobile at 60 along a smooth parkway. I miss all those things and many more, but most of all I miss the person I love more than anything else in the world, my wife.

I miss the adventure of our companionship, what we share, the new things we experience, and the old that we remember, the fun and laughter, the sadness and tears, and an occasional spitfire disagreement.

I miss talking to you, looking at you admiringly, being made to feel like a king by someone who counts, holding your hand, cuddling you, kissing you gently and expressing our love and feeling for each other beyond the measure of words.

I often think back to those two superb weeks in Bermuda. There is so much to look back on, and so much more to look forward to, that sometimes I get very impatient for the time to pass. I know in my heart, though, that God will take care of the time while we, with His guidance, take care of the present. This is the time during which we build and strengthen ourselves into worthy people. Worthy of each other and acceptable to God. When God knows that the current task is accomplished, without the delay, He will swiftly reunite us and our lives will take on renewed meaning.

I love you, Lucy, from the very bottom of my heart and soul.

Your loving, faithful, devoted husband,

Bill

* * *

3 Nov. 53

Dearest Lamb,

Things are going well so far in my new job as (acting) Battery Commander. No strain, no unsolvable problems, but I'm afraid the worst is yet to come. Lt. Weiss came back from a visit over at the 31st Battalion and reported that the new division commanding general is hell-on-wheels in an inspection. Weiss heard that during the general's first inspection he had completely silenced and dumbfounded the captain who was trying to escort him around his battery, and roared through the area tearing things apart, ranting and bellowing and trying to find things wrong. Whenever he found something wrong, he would shout, "What's the meaning of this, Captain?!" Before the captain could answer, the general was off again, looking for something else.

To the best of my knowledge, the best way to handle a person like that is to be as snappy and military as a civilian can, instead of being embarrassed over not-too-obvious shortcomings, and try to blast back a short, fairly logical answer. I'm not half as convinced I'm good at this sort of thing as Capt. Sosa and Col. Moore are, but they evidently believe I'm up to the challenge.

When Capt. Sosa heard about the new general's inspection procedure, he chuckled cheerfully and said, "Enjoy yourself, Lieutenant, while I bask away the happy days in Japan." They all laughed heartily. Then I asked him how he'd like to return to his battery and find himself reduced to second lieutenant, while any remaining battery officers were packing their gear and, being completely useless to the army, transferred as washouts to Alaska. Nevertheless, the Captain decided he will take his chances and left shortly after, in the highest spirits. It's very possible that I talked him into spending half the money he's taking with him on a phone call to his wife.

I'm so glad you had a good time at Cammie's. It always makes me happy when you are enjoying yourself. Did I ever tell you, Lucy, that you are the most perfectly wonderful person in the entire word? I love you with every bit of love that is within me. I cherish and love and adore you.

Good night, wife.

For always and ever,

Bill

P.S. I'm sorry it's a little short tonight, but I must write Chris and Aunt Wawee and it's been a long day.

* * *

4 Nov. 53

Dearest Lucy,

Today has been a little more varied than the most, not necessarily an improvement, but at least different.

From eight till ten this morning we attended our third class and practical exercise in some of the more obscure aspects of fire direction. This is one thing I really enjoy now. Major Guenther was a former math instructor at West Point and he really knows his stuff. He has been acting as coach while we simulate firing some of the more difficult types of missions. He's tough to follow because he is always way ahead of us, explaining fine points and figuring logarithms in his head as he checks our accuracy. I gather all I can from what he says and then re-explain it to my FDC (Fire Direction Center) crew. The result is rather encouraging.

We have another, major artillery Shoot coming up on 24 November. This will be an official Battery Test and we'll be graded on everything we do. I think Baker has a good chance of coming out among the best in the entire Division. At least we've gotten a good start in that direction. After the pending Command Inspection I'm going to begin twice-daily practice sessions for FDC, intense and lasting about an hour.

Enough of that kind of talk. However, I do like to tell you about all the things I'm doing because you're the person in the world who really matters to me and I want to share all my experiences with you. I love you, Lucy, so terribly much that I never can put it into words. You are a perfect, wonderful angel of a wife.

The enclosed Bank of Korea ten-hwan (pronounced "wan") bill is 1/180th of a dollar and is the remainder from this afternoon's shopping trip to Seoul. I'll be just as happy if I never returned to that mecca again. Its present population is 1½ million, down one million from the prewar figure. My impression of Seoul is that of a war-wrecked, packed, poverty-stricken mass of Oriental humanity in broken-down little buildings spread out as far as the eye can see. There are supposed to be some nice urban parts of town, but I had one of our Korean personnel as a guide, and the most magnificent place I saw was the Seoul PX and that wasn't much inside.

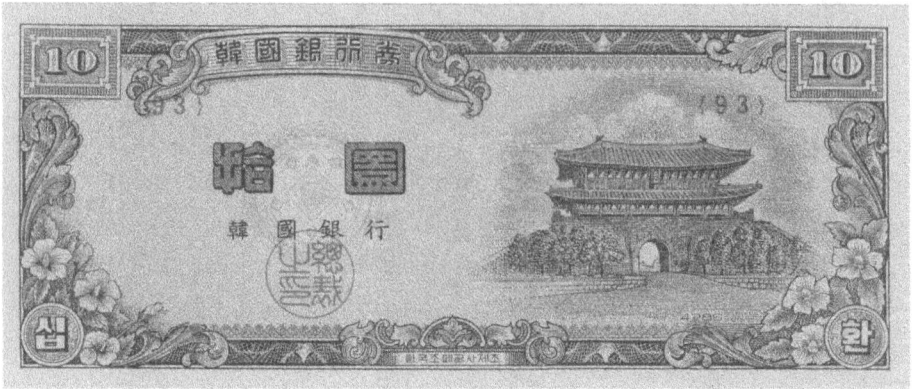

Korean currency mailed to Lucy. Value about 5 cents.

The primary purpose of our visit was to purchase some tablecloths and curtains for the mess hall (hut), which was never accomplished. We toured the innermost backstreets of the crowded city searching for hours, with me the only non-Oriental anywhere in sight.

After finishing the latest film with the shots of your forever-loving husband while back in the battery area, I started a new roll in Seoul. However, the shots you will see are only those of the main drag going into town. In the back-alley sections, I was too busy hanging onto my wallet and camera and trying to keep my driver from running down the mobs, to take any movies.

I have to admit that the very young children are attractive. Either they start walking when they are only about two months old or they are small for their age (I suspect the latter), but the youngsters, who are about as wide as they are high, are out in force. Those about the size of our niece, Rita are trotting about with younger siblings on their backs.

After a two-hour bouncing, jolting jeep ride to Seoul, the return trip seemed even longer under a chilly overcast November sky. I'm tired tonight and tomorrow I take reveille. The old sleeping bag is really going to feel good tonight.

Good night, precious wife. God bless you and guide us and re-unite us as soon as He is ready.

I love you always.

Devotedly,

Bill

* * *

Hi Chicken,

What a tough day, and it's still not over! The Battery Commander's life, in the days before a Command Inspection, consists of a million details. Col. Moore came over this morning and we spent three hours investigating every corner of the battery area while he told me what kind of improvements could be made here and there. He is going all out and will order the other batteries to cooperate in all the construction and digging and painting and beautifying that we're doing. If I want anything the other batteries can't furnish, I'm to call the Col. and he will arrange it.

I've got a bulldozer coming over tomorrow from the Marines. We're building a helicopter landing strip for the General and doing much leveling and grading and the bulldozer is essential. Another of the more essential jobs is building a concrete floor for the kitchen tent.

The Col. stayed for lunch and we had a pretty interesting little bull session. I had a good inward chuckle when he told me that Capt. Sosa had given me an exceptionally high verbal efficiency report a few days ago. I'm sure if Sosa hadn't, the Col. would have kept Sosa here for the Command Inspection instead of approving R&R.

I've been having a good time all day signing and bringing up to date back battery reports and papers. Here's how it looks:

William R. MacIlvaine

2/Lt. Artillery

Commanding

Reading the above sounds very new and strange, but is not as much fun as it might seem. I'm determined to do a good job, not so much for the army because you know I feel about that. Primarily I want to do a good job because of you. I think it's expected of me, and I know you'd be proud of me. Also I want to prove to myself that I am capable of doing a first-rate job when I work hard at it. Remember at Fort Sill when I used to be concerned about the relationship between one's effectiveness in the army versus in business? I knew I was giving a mediocre performance compared with what I felt the best people were doing. Hindsight is sometimes very illuminating. Now that I don't mind the actual job so much, and I appreciate the end purpose, I work hard and am getting results. Nevertheless I also am beginning to realize that a person like Capt. Sosa, with nine years of army experience, should be able to run a battery better and more efficiently than I can, with less than twelve months experience in the army and only three months in a howitzer firing battery.

What it boils down to is that I should quit comparing myself to other people and being so self-critical, go get a civilian job I like, and work hard at it. I'll do well as long as I have a challenge from which I can develop a feeling of personal achievement and success.

I sent Lt. Weiss off to Seoul today with sixty-two dollars from the Unit Fund to complete our purchases. Unit Fund records are amazingly complicated even for the army. The procedure is foolproof to the extent that a battery commander cannot misappropriate funds. For each army purchase stateside, you have to pay by check, get a documented receipt, staple both to a voucher and enter the transaction in the books. Here in this lonely and remote land we don't use checks, but the rest of the procedure is the same.

Late this afternoon Weiss gaily trooped in with all his purchases and receipts. There is only one catch. He had to buy the stuff on the Korean market, exchanging currencies and using hwan. The (possibly honest) little character who wrote out the receipts neither spoke nor wrote English. I am now the not-so-proud possessor of two attractive little sheets of paper on which it looks as if two inked-footed chickens had once held a tap-dancing contest.

I really can't blame Weiss. It was either a matter of accepting the receipts in Korean or not buying the tablecloths.

The only plan of action now is to somehow get the unintelligible papers translated, have Weiss certify both papers, and include the whole works in the records. I hope when our books are eventually inspected, our transaction will be approved. Can you imagine the look on the inspector's face when he turns a page and finds himself staring at two unreadable, scratched-up Korean receipts for sixty-two dollars?! He'll probably sputter for a week!

The other irregular event today occurred when we sent "boysan" out to refill our gasoline lantern after our light bulb went off. He brought the lantern back very pleased with himself and we proceeded to try to get it going. It is usually quite temperamental, but this time it simply would not start. After fifteen minutes of tinkering, I started to take it apart, and to my amazement I found the tool compartment full of gas. Further investigation disclosed that boysan had unscrewed the wrong cap and filled the tool compartment instead of the gas tank. Furthermore, he used red gas (leaded) instead of white gas. Deciding to instruct him correctly, we pointed out his error and he was very embarrassed. Then we took him over to the red gas and told him, "No, this is #10" (meaning very bad). Then we marched him to another drum and told him, "Yes, #1" (very good). Then we filled the gasoline lantern.

After repeated attempts to light the now very lowly regarded lantern still failed, we suddenly realized we had just filled it with Diesel fuel. Boysan rapidly became much less embarrassed over his previous error (but withheld his glee), and watched with great interest as we tried to clean out the gas tank. When we finally filled it with white gas, we almost had the thing going, but we busted the mantle (the part which actually shines). Then, before we had time to contemplate this newest misfortune, our light bulb suddenly blinked on and the whole mismanaged episode ended in a rather enlightened (pun intended) conclusion.

Good night, perfect wife.

I love you always with all my being.

You are the most wonderful, precious person on this earth.

Your loving, adoring,

Bill

* * *

Dearest wife,

Now how in the world does anyone expect us to prepare for in an Inspection when they keep stopping us and giving us preliminary inspections to see how we're coming? Col. Moore I don't mind, because he is always helpful when he comes around and he doesn't expect me to escort him around and make him feel important.

The Division Artillery Commanding General, currently only a bird Colonel named Lester, breezed in this morning with a sneer and proceeded to tell us we were in very poor shape for an inspection, even though we don't pretend to be anywhere near ready yet.

I have heard of this bird before. He is even more infamous than the General. Specialty: ripping up units during an inspection. Col. Moore actually apologized for him after he left. The bird is a stubby little thug with a long hatchet face. He hardly spoke a word, but threw things around that he thought were unsatisfactory. At one point he found some tent poles stacked in an ammo bunker and in his zeal of throwing them out on the ground, he hit Lt. Col. Moore on the shin. It was an exceedingly humorous event, but with great effort I managed to succeed in appearing very serious.

Aside from Lester's obnoxious character, the thing that really burned me was his comment when passing our prized PX: "That shack will have to go." No investigation, no questions, nothing. He just walked by, pointed to it and snarled.

The PX was not only my pride and joy, but the love of the entire battery. We had painstakingly scrounged lumber and iron and built a perfect little one-room store, complete with merchandise displays and counter. It was as yet unpainted and the roof needed more work, but given a couple more days and the General would've been pleased with it, I'm sure.

The next big problem was where to locate a replacement PX. When you're both the Battery Commander and Battery Exec., who do you consult with? It wasn't an appropriate problem for Col. Moore. However, it was a tough decision because it meant we would have to use one of our squad tents, and it would be the one which housed the overflow men from each gun section squad tent. I had to spread out personnel from one tent into already crowded other tents. I hated having to do it.

Aside from the PX deal and a temporary delay in our work, Lester didn't bother me to any greater extent. Almost all his criticisms were of projects that Capt. Sosa had sponsored. For my money, Sosa is a very fine BC, so I believe Lester would have found fault with anyone's work. He is returning again Monday. This time we will have warning and be forearmed.

Still, I am confronted with a million details—more work than it now seems we can accomplish by next Tuesday. The bulldozer does a number one job, but the operator is so exacting that he works slowly. I'll have to use him all day tomorrow and probably Sunday.

I'm also working the whole battery all Saturday and Sunday (à la Lt. Tassie) but I have gotten permission from Col. Moore to give everybody the day off after the Inspection. That is a feat I don't think Tassie would've bothered to venture.

I held a cadre meeting tonight with my seventeen top NCOs and sergeants. Together, they have probably spent more time in chow lines than I have in the army. It went well. I outlined all the plans for the Command Inspection and the work to be done, and I think I'll get a good effort from them all. Morale seems to be reasonably high.

Darling wife, I love you. It seems as if I work every minute of the day, but I'm thinking of you every second. You are an adorable, inspiring, precious comfort.

Good night, lamb. God bless you.
I long to kiss and hold you,
Bill

* * *

Saturday, 7 Nov. 53

Dearest Honeybun,

I wish tonight I could sit down with you and talk for hours, telling you all the problems and what we're doing about them, and generally how Baker, and specifically how your devoted husband, in particular, is progressing.

As far as the Command Inspection is concerned, I'm sure that even if we had an additional week to prepare, we still wouldn't be up to the level theoretically expected. Here is what we are up against: Division and Army staff officers decide on a certain policy. For example, oil drums for our heating stoves must be at least five feet from the tent. They publish a letter advising all units of this regulation. We are issued stoves with enough fuel line to place the oil drum only three feet from the tent. The headquarters units get extra fuel lines from their base supply depot. Lower units can't get extra fuel lines for love or money, and the base supply depot will not give us any. Result: our fuel drums are only three feet from the tents.

It sounds silly, but it's a fact. That is why theoretically we will never be prepared for Inspection. For practical purposes there are a vast number of things which could be done but which no unit would ever normally do except for Inspection. One example of the many hundreds of things in this category is a painted sign in each tent announcing the maximum heat setting on the dial of each heating stove.

These things are possible to be accomplished, but there are so many of them, each with its own problems, that I know we won't get them all done by the 10th.

I personally believe we are working hard and making excellent progress, and I doubt if any battery could do better. Therefore, no matter what the General's reaction, we will have accomplished a great task. Naturally, I will be a lot more pleased [so will the Col.] if the General agrees.

I received your wonderful long letter # 60 from Summit today and two heart-stopping pictures of you (among others). To see you at the desk at Westlands and in the easy chair at Cammie's made me want to take the next plane for Bronxville and then we take a plane for Bermuda or Dingman's Falls or Maine or anywhere, as long as I can hold your hand and look at you for the entire trip. I was lost in the closeness and love and adoration for my perfectly lovely, wonderful wife.

I love you so terribly much, Lucy, that it is impossible to describe. You're everything in life, everything in the world, and my wife.

Good night. God bless you. You have all my love and affection.

With all my love, heart and soul,

Bill

* * *

8 Nov. 53

Dearest Wife,

Two or three words to tell you that I love you with all my being.

I have been harassed today to the point where I can hardly tell you what year it is. Any army problem or trouble you could think of, I've got. Our inspection is scheduled the day after tomorrow, and for my money we are still in terrible shape. That bird Col. Lester will storm in tomorrow, and I know he'll rip us up again.

To top it off, our borrowed bulldozer got stuck deep in the mud early today and has all but buried itself trying to get out. I've been to every army and Marine unit within five miles trying to get a tank to pull it out. That's the only vehicle that can do it. We've had a 4-ton truck and a 2½-ton wrecker working all afternoon to no avail. Tomorrow I have been promised a tank by a Marine outfit. I am interested to see whether the tank or Col. Lester arrives in the area first. If it's Lester, Battalion will catch hell, because they swamped a bulldozer once before and it took three months to get it back in working order.

Can you tell me why they picked MacIlvaine to command a battery in a Command Inspection when the battery has been in this location only four weeks and the 2/Lt. concerned has been in Korea not a significant time longer? They say, "Stay loose," and I'm trying to do that, but what a challenge it is when I've been (acting) BC for only a week.

A more pleasant subject: Early Release. I have found the authorization circular: 7th Army Circular 76 paragraph 2b. I might qualify for release as early as 11 May 1954 if it is approved. I will submit the request letter after I have completed 15 months of active duty. There is no reason to actually expect this will be approved, so don't get your hopes up. God will decide if the time has come for my return. We can hope and pray, but not be sure of getting what we think is best. God will decide.

I love you, darling, most wonderful, cherished wife, and I live only for the day when I can take you in my arms and personally tell you.

Good night, Lucy. I pray that God watch over us and guide us and lead us down the path of swift reunion.

Adoringly,
Bill

* * *

9 Nov. 53

Dearest wife,

Tonight is the eve of the Inspection and we are slowly struggling into shape. With the short time we've had for preparation, I don't see how we can expect any sort of outstanding rating, but we have improved in everything tremendously since last week.

The bird Col. Lester actually remarked favorably on our progress over the weekend, didn't wreck quite as much here as before. He finally left the area, in his highly polished and stylized jeep, with a smile on his face.

We succeeded in getting our bulldozer hauled out by a Marine tank this morning while the bird was here. He didn't ask many questions about the bulldozer and probably assumed it had gotten swamped this morning. I wish I could've gotten a movie of the scene. The right side of the 'dozer was completely buried in water and slime and tilted over at a dizzy 45° angle. It was a very startling sight to see a roaring monster of the land pitifully entwined in the clutches of the deep (or at least in our abandoned rice paddy).

I wish I could go on and recount my every thought and action for today, but I've set reveille for 4:30 tomorrow morning and by that standard it is already way past midnight (actually, 9:30). Tomorrow may prove to be a long, very full day.

I love you, my darling wife, with all my heart and soul. May God be with us and guide us always.

Good night, Lamb, you are ever in my heart and thoughts.

Your loving, faithful husband,

Bill

* * *

10 Nov. 53

Hi Chicki,

This morning at half after nine a tiny dot appeared in the eastern sky, quickly grew to become a solitary helicopter, and gently set itself down on Baker Battery's carefully prepared landing field. Inside the glistening bubble sat an immaculate Two Star General, the Seventh Division's big boss, Maj. Gen. Lionel McGarr. The sole purpose of his visit was to find out whether a new 2/Lt. named MacIlvaine could show him an efficient, highly trained, well-prepared fighting artillery battery.

The responsibility for whatever he found, right or wrong, rested completely on the burdened shoulders of the lowly 2/Lt. Battery Commander. Although everything is technically my responsibility, I cannot take credit for everything that the General might have liked or disliked. It turned out to be, however, a highly satisfactory inspection! We have not received an official rating yet, but know we passed with flying colors. The General made a number of favorable comments, asked several questions which I was ready to answer, and made no unfavorable remarks. I have the unofficial personal satisfaction of knowing that those few points upon which the General commented were in no way attributable to the Battery Commander's or anyone's lack of preparation or effort. Just between husband and wife, you can hold up your head and be proud. But thank God with all humility that, as a team, we made the grade. Without Him, and you for support, we could never have passed.

I love you, my wonderful wife, more than I ever imagined was possible. Tomorrow is the promised day off but it's late now and I'm exhausted. In the morning I'll keep my appointment with Personnel to initiate a request for Early Release.

Good night, Lucy. Always remember how precious and important you are to me. God blessed me with you.

I love you always,

Bill

* * *

11 Nov. 53

Dearest Wife,

This was supposed to be a day of rest. It was for most of the battery, but not for me. I did as much as a regular day, although it wasn't all work. This morning was the usual two-hour class in FDC (Fire Direction Center) at Battalion Hq. Then I stopped in at Personnel and told them I was applying for Early Release. It is so wonderful that the mere thought of it makes me wild with excitement! If it would only become reality! I cannot say I'm optimistic over the chances. It is a long shot. But final approval or disapproval will come from the Department of

Army in Washington. Our theory at this point is nothing ventured, nothing gained.

* * *

I quit writing last night in increasingly lowered spirits as our light bulb, then heating stove, and finally the flickering candle gave up the ghost, one by one.

Getting back to my activities yesterday, I drove over to the 633rd F.A. Battalion (ROK) to visit McAllister. Remember I told you he was an advisor for a new Korean Battalion just being organized and trained. It was a very colorful experience, but I wouldn't want his job for anything. He gave me a comprehensive guided tour of the entire unit.

I couldn't believe it until I saw how it was done. Tents are dug into the ground so that only the roof and upper half of the sidewalls are exposed, thus eliminating drafts. Then straw mats and one blanket per man are laid on the ground and the men sleep in rows of fifty, on either side of the 20' x 40' tent.

The chow consists of two dishes: rice and kimchi, with the addition, a few times a week, of fish or chunks of pig, which get tossed in.

The Korean 633rd prepares their food in five large iron cauldrons (a.k.a. 55-gallon oil drums) set over five low earthen ovens. Three of the cauldrons contain rice and two kimchi. This is a highly colorful sight and it's most interesting to watch the cooking procedure. The rice is snowy white and the kimchi bright green. Water for cooking is procured from a nearby stream, undoubtedly polluted, and all the chow (i.e., both the gourmet entrees) are stirred with an old rusty shovel. I wasn't tempted to sample the offerings, but I'm going back as soon as I can to take a movie.

Today was very chilly and a gray sky seemed to threaten snow, but it never quite materialized. Tomorrow we will be issued our winter parkas and waterproof thermo boots, and start wearing our Siberian caps. We now even have heaters in a few of the vehicles (but no side curtains yet).

Unless it gets a great deal cooler than I've ever seen (and it could), we should do very little shivering this winter.

Good night, my darling honeybun. I love you faithfully, forever, with the greatest and most powerful affection. You are my life, my wife, and I cherish you.

God bless you and guide us, and if He finds we're ready, bring us together swiftly.

I love Lucy,

Bill

10
Gunnery with a Purpose

13 Nov. 53

Hi Lamb,

I just now asked Weiss what the date was. "The thirteenth, the third day after the Inspection," he said, and that sums up very candidly the way we feel now that it's all over. Before the Inspection I rushed around, non-stop planning, advising and supervising. Then the anxious moment arrived and, in the course of a few hours, passed. Finally we received the word of our excellent result. Afterwards came a tremendous let-down, but it wasn't as relaxing as we anticipated. Now after three days we are getting more or less back to routine.

Capt. Sosa returned late last night looking not too happy to be back, but still nourishing high hopes that his release will come through any day. He reported most of his time and money was spent shopping, sleeping and eating thick sirloins. He reported that his only conquest consisted of rebuffing some major who tried to requisition his jeep on the return trip from Seoul to our battery position.

Our last FDC class for the three firing batteries of the 49th F.A. Battalion was completed this morning. It consisted basically of a howitzer firing registration on a known point, but with the target out of sight, so the Forward Observer is unable to make aiming corrections. The problem involves computing muzzle velocity in feet per second and using weather correction tables to refine an exacting trajectory and direction. For the first hour, the entire class was completely lost.

About halfway through the second hour I began to understand how the principles applied, and when we got to the last exercise of the day, our Baker Fire Direction Center team shifted into high gear. We finished the problem ahead of the other two batteries and announced that we were ready with the gun data commands even before Battalion FDC had come up with the answer. Therefore I was quite chagrined when the Major came over with his previously computed data and announced that we were a good 300 yards off target.

After some silence he began checking our data against his own. Then he got out his slide rule and started figuring logarithms in his head again. Finally, he announced that Baker had the data right on the nose! Fifteen minutes later, after we all had packed up our plotting tables and equipment and were trooping back to our respective batteries, he was still trying to figure out where he made his error. Nevertheless, I attest that the Major is a whiz in the FDC, and at math, and a great Battalion Exec. Officer.

The date for our crucial field firing for the Battery Test has been set and comes up on the three days before Thanksgiving. We only have two weeks to practice and go over all we've learned, but I have a feeling Baker is going to do well.

I received two letters today from my most perfectly terrific wife. I'm particularly proud of you and impressed with some of the things you say and the insight behind them. I also enjoyed especially your reading of the lad with the 500 hats and your discussions with the six-year-olds on helicopters and trajectory. You'll be the most perfect mother of our four wild youngsters the world has ever known.

You are my most charming and wonderful cherished wife. What would be more wonderful tonight than a few hours at the Silver Spoon, or 42 Street, or The Mixing Bowl, or Danny's. We would dance and talk and laugh together. There are so many things I want to talk to you about, places I'd like go to with you, new experiences, and to express in person the depth of our love together. I'm waiting with my every hope and prayer for our reunion.

God bless and guide us both and grant that I may return soon. Good night, dearest wife. I love you ever faithfully, completely, and forever.

Your adoring husband,

Bill

* * *

14 Nov. 53

Dearest wife,

This has been a very lively Saturday. The day started off very quietly, with very little for me to do me to do until Capt. Sosa and I made our inspection at ten. I got up at the usual early hour nevertheless, to take advantage of the (seldom seen) fried eggs which Weiss reported were on the breakfast menu. We have had thick, rather unpalatable pancakes (known as gag pads) every couple of days and I have gotten to appreciate greasy fried eggs as a rare and delightful luxury.

After the inspection, my Chief of Firing Battery reported that the lone tree on a nearby hill which serves as one end of our Orienting Line had mysteriously disappeared. The Orienting Line is used as an alternate method of determining direction when we lay the battery and it is painstakingly surveyed in by Battalion. Evidently some uncaring, uninitiated soul decided that tree would serve him more satisfactorily as cut firewood and took an axe to it. The tree was over in the direction of Headquarters and Able Battery, so I'm sure the culprit wasn't from Baker, nor is it likely any civilians are infiltrating this desolate, deserted outback. However, Battalion is in quite a stew and tomorrow will have to survey us a new Orienting Line. I hope they have sense enough this time to adopt a more durable object.

After lunch Battalion donated the use of a Quonset hut, and each battery supplied a gambling table and operator, in an effort to raise $2,000 for support of an orphanage in Seoul. The turnout was enthusiastic, though I think the men's motive was directed more toward personal pleasure than any philanthropic urge. The significant attraction was a plentiful supply of G.I. beer.

I spent most of the afternoon spinning a roulette wheel and raking in piles of plastic chips. My job was a sort of combination between a Monte Carlo croupier and a circus barker. It was a very rare experience until my voice gave out.

Financially, the carnival was a roaring success, literally. I haven't seen the numbers, but I'm sure they've collected at least a thousand dollars. As far as the principle behind the party, I'm not too sure that I would agree, although it is probably the only way such a sum could have been obtained in so short a time.

The biggest mistake, or at least the most obvious, was an overabundance of the brew. Some of these young enlisted gentlemen have a few beers and begin to believe they are either Tarzan or Joe Louis. We've already broken up several fights, and I had to take one groggy gent to the medics with a swollen eye and a bleeding cheek that required two stitches. While I was at the medic, a lad from Charlie Battery was brought in with the same condition. Battalion learned a lesson tonight about controlling beer supplies and organizing gambling parties.

All is quiet now. I'm OD tonight, as I will be every night for a week, because Forward Observer Lt. Weiss left for the hill this noon. I don't mind the evening duties half as much as I do taking reveille every morning. Would you care to punch my chaplain's complaint card?

I remembered today you asked me about my Tiger Inn dues. We'd best pay this year's dues of $10. I don't remember paying any dues before, so if they ask for last year's dues I'll hope you pay that too.

Also, please send a dues check payable to Sigma Xi, Scientific Honor Society, Princeton , for $3 and addressed to: H.D. Holland, Geology Department, Princeton University.

I was so immersed and fired up with this Command Inspection that I forgot completely about football and the Harvard game until someone told me Wednesday that Princeton had piled up six big points and Harvard had bitten the dust. Never did I imagine in my wildest dreams it would ever be possible that my involvement in army activities would trump my interest in football! But it finally happened!

In about five hours Palmer Stadium will start to take on life again as the Yalies make their bid. Would I ever love to be walking out of Tiger Inn, through the crowds, down the path between Cap and Cottage, with all the noise and excitement and fun of being with you. You know, Love, you might, at long last, even talk me into buying you a hot dog!

Good night, Lucy, I love you passionately, affectionately, tenderly. You are my wonderful, perfect princess of a wife. God bless you.

Devotedly,

Bill

* * *

15 Nov. 53

Dearest Wife,

For some reason I'm exhausted tonight. I hardly did anything productive all day long, so maybe that's the reason.

This morning at 8:30, with one ear open and the rest of me asleep, I heard Capt. Sosa tell "Papasan" (more about him later) to bring some coffee up to the BOQ. Half an hour later as I struggled with my sleeping bag zipper, Papasan returned with a large, battered cardboard box containing everything on the breakfast menu complete down to the peanut butter, jam and salt and pepper shakers. Room service is delightful on a gray, cold Sunday morning!

Papasan has probably worked for Baker Battery longer than anybody here. He is said to be a former school teacher who toiled and suffered at menial labor under the Japanese occupation of Korea, starting over twenty years ago. He is elderly, gray haired and stocky. His primary task seems to be mess steward (if the army had that navy job description) for the officers of Baker Battery. His command of English seems to consist only of saying "Yes sir, yes sir," with a bow from the waist. When he cannot get something you've requested, his response remains the same, "Yes sir, yes sir," except it is then followed by "Hava-no," accompanied with another serious low bow. I have never heard him say "No sir."

We've got a new chaplain. He's a big, energetic, forceful man in his late 30s and he'll be a vast improvement. He came over to Baker Battery just before evening chow and we talked about the war and the army and faith and religion. He showed me a picture of his wife and children and I responded with your beautiful picture. He said he preached his first sermon at age sixteen and I told him you had done the same at age seventeen.

As he stayed for dinner and in later conversation, he remarked that he was surprised that in his experience so far with the five artillery battalions in the 7th Division nobody told any dirty jokes. It's very true, but I never noticed it before. I couldn't explain exactly why. Perhaps for the married men, the physical separation from their wives involves almost a sacred, intimate longing which doesn't seem appropriate to joke about. For the single men, I guess, the ladies seem so distant that sex is a discouraging thing to be reminded about. As a matter of fact, I don't think I've ever heard any jokes of any type over here.

At most of the parties we stand around and drink beer and talk about what we've seen and what we've been doing and the two types of "R". They include the Double "R" as in R&R and the Big "R" as in Rotation. Both amount to about the same thing: getting your aRse out of Korea. (Now I've just contradicted myself. I did hear that quip at a party.)

By the way, I got a fruitcake from Aunt Wawee today into which the Capt. and I have already started. It is #1.

Did I ever tell you that you are the dearest Chicki in the whole wide world? Well, you are. I'm starting to get punchy, so it's time for bed. Good night, angel, I love you more than I ever imagined possible.

Love and kisses,

Bill

* * *

Dearest Lamb,

Be it known that for today (but only for today) you are to regard yourself not as a lamb, but as a black sheep, and additionally, quite un-wooly. Want to know why?

In the first place I thank God that your letters 67, 68 and 69 did all come in one batch, otherwise I would have been awfully discouraged, knowing how forlorn you were. I understand why you sometimes get so discouraged and why you wrote as you did in one of those letters.

This is the most important thing, Lucy: you and I are husband and wife, irrevocably for ever and always bound together as one. There can be no halfway or holding back or partial trust if we are to have full and complete love. We both have to be open and let ourselves go completely, one for the other.

You and I and God all know that I will return before long. I pray He will bring me out of Korea at the latest in early July. I know only too well how discouraging and frustrating and lonely it is to be apart and how encompassing are the connotations of those three words. Usually when I feel the worst, I am reminded of one word: character. The more difficult the ordeal through which you navigate, the more strengthened is your character when you emerge.

Now it's my turn to apologize. Please forgive me for all the oration. It's not well expressed and it may not be exactly what I'm trying to say, but I hope at least you get a vague idea.

I drove over to Base Camp again after completely searching the local PX's. Result: I still haven't been able to find you a Christmas present that is halfway good enough. I'm pretty certain now I won't be able to find anything that you will really like until I go on R&R. However, I'm still trying, and I'll get you the nicest thing obtainable, so you'd better not stick your nose up at it. Ha ha.

Please tell all the families that their gifts will have to wait until I get to Japan.

Thanks for the pictures. Are you kidding? I wouldn't think of throwing them away. You are such a loveable Lamb (you may now once again consider yourself a Lamb, white and wooly).

We got our last winter issue today, fur-trimmed parkas. If I put on all the winter clothes I have, only my eyes and nose would be exposed, I'd weigh about 15 pounds more, and if it were 60 below, I'd probably be uncomfortably warm. Oops! Maybe I'll get a chance to prove that statement.

Goodnight, lamb chop. Remember how terribly much I love you and that you are the most wonderful, perfect, darling wife in the world.

I love you, I adore you,

Bill

* * *

18 Nov. 53

Dearest White and Wooly Lamb,

Enclosed is a fairly typical menu for your review and appraisal. Objectively speaking, it looks as if we eat high on the hog. Actually, the difference between this menu when prepared by the Ritz Carleton and the way it is served here is a difference so profound it must be experienced to be believed. But those hot biscuits! When you break one open, a cloud of steam rises in the air. This is a new addition to the menu, and I've told Sgt. Glaze to keep up the good work. Now I'll have to start thinking about that stupid waistline again.

```
                    BATTERY "B"
            49TH FIELD ARTILLERY BATTALION
                    APO    7

                                        18 November 1953


                    * MENU *

BREAKFAST

Grapefruit Segments
  Dry Cereal
    Whole Milk                  Note:  Save chow for One guard at each meal.
    Creamed Beef on Toast
      Jelly
      Oleo
        Coffee


                DINNER

                Grilled Liver
                Fried Onions
                  Boiled Potatoes
                  String Beans
                    Bacon
                    Hot Biscuits
                    Jelly
                      Peaches
                        Coffee


                                SUPPER

                                Fried Chicken
                                Giblet Gravy
                                  Mashed Potatoes
                                  Buttered Corn
                                    Bread
                                    Oleo
                                      Grilled Pineapple
                                      Coffee

    NOTE:  This menu is subject to change without notice.


                                    DANIEL L GLAZE
                                    SFC  Mess Steward
```

49th Field Battalion Menu.

I'm surprised that Bob Griffin reported to Cammie that they had a big war scare in his sector after the first 90 days of truce. There was very little speculation of that sort around here. After reading Pres. Syngman Rhee's statement on the truce, I can agree with him on one principle only. Korea should be united and free. However, as far as his reasoning about stopping Red aggression by now conquering all of Korea, he's taking us further than I'm ready to go. The United Nations has already accomplished the limited task which they initially attempted, that is, an armed resistance against Communist aggression and the defense of South Korea. North Korea was already ceded to the Communists by agreement after World War II.

Luxury is a home-made door on your BOQ.

Even though Rhee still wants all of Korea, I cannot believe he is so out of the control of the U.N. and U.S. that he could engineer a resumption of hostilities here. The negotiations will resume painfully slowly with many seemingly hopeless deadlocks, but I think and pray they will continue to keep us one step ahead of all-out war again.

Talking about Rhee, our old, tough, ex-airborne first sergeant has gotten a puppy.

Meet and Greet "Syg."

"Syg" contemplates chewing my thumb.

He is about eight weeks old, about ten inches long, and six inches wide. The name is Syngman, known by the troops as "Syg." The dog is ignorant of the word, housebroken, and has taken a fiendish affection toward the BOQ. I'll get a movie of the two of us leading a dog's life in my next sequence. Syg is very cute and furry and looks as if he might be part police dog. Time will tell. He takes an awful beating around the battery. Everyone who sees him either pats him, or growls at him, or playfully pushes him around.

Heading out for a Shoot and a playful "Syg."
Video Link: http://lovelettersfromthefront.com/videos

At this point my longing and love for you are so over-powering that I feel like going AWOL and hitching a flight away from all the loneliness and heartache of separation and appearing in an instant by your side. I don't think it will take long before you'll be so accustomed to having me around that you'll wonder if we ever really have been separated by the miles.

God and our great love will always keep us close.

Goodnight, my darling wife. In a few minutes I'll be talking with God and praying for our guidance and swift reunion.

Adoringly,

Bill

* * *

Dearest wife,

Wow! Was it cold last night. The thermometer registered 10, but it felt like 10 below. Inside the sleeping bag with the stove turned on low it wasn't too uncomfortable, but of all nights, I woke up at 3:00 and decided I wanted to trot outside for a few minutes.

It was a tremendous effort and when I put my bare feet into a pair of icy boots it was like falling into a tub of ice water inside a deep freeze.

Clad only in my long johns and unlaced boots, I stumbled from the tent running at top speed and returned in even greater haste.

Tonight seems only a little less frigid, almost as if the beautiful full moon directly overhead were shedding a little warmth as well as light.

I got your package of Charms and peanuts and gum and lollipops today. You are so sweet and wonderful and thoughtful and I appreciate very much all the many loving things you do for me. Capt. and I started out on the lollipops right after lunch. I know we'll make a big hit with the troops, walking around with a lollipop sticking out of our mouths.

It's late now because I argued a court-martial case tonight as defense counsel. The defendant was a three-time loser. First, he broke restriction twice in the States, then he was AWOL for over two months. Tonight he was up for Drunk on Duty. I did my best to get him a light sentence, but he got 3 months confinement and was fined 2/3's of his pay for 6 months. My first venture as a defense trial lawyer was none too successful.

Goodnight, beautiful wife. I love you with all my heart and soul.
God bless you, encourage and guide you.
I love Pooh Bear,
Bill

* * *

Dearest Wife,

For the first time today since Sasebo, Japan, I got a chance to sack out in the afternoon. I crawled into the comfortable sleeping bag at 3:30 and got up just in time for evening chow!

After chow we saw the movie "Monster from 20,000 Fathoms." Strictly grade B, but enjoyable after all the western shoot-'em-ups. After we returned to the BOQ a great discussion arose as to the possibility of sea serpents, then flying saucers, and somehow this worked into politics. We dealt at length on the wisdom of subsidizing farmers, then hit on world trade, then government, and evolution of government, and evolution of man and finally, religion. We finally decided that religion is the only thing that can guide mankind toward harmony in the foreseeable future. Most agreed it would take a major intervention by God to bring the peoples of this world into harmony and peace within our lifetime, or even that of our children or grandchildren. However, I believe God holds a different relationship with the world; instead of viewing us as a collective mass of mankind, God knows and loves each of us individually and seeks us out, interacting with each of us personally, as responsible individuals—accountable to Him.

The discussion was absorbing, animated, and at times became quite enthusiastic. It was interesting but wholly theoretical, because none of us is well versed enough to advance much more than ideas off the top of his head.

The cold rain is now pouring down in a steady cascade and Sosa and Weiss have turned in. So here I sit by candlelight again, with my thoughts of you and my love and my loneliness and my desire for your companionship.

I love you, Lucy. I need you, and without you my life is only half complete. The only redeeming part of this separated existence is that we are always building and learning and maturing so that we can be better people, a better husband and wife, and better parents and then even grandparents. It's said, if one is not always moving ahead, you are slipping backwards.

I don't think this period of separation will accomplish our goals by any means, but it has at least strongly reemphasized the basic rock-bound foundation of our love. It has given us a greater and more complete faith in God and in each other. It has matured us in many respects and given us the desire to work together toward each other, for each other. We are one person living together, experiencing together, loving together.

I love you, Lucy, my thoughts and prayers are always with you. God be willing that our reunion be swift.

Goodnight, precious lamb,

Bill

* * *

22 Nov. 53
Sunday

Dearest Lamb,

I spent the entire day in the back of an open jeep bouncing and jolting over eighty miles of cold, rough dirt roads. What a life! Even with my parka and my winter mittens I was frozen. Next time I'll wear more underneath. I haven't gotten my thermo boots yet, so the feet were numb as a board most of the day.

We stopped at "I" Corps Hq. for lunch and ran into none other than Tim Sick, lately of Tiger Inn. He's been here since March and is now teaching at the "I" Corps NCO academy. He expects to get out after nineteen months, says there's a much better chance if you are with Corps Hq. rather than in the field with a Division. For some reason officers are critically short now in Division Artillery, although we are way over-strength on EM. I hope last summer's BOC classes begin arriving soon for the sake of my Early Release.

Time alone will tell the result. Keep hoping and keep praying. It will be God's will whenever I get to come home. I only pray it will be soon.

The doggone lights went out just as I started writing, and with Weiss and me now sharing one lousy candle, it's so dark I can hardly see the page.

I love you very dearly, angel. I dream of you and think of you and your love always.

Devotedly and Adoringly, Bill

* * *

23 Nov. 53

Dearest Chicken Pot Pie,

For some reason today has been more fun than any day I've spent since I've been in Korea. Tomorrow we leave for our assembly area about forty miles east, near the area where we fired our last Shoot. The following morning we fire, pack up, and return in the afternoon. The next day is Thanksgiving.

Today all three of the 49th Bn.'s firing batteries have been making their last-minute feverish preparations. We've been at work over here in Baker, but we officers of Baker are playing it very cool.

The working atmosphere here is really great. There is none of the feeling as at FARTC (Field Artillery Replacement Training Center) at Ft Sill that you have to avoid or hide from the Colonel. We don't engage in "make-work" projects. The Colonel very rarely comes around snooping, but if he does and happens to find us in the BOQ having a bull session or resting, old Capt. Sosa says don't let it bother you. As long as we continue putting out excellent results, the Colonel should have no gripes.

Baker Battery. We live with mud.
Video Link: http://lovelettersfromthefront.com/videos

That's typical of Sosa, who is very easy going, with twelve years of army experience and a top "7" on his last efficiency report. Minimum wasted effort and maximum results. Between periods of enthusiastic, concentrated, productive effort, we relax and make fun of the army and our sorry, unhappy plight.

We laughed all through lunch today. For the second straight day we had hamburgers, which I enjoy but Sosa can't stand. He sputtered and fumed while Weiss and I dove in hungrily. Finally he began lecturing us on some really fine dishes served in Puerto Rico. One which he described at length was stuffed cheese. "Using one of those round red Holland cheeses, you dig out the interior and stuff it with dice-sized tidbits of chicken mixed with onions, peppers and the trimmings. Then you peel off the red outer covering of the cheese and put the preparation in the oven for a few minutes until it's heated through, and the cheese is soft and partly melted." He finished his dramatic and convincing oration, sat back very pleased with his presentation, and awaited our reaction. Weiss's only comment was "And Captain, about the cheese that is scraped out of the cheese to make room for the stuffing, I suppose you use that to stuff the next chicken?" I howled so loudly that all the E.M. in the (Quonset hut) mess hall stopped eating and turned around to see who and what was causing this hilarious disturbance.

A friend of Weiss' called and announced his Early Release had been approved and he was leaving today. His departure plans immediately brought up the same subject about which we tirelessly expound every day.

We don't talk so much about what our possibilities are, but rather what a shame it will be when one of us (the speaker) has to leave the other two behind in this wonderful and inspiring corner of the globe, while he takes a tiresome, boring, long ride back to the States.

And so it goes; we are not so much bemoaning our fate as making fun of it.

Thursday, Thanksgiving Day, whether or not we get the day off, we have decided to borrow shotguns from our battery interior guards and go pheasant hunting. This area abounds with the birds so we shouldn't come back empty handed. We will have turkey for dinner and pheasant for supper.

The Capt. brought out his service ribbons this afternoon so that we would all know the correct uniform and decorations to wear when we start home "next week." I found to my surprise that I've already earned four and possibly five decorations and perhaps one battle star, according to existing regulations. At the end of our discussion it was unanimously agreed that the army could take all its decorations and... (well, possibly burn them) if they would send us home tomorrow.

I'm glad my letters are arriving regularly again after #53 and #54. However, it sounds like I may have put my foot into it when I invited you, during that phone call, to share my sleeping bag with me. At least in the sleeping bag you wouldn't be able to crowd me out in the cold like you enjoyed doing while occupying more than your half of the double bed!

My wonderful Chicki, I love you so tremendously! How can one person admire and adore another so completely? You are a precious, wonderful angel of a wife and my thoughts and love and prayers are always with you.

Goodnight Lucy, with love and kisses.

Your faithful, devoted,

Bill

* * *

24 Nov. 53

Dearest Chicki,

We pull out in a matter of seconds. I love you dearly!

Love and kisses,

Bill

P.S. Returning from Btry. Test tomorrow night—wish us luck!

* * *

25 Nov. 53

Dearest Chicki,

You are now talking to one very tired but highly satisfied 2/Lt.

Even the Division Artillery C.O., Col. Lester, sported a wide smile as he observed Baker in action. We won't get our official score until next week, but it has been estimated that we rated among the top in Division! Col. Moore was greatly pleased with our performance and told me that I did a Number One job. Said I reminded him of an "old (regular) army" Exec. That is high praise!

Preparing to shoot.
Video Link: http://lovelettersfromthefront.com/videos

Capt. Sosa and I have decided we might enlarge the sign on the hillside by our battery entrance, and make it more descriptive. How about "BAKER—BELL'S—BEST," adding the phrase "BY TEST." If we do turn out to be best in Division, we'll incorporate that improvement.

Firing high angle.

Video Link: http://lovelettersfromthefront.com/videos

I'll tell you more tomorrow, perfect wife. Right now I can hardly keep my eyes open.

Goodnight, Lucy. I thank God for His support and backing today and also for yours.

You are an adorable angel.

My complete love,

Bill

11
Not All Work

26 Nov. 1953
Thanksgiving Day

Dearest Pumpkin,

Tonight I was going to write you a good long letter telling you all about our Battery Test and Thanksgiving Day and pheasant hunt in detail, and answer your last three typically wonderful letters.

I wrote the date and Dearest Pumpkin (in honor of the occasion) and the lights went out. That was an hour ago. Since then I have searched the battery area for illumination, worked for half an hour over a Coleman Lantern that would not start, and finally lit one lousy candle. In the meanwhile the generator went on and off several times. By now I'm so darn grumpy at the whole situation that I'm just going to give up and go to bed. And the hell of it is that I've got so much to talk to you about!

I'm enclosing the Thanksgiving menu. The meal was good but couldn't begin to compare with the best I ever ate.

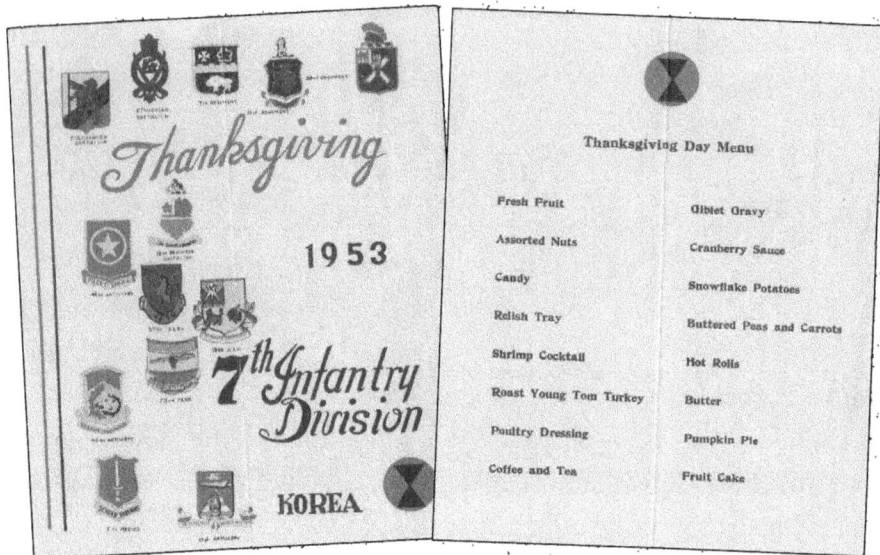

Thanksgiving

1953

7th Infantry Division

KOREA

Thanksgiving Day Menu

Fresh Fruit	Giblet Gravy
Assorted Nuts	Cranberry Sauce
Candy	Snowflake Potatoes
Relish Tray	Buttered Peas and Carrots
Shrimp Cocktail	Hot Rolls
Roast Young Tom Turkey	Butter
Poultry Dressing	Pumpkin Pie
Coffee and Tea	Fruit Cake

I haven't forgotten our first Thanksgiving dinner you served this day last year. That's my idea of a #1 meal. How can one Chicken Pot Pie be such a Lamb by cooking a turkey? I'm even including your cornbread stuffing in my praise! (You'd best file this letter in case of a stuffing disagreement next year. I still like chestnut stuffing.)

The Thanksgiving "hunt" was great sport even if there was only a single opportunity for a shot. Too bad we don't have a hunting dog for a pointer ("Syg" is totally untrained). Somewhere along the trail, I unwittingly flushed a pheasant from a bush only inches from my toes. It exploded upward and outward with the sound and fury of a grenade. By the time my shock subsided and I clicked off the safety, the pheasant was high in the sky, out of range, and I missed.

The Capt. and I and Weiss walked for miles up and down the dried-up countryside enjoying brisk exercise and chilly late autumn air. Since it is remotely possible the area had once been mined, and out of respect to the Capt.'s rank, we deferred the lead of our file to him and were heedful to walk in his footsteps, besides taking care to remain a goodly number of paces back.

Goodnight, precious wife. My love and complete devotion are with you now and always. God bless you.

Your still grumpy, but always and forever adoring, faithful
Bill

* * *

Dearest Lamb,

At eight thirty this morning I set out with my nose pointed eastward on a twofold mission. It was comparatively comfortable bouncing along bumpy roads in Capt. Sosa's heated jeep, but my venture took the entire day and I finally arrived back in the battery area after four this afternoon.

My primary mission was to finally, without further delay, find your Christmas present. I was bound and determined not to return empty handed. Now I've returned with two gifts and a brilliant idea for a third, which I can arrange with another excursion. I hope by now you're getting profoundly curious. I'm hopeful you will like what I've gotten. I found it impossible to pick and choose at any one destination. Rather, I was seeing something almost suitable in one location, and then piling back into the jeep and searching the countryside for the next possibly promising place.

I got one present in the 7th Div. Hq. PX and the other in a PX over in the Commonwealth Division Area. The quality of both presents is top notch and the spirit and love and care with which they were selected is just a small indication of my overwhelming love and dedication for the most wonderful and precious person in the entire world.

I'm going to scrounge up some lumber tomorrow and make a wooden box in which to pack them so they can go out in the next airmail. I haven't had more fun "since da hogs ate ya uncle"!

We celebrate Thanksgiving with friends.
Video Link: http://lovelettersfromthefront.com/videos

The second part of today's effort was to locate a replacement part for our broken-down little gasoline engine that powers our battery's electric generator. We can't go through regular supply channels because we are not authorized to have a generator in the first place. I finally got the part, through the aid of Capt. Sosa's brother in Service Battery, but found upon my return, to everyone's dismay, the part won't fit. Tomorrow we'll send somebody over to the 71st Signal Company and see if we can beg, borrow or steal another part. In the meantime we are reduced to using candles again.

My movie making is continuing on schedule and I now have completed all but four feet of my second reel for November. I'm glad you liked the last one so much. I can't wait to see them myself and narrate in person. I took a shot of the mess hall (Thanksgiving Day) and hope you'll be able to see inside with enough detail to make out some Korean youngsters at dinner. We invited the families of our Korean personnel. One little guy in particular gave me a hard time. He's probably the only one you will be able to see. Every time I would laugh and wave at him he would smile, and every time I started to take his picture he would get very curious and look serious again.

Taking a stroll to deliver the payroll.
Video Link: http://lovelettersfromthefront.com/videos

Incidentally while I was at Div. Hq. I drew a check for $350 payable to you and mailed it from the Finance Office in a big official envelope. It should arrive in Summit the same day you get this letter. I hope you will use it to buy that suit you want, and anything else you'd like to have.

The Battery Test: Although the results are still not official, it's common knowledge that we beat the daylights out of Able and Charlie. It wasn't even close! Much of the individual credit has to go to Capt. Sosa. He had every job and every action planned out in advance in detail so that every member of the battery knew exactly what he was supposed to do and when. And still there were a hundred things that could have gone wrong. We were graded on Speed, Accuracy and Procedure. A little error anywhere along the line could have messed up the problem.

The Test started as we waited in a camouflaged assembly area fifteen minutes' drive from the firing point. There an umpire met us, gave us maps, a direction of fire, and the enemy situation. Then the umpire clicked his stopwatch. Off went the FO's with another umpire to establish an OP, and off went the battery to get into position and start delivering the requested fire. Starting off, we were allowed 45 minutes to pull in our perimeter defense, hook the guns to our vehicles, move out onto the road, travel to the new area, occupy the position, lay the battery parallel, set up FDC with the new muddy location maps, establish communications, unload and uncrate the ammunition, set up a new perimeter defense, contact and receive from the FO's the target data for FDC to translate into gun commands, adjust (using two guns) our fire onto the target, and finally fire two volleys accurately on the target using all six guns (Fire For Effect).

Firing and flaming also Capt Sosa, the Lt. Col and Maj.
Video Link: http://lovelettersfromthefront.com/videos

We did it in 39 minutes. The remainder of the Test consisted of shooting various types of firing situations, running a survey and laying wire so that telephone could replace radio communication.

All of the many sub-phases of the problem were individually timed and evaluated as well as the overall result of our activity.

There was lots of top brass on hand to observe, and I really kicked up the dust [mud] with my hustle and enthusiasm and gave them a show for their money. For every round we fired, I personally checked the firing data in Fire Direction Center, then ran down to the gun positions, shouted out the gun settings keeping eye contact with the crew Chiefs, and then, when all reported ready, ordered, "Battery, Fire." All the guns firing in unison, exactly at one time, sounded like a single shot. Time was crucial to our success, so it was necessary to shake a leg.

Everybody was wildly approving of our results and I'm still hearing stories about it. At the Bn. Officers Club tonight Maj. Guenther introduced me to a visiting captain as "the Executive Officer at Baker Battery who did everything except guide the shells to the target after they left the guns."

I have gotten tremendous personal satisfaction out of the results of our Battery Test, but I try not to let it show, except of course to my other half. I feel very strongly that our success was due almost completely to the powerful backing of God and my wife. We can both thank God by trusting in Him and leading the kind of lives that He expects of us. The best enduring thanks that I can give you now is my faithful, complete, enduring love and adoration.

You are the sweetest and most lovable white wooly lamb that ever lived.

Goodnight, Lucy. I love you.

Your devoted,

Bill

The way to stay warm is keep moving.

* * *

Sunday, 29 Nov. 53

Dearest Chicki,

I never seem to have a chance to write during daylight, and this single-candle eyestrain in the night is nothing but #10. I wish I'd written you earlier today because I was in a positive and energetic frame of mind. Then I lit a candle and started writing the parents unsuccessfully. I started off a letter to Mom and Pop, but after one sentence that took about half an hour I tore it up and abandoned the task in frustration.

Anyway, Sunday, today, began with a good warm quiet morning and we slept late [until almost 8:30]. I received the home church bulletin, a letter from Mom, and four letters from you! I'll answer them tomorrow.

After lunch we had an ultra-rare and unexpected visit from a couple of civilians. They were the Korean version of traveling salesmen. Their product was photography, delivered by an enormous, ancient, old-fashioned box-like camera. I spoke with the First Sergeant, who turned out the battery for a group picture. Then for two dollars, I had a picture taken of me standing on the steps in front of the BOQ. They said they'll return tomorrow with the prints. So tomorrow I'll mail them along.

Later, Weiss and I jarred and jolted off to church. It was a very good service by a new chaplain, Weaver, the character I wrote you about ten days or so ago.

After church it was time for the weekly shower, one of the greatest pleasures of life. Then feeling refreshed and revitalized, wearing all clean duds, I took off for Service Battery, where they have a machine that wire-banded my wooden crate. However, it took two hours before I finally got the job done and, at long last, put your Christmas present in the mail!

In my best duds - ready for church.

I stayed for supper and finally arrived back at Baker around seven.

I understand completely, from your letter, how you feel sometimes when it just seems that the only thing satisfactory is to sit down together and talk about everything and about nothing for as many hours as we can keep our eyes open. Do you realize fully how terribly much I miss your companionship and how terribly much I adore you and how close I always feel to you?

I think, except for the day of our parting, the time currently is the toughest of our separation. We've been apart long enough to be totally aware of the emptiness of our lives apart and yet not quite long enough to be able to begin counting the days or hours that will bring us swiftly together again.

This is the timeless age between departure and arrival. Because it is the most discouraging time, it is the time during which we must muster all of the courage and character that we possess, trust perfectly in each other and above all have complete and active faith in God so that we may follow confidently along the path which He is carefully leading us, without stumbling.

The great news: Results of the Battery Test are still unpublished, but we today found out officially that Baker [that's me] of the 49th Bn. scored second-highest of the dozen or so artillery batteries of our 7th Division! One battery, in the 47th Bn., got a couple more points than we because on the first mission fired, their rounds landed in a pattern that covered the target somewhat more evenly than ours. Aside from that, both the two top batteries performed in much the same manner and score. I don't know who the other battery's Exec. is, but I did hear today that old bird Col. Lester has been saying some complimentary things about me up at Division Hq.

Will they give me a raise or promote me? Hell no! They'll just expect more of me and Baker next time we fire. I wish I were a civilian and had you in my arms.

I love you forever, completely.

Goodnight, favorite wife. Bill

* * *

30 Nov. 53

Dearest Wife,

Groan and still more groan. We are now down to our last candle.

I tried two more likely places today in a renewed effort to scrounge up that part (connecting rod) to repair the engine of our generator. No success, but I did get a lead which I'm hoping may be the answer. An officer at the U.N. Munsan Warehouse told me I might have some luck with an Engineer Maintenance Company about 30 miles to our rear. Tomorrow I'm sending out a mechanic with the broken part, and in the meantime cross your fingers that they can locate a replacement! We have even gone so far as to order the part from the Sears Roebuck catalog, shipping from the States, although it will take weeks before it arrives.

The Korean photographers returned with their wares. Enclosed is the picture taken yesterday. Because I'm standing on a step, my legs and feet look double sized. As OD, I'm wearing my forty-five pistol and the red scarf, but they don't show up at all. I'll have a better picture taken in a couple of days.

The photographer gave me these pics free, since because Sosa wasn't here at the time, I was the officer who gave the permission to work in the battery area.

I finally got a letter written to Mom and Pop tonight, so it's late now.

I love you, Lucy, completely, always.

Your devoted husband,

Bill

* * *

2 Dec. 53

Dearest Wife,

Hurrah! At long last we are existing in an environment of brightly lighted glory! No longer doeth a flickering circle of candlelight poorly penetrate a murky, fathomlessly gloomy tent!

Another kind of gloom has replaced the darkness. As I expected, last evening my poor Early Release application landed back into my tight little fists, "not favorably considered at this time due to the critical shortage of officers." So it is now my plan to wait a month or, until we start getting in more officers, whichever happens sooner. Battalion has gotten a 2/Lt. and a Capt. in the last two weeks, so maybe they are on the way. Our other possibility, which also includes watchful waiting, is the expected new circular for Early Release for Category IV, which should come out this month.

I'm sorry I can't be more definite with my news, but you know the army. Happiness will probably arrive very suddenly when we're not expecting it. In the meantime we must have patience. I know that's hard, but there is no alternative—patience, faith in God and hope.

I hope you will forgive me for not writing last night. I was feeling low then, and I still do for various reasons. Most pressing is that harassment has been steadily increasing all the way down the line. We, as a battery, are less on our own and are becoming more and more subject to controls such as training schedules, inspections, and officer classes which are decreed from the top, down through the chain of command, and which we receive from Battalion. We are slowly losing the informality of a combat outfit and taking on the aspects of a garrison-type unit.

Talking about combat, this still officially is a period of combat (with combat pay). Yesterday Capt. Sosa wrote out an efficiency report for me to cover my first two months as an officer under battle conditions (officially, hostile fire). He wrote out a wholly complimentary report and gave me a 6 (out of 7) for an overall rating! I'm delighted with that report, even if currently the only hostile fire I'm experiencing is the flame of the candle sputtering and dying out.

Do you know what just happened? That damned generator just quit! Going out to investigate.

Back again. It's not too bad. The engine blew a gasket, but we should be able to get another tomorrow from the Battalion maintenance shop. It's just one more night in darkness. I need cheering up.

McAllister just called. He had been on R&R for a full 17 days instead of the usual week in Japan, plus the two days in transit. He was being carried as AWOL in his Battalion, and he wouldn't tell me over the phone what the reason was for his long absence. He is not the type who would lose his head, or get thrown in jail, or do anything scandalous, so it will remain a mystery until tomorrow.

Another bit of local news. We are going out to the field (as if we weren't there now!) on 14 December for five days of firing and our Battalion Test. We will return on the 19th. From then until Christmas this 2/ Lt. is going to take a self-appointed vacation.

You know, Lucy, the greatest pleasure I have in life is loving you. I shall never stop wondering how one husband can be so lucky as to have such a wonderful, beautiful, smart and adorable wife. I am so overcome with love that I almost feel rash enough again to offer to share my sleeping bag with you! Best I quit and turn in.

I love you so. God bless you, Wife. Good night.

Your faithful, adoring and overwhelmingly in love,

Bill

* * *

3 Dec. 53

Dearest Love,

How did you ever in this world guess (I'm grinning) that we needed a Coleman Lantern?! Your terrific package arrived this morning and everything it contained was something I had wished we had. The Coleman Lantern with the extra gas valve and spare mantles was top priority. Baker's makeshift gasoline engine-powered electric generator is still running in a hit-or-miss fashion, so the Coleman is now our dependable light source. Many, many thanks. Also, many thanks for the little Primus water heater. We haven't fired it up as yet, but I'm familiar with them and know it's a Number One machine.

The knife with all the Swiss blades is something I've been planning to buy, but I haven't seen any around. And then you sent me one! You are one smart Chicki.

Let's face it, you couldn't have sent a better package of things I really wanted if I had actually asked for them item by item! What makes you such a smart old white woolly Lamb? What makes me love you so!!

We got a great little training gadget at the Battalion Hq. yesterday. It's called a Bishop Battery and consists of three miniature howitzers mounted on a platform. They fire one-inch steel balls by compressed air up to a distance of 80 yards. They employ the regular sighting instruments from the 105 mm howitzer and because they are very accurate we can practice every procedure of actual firing, except exercising the gun crews.

I spent an hour this afternoon playing with our new toy. On a level area sawdust was spread on the ground, then tin cans were placed in the target area. When the steel ball landed in the sawdust it kicked up a little puff of dust. A Forward Observer with binoculars occupied a little rise nearby and, using the ratio of one yard in the target area to 100 yards in a real target area, sent his corrections to an FDC (Fire Direction Center) set up near the guns. FDC plotted each round using the FO's corrections and, also by telephone, sent their commands down to the guns. The guns then entered the revised settings, fired, yelled, "On the way" to the FO, and awaited the new corrections.

Great sport! We fired two Precision Registrations and an Area Mission. The procedure was exactly as if we were firing live 105 mm rounds except that each round didn't cost the harassed taxpayers $37 apiece.

As Battery Executive Officer, tomorrow I drive over to the 47th Bn. for an all-day class for all 7th Div. Artillery . Does a class on howitzer maintenance sound exciting? However, I'm rather interested in meeting the other Execs., and especially meeting and comparing notes with the one who (ever so narrowly) edged us out on the Battery Test.

Loved that fur trimmed parka.

McAllister stopped in today and it turned out that he had gotten intestinal grippe on the last day of his R&R, along with two other officers. All had eaten their previous meal at the same restaurant. All three went together to the hospital for a week. In a streak of good fortune, on the last four days he was given a pass each evening. Says he had a fine time and wouldn't mind having to spend another extra week indisposed in Japan.

It sounds like a good escape from Korea, but I'd rather make the escape by flying all the way to New York!

I love you, Lucy, with a great and longing devotion. You are my very favorite wife.

Good night, pumpkin. God bless you.
With a hug and kisses,
Bill

* * *

Dearest Pooh,

The Coleman Lantern is proving its worth a hundredfold again to-night. That new connecting rod, you remember we procured for the gen-erator, broke in the same place as the old one. And after only one day's use! It must be due to the faulty design of one of the adjoining parts. The next question was how to get another engine to replace the little one-cylinder engine that powers the generator.

After much discussion, one of our mechanics remembered that about four months ago we had to dispose of an extra jeep engine which we possessed, but was unauthorized. Because a command inspection was imminent, what did some lamebrain do but bury the thing! Luckily, he was smart enough to remember where we left it. The location was our battery position three moves ago. So we sent out a detail to search for the buried treasure. And lo-and-behold, they returned with a long-ne-glected, grubby, four-cylinder jeep engine. Inspection revealed the parts still move, so our next step is to tear it down, clean it up, rebuild it, cross our fingers, and engage the starter.

If it works, we have a super powerful generator engine, for which replacement parts are no strain. If it won't work, there is a chance we can arrange a trade for an engine which has been turned in for salvage. The future looks bright (you may disregard pun). However, regardless of our bright future (continue disregarding pun), I can foresee what will happen. Having such a mighty four-cylinder engine, some happy young lad will open it up full throttle and instantly burn out the fragile gener-ator and all our makeshift electrical wiring. The Coleman Lantern re-mains a great comfort.

This morning, in the chill of a gray dawn, we drove over to that Howitzer Maintenance Class that I mentioned in an earlier letter. What a farce! Scheduled from 8:00 to 5:00, officers were required to attend only the first 20 minutes. We three 49th Battalion Battery Execs. managed to kill most of the morning discussing gunnery with the other officers. It was a pleasant, interesting group, but I can't say I was overwhelmed with anyone's display of unusual insight on the subject.

This afternoon was spent back at battalion shooting fire missions with our new little toy. Much fun was had by all because everyone could see the rounds land. I divided the Baker group into six sections, each of which had their turn at the guns. I think the training value was high, because being a compact setup, everyone could actually observe and appreciate each other's job and each phase of the firing procedure. I wish you could've been there. Although if you were, I doubt either of us would have gotten much out of the exercise. You could rather easily have diverted my attention!

These Christmas mails have really slowed up and are most irregular at this end of the line. I haven't gotten a letter in four days now, but confidently expect to get a stack tomorrow. You must be receiving my letters in the same fashion.

You're constantly in my thoughts, Lucy. In everything I do or see, or hear, you are beside me. I love you passionately with all my heart and soul. We are very close. God bless you and guide us and bring us together again quickly

Good night, my love,

Your devoted,

Bill

* * *

5 Dec. 53

Dearest wife,

Today is the birthday of the 7th Division (Activation Day) and was supposed to be a day off duty. We went to bed last night looking forward to a day of complete vacation. Because there was no reveille to be paged for, I left the telephone hanging over on the tent pole instead of under my cot.

At ten after five this morning the phone rang. I reached out of my artic sleeping bag through the opening for my face and sleepily groped along the rough wood floor. No phone. Then I pulled my arm in, remembering the phone was hanging on the tent pole about eight feet away. My hand was already chilled from that short exposure to the cold air. I lay still, hoping perhaps it was a mistake and it wouldn't ring again. That allowed four more seconds of comfort. Then the phone buzzed again. I am the closest, so it was my problem. I struggled up, staggered across the icy floor, fumbled with the receiver and growled, "Baker Five, Lt. MacIlvaine, Sir!" It was battalion switchboard. Battalion had called to inform us that the men from Baker who were to march in the Activation Day Parade were to wear field jackets for the truck ride over to Division Headquarters. I muttered something and hung up. Then I mumbled something to the Capt., who was half awake now. He mumbled something in return and I got back into my recently abandoned sleeping bag for renewed snooze. Question: Who in his right mind would take a two-hour open truck ride in below-freezing weather and not wear a field jacket?

At 8:30 I was still sound asleep when the phone rang again and I was summoned to Battalion to supervise another moneymaking gambling session for our orphanage. That's how my morning-off was spent.

This afternoon was more relaxing. However, at three, again the phone rang. This time with a challenge to all comers from the Col. to match his .45 automatic pistol skill. With all proceeds going to our orphan fund, we each put up a dollar and fired three shots. Then the Col. fired three. If we outscored him, we won five dollars. We'd get no rounds to zero-in the sights, or for practice.

Contestants were firing a mostly unfamiliar weapon (the carbine is standard) and the Col. only lost to one person in the battalion. Even considering his advantage, he proved to be a very good shot. It was good sport. I've fired the .45 before and when I got my first two shots in the bull's-eye, then the third in the first ring, I was sure I'd won five dollars. This time around, the Col. put three in the bull's-eye! The orphan fund came out the winner.

Tomorrow I should be getting a handful of mail. I got your letter #84 today and I'll talk more about it tomorrow.

Good night, Lucy, you are an angel. I love you very dearly.

Your sleepily always devoted,

Bill

* * *

6 Dec. 53

Good Evening Chicki,

We had the hottest, best, golden brown rolls for supper tonight that any home kitchen has ever turned out. They were so good I went to the kitchen and personally complimented our rather shy baker. Together, the Capt. and I finished off an even dozen. We had traded with the 1st Commonwealth Division (British) for a can of real Australian butter. With that and apple jelly, I bet I put on few pounds. A half an hour later one of our truck drivers returned from Base Camp (U.N.) and brought the Capt. and me three pints of ice cream. We had just finished that when the mess sergeant entered out BOQ tent with a plate of fried pheasant. It looks very tasty, but I haven't the courage to even take one more bite of anything.

I remember your writing of Griffin's report that many "moose" were lurking in the countryside around his area. BAKER—BELL'S— BEST—BY TEST had its first reported incident the other night. As you might imagine, about 99.44/100% of those not-so-lovelies are infected and therefore the V.D. rate among soldiers is something to be reckoned with. Higher Hq. is always very concerned with a unit's V.D. rate, since it is supposed to reflect the state of discipline of the unit. Since discipline is a command responsibility, all unit commanders are very interested in apprehending and turning in any and all local prostitutes.

The First Sergeant came into the BOQ the other night and announced that the Sergeant of the Guard had captured a moose and her Korean "business manager" who had come up to the back barbed wire fence and were attempting to drum up a little trade. Our first move was to call the Bn. Duty Officer, who called the MPs and informed the Colonel. From then on, we had performed our duty and could simply wait until the MPs arrived and took the two off our hands.

I was a little surprised, therefore, when only a few minutes later the Colonel walked into the BOQ and wanted a first-hand account of recent happenings. After we explained the details of the apprehension, he said, "Bring the prisoners in." He wanted to interview them. We called the Sgt. of the Guard and presently he entered with the moose and friend. We also called in our interpreter. Although the First Sergeant declared she was exceptionally attractive for a Korean plying the trade, it was difficult to conceive of her as a female. She was about four and a half feet tall, thoroughly unattractive and dumpy, and attired in baggy trousers made from a heavy G.I. blanket, and a fatigue jacket. Her friend looked like an Oriental version of Al Capone.

The Colonel was fascinated. Although his questioning was strictly a line-of-duty performance, you could see he was as curious as a six-year-old on his first visit to the zoo. The rest of us in the BOQ probably also shared that kind of interest.

When the MPs finally arrived, the Colonel turned over our two prisoners with a great flourish, the way I would have handed over a Russian MIG if I discovered one had landed in the battery area. The MPs obviously weren't impressed. One told me, out of hearing of the Colonel, that they picked up an average of ten a day.

We announced in formation the next day that the lad who reported the presence of the moose would be given a day off. I can imagine what will happen next. All our troops will be scouring the countryside for moose to turn in so that they can earn a day off! Could be rather more rewarding than collecting box tops, don't your think?

The First Sergeant managed to obtain another generator today, but without the gasoline engine. So now we have two very scarce generators but nothing yet to provide power for them. The (once buried) jeep engine is still in the process of being rebuilt. The Coleman Lantern remains our constant guiding light.

You know, I was thinking tonight that I have been on the army payroll now since 21 March 1950. That's almost three years and nine months, including enlisted reserve time while in college. Although the majority of that is not active duty, and thus relatively unimportant, it might be a good idea to stress my total length of service in my next Early Release request.

Still no more mail from you. My latest received letter was written the evening before Thanksgiving and mailed from Summit, #84. Of course I loved your pictures!! Any and all you can send me of your beautiful self are tremendously desired and appreciated. You should know, Chicki, that I love you so much that I'd love to have all the pictures taken of you. I hope you got some on Thanksgiving.

Why do you say you are so afraid that your world, life, and everything you love and trust implicitly will vanish? Is that worry about my safe return? From a coldly logical point of view, even in the quite doubtful possibility of renewed hostilities, I can see no need for concern. I am just as safe here as I would be among the perils of everyday living back home, and much safer than crossing the street, mid-block, in Manhattan. Besides that, our lives and welfare are completely in the hands of God. He will watch over us. He will make no error, nor will He forget us for an instant. How much safer can a person be than when protected by the most powerful might in this world, or any other. Lead your best, faithful and honest and courageous life, and God will take care of the rest.

I love you, Lucy, with all the feeling and tenderness and respect and devotion that are within me. You deserve my very best, and I try hard to live up to your wonderfulness.

I constantly think of and long for you in the fullest sense of our overwhelming and complete love.

Your faithful and adoring husband,
Bill

* * *

Dearest Angel,

I'm sorry this is just a note tonight, but we had an officers' meeting at Bn. Hq. which lasted almost two hours and I'm bushed.

We will be setting out in earnest on a basic-type training schedule, which does nothing to excite or motivate me, and a new character from Bn. will be inspecting us regularly. He is disquietingly R.A. We go out for our big Bn. Test Monday and return that Saturday. I have hopes that the program could dissipate after that, but it doesn't seem too likely. I guess I need your cheering up tonight as usual, and also a good long backrub.

I love you with all my heart and soul, my wonderful wife, and I need your comfort and companionship and attention and care.

How lucky can one husband be to have someone who loves and cares so much for him? I appreciate you and your love more, Lucy, than I think you have ever imagined.

God bless you and encourage both of us, make us strong and decisive, and lead us together swiftly.

Goodnight, precious wife.

I love you,
Bill

* * *

8 Dec. 53

My Love,

Some items of interest for today. First thing this morning, around 0830, in walks the Bn. Operations Officer to inspect our training. Captain Dillender, is a good, hardworking, constructive type of individual. He doesn't believe in R.A. for the sake of R.A. When he wants something done, he tells you why. It sounds very reasonable and we get it done. Capt. Dillender's aim is to make the 49th Bn. the best shooting unit in Korea. I'll go along with him on that all the way, while also we make Baker the best shooting battery in the 49th Bn.

His assistant, 1/Lt. Anderson, came up through the ranks. He is likable enough to talk to, but he's the character I mentioned last night who is dangerously R.A. He's almost a fanatic and the army is his god, while the regulations and orders are his bible.

So far we haven't clashed outright, although I know my attitude of somewhat-good-humored tolerance doesn't endear me to him. As long as everyone knows we are producing the goods in Baker, any inspection gripes he may have won't throw any weight at Bn. Hq. Comparing the differing methods that Capt. Dillender and his assistant employ to perform their duties is an eye-opening lesson in leadership for me. The "carrot" is working better than the "stick." However, I can see that at times a combination may be required to get the job done.

That's enough on personalities except for Syg, who is now called Devil. We were romping this afternoon and one of his baby teeth gave me a cut across the end of my finger that could have been made by a razor. He's not a dog to trifle with. No one teaches him anything but roughness, and when he gets a little bigger he will probably make it very unpleasant for strangers. I'll remember to stay in his favor.

Did we ever have hot biscuits tonight! Flaky, golden and crisp around the edges. The Capt. had finished dessert and left and I was still eating biscuits. Don't worry about my waist, sweetie, while we are apart, but I have a feeling I could gain weight on your cooking when I get home. Maybe you'll have to put me on a diet, or maybe you'll decide you don't want to.

* * *

Money Matters Finally Explained:

Month	Payment to Me	Allotment to You
July	In Full	None
August	In Full	None
September	In Full	None
October	Partial	$250.00
November	Partial	$250.00
December	Partial	$250.00

For July we were paid as usual at Ft. Sill. For August, I was paid at Camp Stoneman and sent a check to you from Stoneman. For September I received my regular pay, but I saved here and there from previous months and by the time I got around to sending it to you, I had accumulated $350, which I directed Finance to send to you. Then my $250 automatic monthly allotment to you started.

I have received your letters up through Thanksgiving. The last four have distressed me because you sound as though you are so terribly unhappy when you say you are so lonely and want me to come home. Golly, sweetie, if I were given half a chance I would be home in your arms in 72 hours.

It doesn't seem to me it's a good idea emphasizing how we feel so lost and lonely (as if we could help the way we feel) and that we feel alone because no one around us understands fully the hardship and unhappiness through which we are going. After all, you and I both understand it, and since no one can fully understand any of the joys or sorrows that we share together, why should we worry if they can't understand the pain we feel from our separation?

Look at it this way. I have been chosen to perform an indispensable job. I'm not flag waving, but somebody must be here. I happened to be at the right place at the right time with the right qualifications and I got the job. I wish it had been somebody else, from a personal viewpoint, but it wasn't, and I justly can't complain about it. Others have had to do this before and others will have to do this in the years to come. Right now it's me. How many of those happy families that you see in the department stores had husbands or fathers away in Korea or in WW II, some for as long as three years or more? They must have felt the same way then as you do now.

What I am trying to say is that our hardship now is not new, nor is it unique. It is our share of the burden that must by carried, with God's will, for all free people. You should be proud, and grateful that you and I are carrying a share that, while larger than some have been called to carry, is far less than many others' burdens.

Don't despair or count the hours or days or wish me back before I can return, but live each day with confidence and assurance that we both are doing an important job, in the unshakable faith that God, when He knows the time is ready, will swiftly and surely return me to you so that under His guidance we may resume our lives together.

After starting off this letter as an exhausted fellow, I ended up not being able to stop writing. I hope I haven't bored you with all the bull, but every once in a while not being able to talk to you in person causes me to more fully put down my thoughts on paper.

How can I love you so much? I need your companionship and your ideas and your love.

Goodnight, precious wife. God bless you and guide us both together again safely and swiftly.

Your ever adoring husband,

Bill

* * *

10 Dec. 53

Dearest friend,

For some unknown reason I started thinking tonight what would be fun to do when I get home. In the first place it's all decided that we are going on a second honeymoon. Now the question is where? The pesky trouble is that there are a load of variables as yet unknown. Will I arrive in the States in March or late July, or sometime in between? Will I stay only a few hours in San Francisco or Seattle, or will they hand me my travel pay and send me flying off to New Jersey? If they do hold me over on the Coast, which I doubt, I'll get on the phone and you can hop the first plane to California and meet me at the Mark Hopkins about ten hours later.

If I come straight to New Jersey, I hope they discharge me within a couple of days and then we'll leave immediately. If it's still wintertime, what do you think about going south? Bermuda, Florida, or maybe the West Indies. If it's getting later, in warm weather, perhaps the Pocono's or Maine, Canada or the Thousand Islands. And then there is still Bermuda.

I've been sitting around here thinking of hundreds of places and I'm very undecided, except for one thing. I know that being with you again alone, wherever we are, will be the greatest, most magnificent paradise and the most wonderful experience imaginable.

Chicki, I LOVE YOU!!

I got a package from you today mailed from Summit on November 2nd. So keeping one eye shut, I opened the outer box and saw what I can safely identify as Christmas packages. I quickly repacked the box and put it out of sight behind my homemade "bureau," still with one eye closed. I can thank you now for being such a wonderful and thoughtful wife and I can tell you I love you and you are a darling to send me some (suspected) Christmas presents, but I refuse to say another word until I open them on Christmas morning because I really shouldn't be aware I've gotten anything. I bet you are going to prove to be an un-wooly Lamb and a party-poop and open my package as soon as you get it!

I took a shower today for the first time in recent history and that explains why I'm feeling chipper. I've also been doing some hard drinking on a can of straight California orange juice. Not too bad, but I'd rather have some frozen Snow Crop.

By the way, I was pleased to hear you are not giving the impression of moping or self-pity. Some of your letters sounded awfully dejected, but I'm glad that's not the way you've been spending your days. Sometimes if you act upbeat, you can actually make yourself feel more cheerful. (Forgive my relapse into bull again.)

Do you realize that you're keeping me up late? I'll love it when I get home, but tomorrow I've got a reveille formation.

Goodnight, precious, desirable, beautiful Pooh Bear. I love you with a fire. I want to kiss you and feel you warm and soft and responsive next to me.

I love you with all my heart and body and soul.

Your faithful, adoring,

Bill

* * *

10 Dec. 53

Dearest Lamb,

We're having a bit of a cold snap and the Capt. is ready to move out, back home to Puerto Rico. I'm ready to move out to a sunny beach, a warm blue sea and frothy rolling surf, with seagulls circling overhead. Here's an idea how cold it is. Inside our tent I picked up our wash basin this morning, which was left full, on the floor, in the center of the tent, and actually had to chop the ice out of it before I could fill it. Not a thin sheet of surface ice, mind you, but a chunk, frozen solid right to the bottom.

You can't imagine what kind of fun it is (not) to hop out of a warm sleeping bag in the dark, into the subfreezing atmosphere, so early in the morning. As a matter of fact, there is not even a hint of dawn then, and the moon and stars are still shining brightly.

If I had not gotten used to this life gradually, I'm sure I'd now be much the worse for wear. However, in reality it's not as bad as it sounds. Something interesting is always coming over the horizon.

I also received a big exciting-looking Christmas box from Mom today which will remain unopened. I'll thank her tomorrow. I also received a box from Aunt Wawee of canned goodies and paperback books. #1. It occurred to me, and I'm only guessing, but I'll bet she remembers from the last war, and perhaps the one before that, how the Doughboys must have appreciated letters and packages from home. I'll write her tomorrow.

We're talking about cutting a tree, if we can find one that's halfway acceptable, when we return from the field. Then with all our treats from home, we'll really throw ourselves a bang-up party.

I'm always thinking of you, Lucy, and am constantly with you in my heart.

I love Lucy,
Bill

* * *

13 Dec. 53

Dearest Wife,

Last night was the long-awaited grand opening of our Bn. Officers Club. It was built on the style of a Korean hut, with mud walls and a thatched roof, and is totally bare inside, but does have a rustic fireplace and a primitive kitchen attached.

For the grand opening the local hot-shots (all the Bn. Officers) were commanded to attend and all the surrounding big-shots were invited to attend. The Div. CO, Gen. McGarr, the Div. Arty. CO, Col. Bandie (who replaced Col. Lester), and all the other Bn. CO's all arrived for the festivities.

We had steak for dinner, drinks were free, and we even had a string combo to play for us. It was a very informal gathering during which we sang Col. Bandie and Gen. McGarr into the Bn. You may recall me mentioning the song which is used for the initiation. It is thoroughly uncomplimentary and ends up calling the new member a horse's muffin (muffin translates it politely). The song was sung by all with great fervor. It was the first time this Lieutenant ever heard a General called a horse's muffin to his face and take the risk of perhaps being shot at sunrise.

After the General left, the party got exceedingly enthusiastic, and a few of the Lieutenants and a Captain started a square dance with Col. Bandie. It was quite a sight to see the big old blustering ox join hands with a couple of 2/Lt.'s and dance around in a circle.

After the two of us had consumed at least a couple of martinis, I had a private conversation with the Catholic chaplain (a captain) wherein I tried to convert him into becoming Presbyterian. I wasn't a bit successful, but we had a good, animated and friendly discussion. By nine-thirty, feeling no pain, I called it a night (the party started at five).

Groan, did I ever feel terrible today! Last night's blast will last me for several months to come.

Tomorrow we leave for the same general firing area where we fired the last two Tests. On Friday, like Douglas MacArthur, we shall return.

Our six 105 howitzers were kept ready for instant action.

Today the weather was just like a balmy day in May. I wish it would stay that way for another five days while we're out and about, camping.

Goodnight, precious Chicki. I'm headed for that #1 piece of field equipment, i.e., a sleeping bag. Is it ever going to feel good!

I love you, Lucy, with all my heart, body and soul. God bless you.

Your adoring, faithful, and pooped,

Bill

12
Frozen Fields

14 Dec. 53

Dearest Lamb,

We are now enjoying ourselves, camping amidst the pleasures of outdoor life. Actually, we are not much more out-of-doors than we were when home in our battery area, since we are still living in a squad tent (but with a dirt floor) and two stoves that sometimes can be coaxed into actually providing heat. This expedition is for the Battalion Test.

We left our battery position about one this afternoon and pulled into this bivouac area shortly after 3:30. The next two hours were spent setting up tents, unloading ammunition and relocating our belongings. Then chow, followed by the Colonel's conference with all the officers, followed by Capt. Sosa's conference with all our Chiefs of Section. Everybody now is supposed to know all the details of tomorrow's operation.

Tomorrow's operation is the calibration of all eighteen howitzers of the Battalion. We'll arrive at the firing point at seven (after arising at five) and line up all three batteries with the guns placed hub to hub. The point of the whole procedure is fire each weapon, one at a time, with the same data and plot how close to the target each round lands. We can then compute individual corrections for each gun which enable us to shoot more accurately.

The weather is holding up for us very nicely, no rain or mud in sight and no subfreezing temperatures.

Good night, favorite wife, tomorrow is going to be a long day! I love you completely, always, and hope you are having a grand vacation. God bless you.

Your devoted, adoring,

Bill

* * *

15 Dec. 53

Dearest Wife,

I mentioned in my letter last night that it didn't look like rain, so of course we were safe from mud. Ugh—let me tell you how we fared.

We started off in convoy this morning before daylight under a chilled, starry sky. Before we had arrived at the firing point the blackness gradually lightened, revealing a white, frosty landscape and a gray sky. The twisting, much-rutted dirt road was a frozen track, rock hard, as we slammed and jolted and bounced along, passing between serene fields of high, uneven grass, silver coated and looking much like feathery down.

Some time after all the batteries had arrived at the firing point for calibration, some of the trucks were still stuck. The area about the size of a football field had been previously used in warm weather, evidently in a pouring rainstorm, and now from one end to the other, the field was a mass of deep, irregular, frozen, crisscrossing furrows. At noon the sun came out in earnest. The thermometer then rose to about 40° and we spent the rest of the day in ankle-deep mud and mire.

We were wearing our Mickey Mouse rubber boots, so while it was clumsy navigating with these oversize insulated gunboats, the feet stayed dry and warm. The only difficult feat was moving the feet, because with each step the mud closed over the foot and held it like a vice.

After standing and walking all day, with the exception of a fifteen-minute sit-down for chow, we finished firing and arrived back in our bivouac area after dark in time for a late supper and the officers meeting. Then came our Chief of Sections meeting and now it's the weary end of a fourteen-hour working day. The Battalion test begins tomorrow.

I wish I could write the families. I owe everyone letters, but I can scarcely muster the energy to write you!

I love you, Chicki, with all my being. I miss you and adore you. I hope and pray you are enjoying yourself. Have a good time and remember I'll be home before very long.

My complete, eternal love,

Bill

* * *

16 Dec. 53

POSTCARD

Dearest wife,

Greetings and cheers from your pumpkin. I am writing only a card tonight because I'm so utterly exhausted I can barely sit up, much less keep my eyes open. Tomorrow we arise an hour later than usual, so that's what you'd call good news! In these first two days we fired half our six-days' load of ammo. I am, however, looking forward to rest and relaxation during my up-coming self-styled Christmas vacation. I am also looking forward to opening all those presents waiting for me back in our battery area!

While I am on the subject, there is something else I am looking forward to with the greatest anticipation: being with you, Chicki, what else! Darling, I'd write longer if I could, but my eyes are starting to close. I'm flat on my back now, comfortable and relaxed, with that physically depleted feeling.

I also feel disheartened about not writing everyone and sending cards for Christmas. Please do explain to everybody how I am out in the field and going all day and half of each night.

Good night and Merry Christmas, precious Lamb. Ahead is going to be the best and happiest New Year we've ever had—we'll be together again!

God bless you.

I love Lucy,

Bill

* * *

19 Dec. 53
POSTCARD

Dearest wife,

Things didn't ease up as I thought they would when I wrote the day before yesterday on the other Christmas card. Each day became harder than the last because we were more exhausted every day.

I think the battery hit its peak of efficiency and spirit on Thursday. On Friday we didn't quite show the same fired-up performance. Today was the official Battalion Test. I was so pooped and somewhat let down after putting so much into the previous days of firing that I was more methodical than previously, when I put on the gung ho show, charging around and shouting, during the Battery Test. It was obvious that Capt. Sosa and everyone else felt the same way. At any rate, we had practiced so thoroughly that it went very smoothly. Only one battalion in the Division had passed the Test when we went out to take it. We were the last to shoot, and I know we got a highly respectable score. The question now is did we beat that battery in the 47th Battalion? It's probably close.

It certainly was good to pull into our battery area tonight and feel the clomp clomp of a wooden floor (warped, rough and drafty as it is) under your feet. I've now got your letters through #100! More about them tomorrow. All I'll say tonight is that I am more pleased and proud of you than ever. You are the smartest, most perfectly wonderful wife a person could ever pray for.

I love you tonight with a flame and devotion that can't even be dimmed by fatigue. I've never been so exhausted in my life and I've never loved you more adoringly than I do at this very minute.

I hope you had lots of fun Christmas.

I love you always, Lucy.

Your faithful and loving,

Bill

* * *

20 Dec. 53

Dearest Chicki,

Today I took advantage of the day of rest and slept until 8:30, after which I spent most of the day relocating all my personal gear which had accompanied my trip to the field. The Colonel said tonight that it is quite likely that the 49th scored a point or two higher than the 47th, thus we possibly came out top in Division.

Bringing Christmas to Korean children.
Video Link: http://lovelettersfromthefront.com/videos

I'm still dog tired, and to top it off I feel as if I'm getting a good head cold. That's why I'm not writing you a decent-length letter tonight. As in past times when I feel unhealthy, I'm taking a couple of those hay fever pills. They've always worked wonders. Tonight will be the real test.

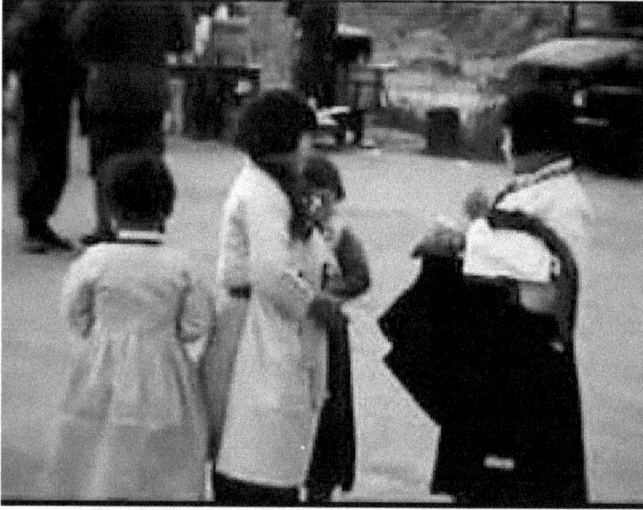

We hold a party for the children.
Video Link: http://lovelettersfromthefront.com/videos

Goodnight, precious lamb. God bless you. I love you completely, with all my heart, body and soul.
Your devoted,
Bill

Two little girls get their first Christmas gift.
Video Link: http://lovelettersfromthefront.com/videos

* * *

21 Dec. 53

Dearest Lamb,

Tonight it's cold and the sky is sparkling clear, with a full yellow moon bathing the landscape and making the ground look as though it were covered with a thin coating of snow. We haven't yet had a snowstorm worth the mention. A few weeks ago we actually saw a few flakes floating down for perhaps a half hour.

We are getting a white tent liner shortly, which should help keep out the winter cold as well as light up our dark interior. In the meantime I am moving my cot within two feet of the stove each night and still get chilly toward morning. One of our stoves is working in #1 fashion. The other is shut off to conserve fuel oil.

We're still without lights, waiting for the parts to repair our jeep engine, so you can guess how much use the Coleman is getting! It runs day and night and is absolutely indispensable. I can't imagine how we'd get along if it weren't for you and your thoughtfulness!! While I'm on the subject of the Lantern, I would appreciate your sending me about 30 extra mantles and an extra injector (Part number T66). Murray Hill 2-3600. The Lantern is (Model) Type 200A. I could also use a couple of pairs of those sponge rubber inserts that fit inside my boots. Boot size 10 extra wide.

A Red Cross man came around yesterday to break the news to one of our men that his father had died suddenly. The army has denied the man an emergency leave and I was very surprised to learn that this is the case in all problems of this type. It seems a little hard hearted to me, but the way the army figures it, unless there is some reason for which the son is especially required, once it's already happened the son's presence wouldn't help.

We are putting the finishing touches on our Bn. Officers Club now, putting in a gravel walk and planting evergreens around it. I think I told you about it once before. It is Korean in design, built by Koreans, and has mud walls, a fireplace and a thatched roof. It's now painted green and equipped with electric lights and a cement floor.

You should be cheerfully rebuked for thinking even for a second that my Christmas shopping for you was more pathetic than humorous. I've never had more fun shopping for Christmas in my life than this year, because I never before wanted to please anyone so much! You would have laughed heartily if you'd seen me bouncing and careening along all those dirt roads, hanging on to my G.I. Siberian "fur" cap—a modern Santa Claus in his jeep!

Your Spring Vacation plans in Florida sound great. I only hope and pray I'll be home in time to disrupt them. No news on that score and no local changes as yet. It's in God's hands and He won't play the ace until He is ready. All we can do for the present is trust and have faith in Him.

Thanks for the Santa candle and the striped sock. I'll save the sock and we'll hang it by the mantle next Christmas in anticipation of our first youngster.

Goodnight, chicken pot pie. I think I love you more with each passing second, although I know I love you more now than I thought humanly possible.

My thoughts and prayers and devotion are always with you. God bless you, Lamb.

Your adoring,

Bill

* * *

Dear Mom and Pop,

After spending all of last week out on the firing ranges on our Battalion Test, we are now back home camping in our semi-permanent area near Munsan. In case I haven't mentioned it before, since 10 October we have been located about eight and three-quarter miles southeast of Panmunjon, about two miles south of Freedom Bridge and between 500 to 800 yards east of the dirt road leading to the bridge. The countryside surrounding us for five miles in any direction is relatively flat, with many low, lightly vegetated hills and much intervening flat paddy land. The paddies look brown and desolate now. Some have been drained, but all still show row after row of the cut stalks which were chopped off an inch or two above what is now ice or frozen mud. The hills are somewhat more colorful, with many low evergreens sprinkled among the brown shrubbery.

Besides the pheasant and grouse there is another bird much like a starling. But the most abundant is a striking black-and-white creature about the size of a crow, with a slightly larger tail. Whatever they are, they are plentiful. Anytime during the day, wherever you are, if you stop and look for a minute or two, you can see one or several perched in a tree. I have yet to hear them make a sound.

So far, no snow. We must be located in a warm pocket. Fifteen miles south there is snow on the ground, and we can see snow on the hills to the north. Here, the temperature can get down to 10° at night, but occasionally in the afternoon the sun is hot enough to partially thaw out our frozen mud.

Probably the most important factor in our relative warmth is protection from the wind from the north. With or without the wind, regardless of the extreme dampness in this region, when wearing our winter clothing we can operate in temperatures in the low teens without undue discomfort.

Out on the firing ranges it was a matter of having our trucks stuck in deep, ice-hardened ruts in the early morning and mud in the afternoon. I wore Mickey Mouse insulated rubber boots constantly. Added to their weight of several pounds was about five pounds of mud, which clung like glue to my boots and resulted in a sensation of walking with leaden snowshoes.

The 49th pulled through the Battalion Test in very fine style, with my Baker Battery turning in a near perfect contribution to the main effort.

As far as infiltrating North Koreans are concerned, I haven't heard of any in this sector. If they could get through the Marines in front of us, they would have to cross one of several heavily guarded bridges that span the river two miles north of us. We have a barbed wire perimeter around our battery area and two 24-hour guard posts. In addition, we have four walking guards during the hours of darkness. Any person who refuses to halt-and-identify at night runs great risk of becoming a target.

Although our range firing is done in North Korea, it is about 40 miles to the east and still miles south of the "cease-fire" line in that location. The "Bull's Eye" range is located in the rear areas of the 25th Division sector. The Chinese can't see or hear us, and if they are aware of our activities, they probably don't take any interest in them.

I'm glad you are enjoying the movies. I can't wait to see them myself. The one I'm working on right now begins with our preparations for movement out for the recent Battalion Test. I was so busy once we arrived that I didn't take another shot. Tomorrow (Christmas Eve) I'll drive over to an orphanage a few miles to the west and get some movies of our Battalion distributing $2,000 worth of food and clothing which we collected in the past month.

Preparations are coming along for Christmas. We have a decorated tree in the mess hall and I am saving my presents to open on Friday. I hope you had a joyful time on Christmas. I will be thinking of all of you especially then.

Affectionately,
Bill

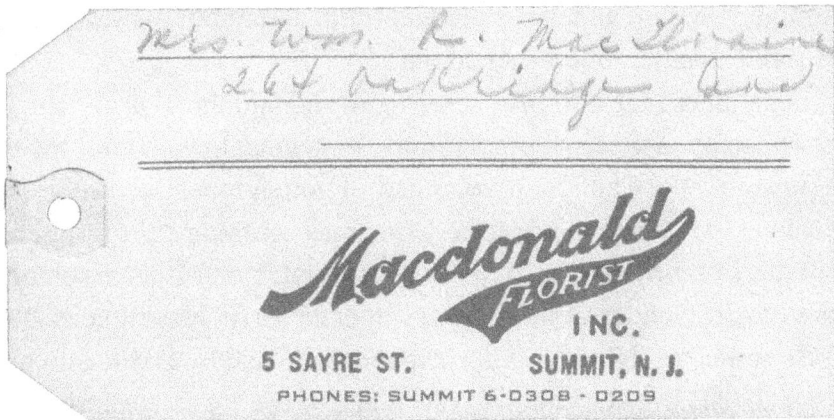

I'd arranged delivery of a dozen roses for Lucy at Christmas.
My parents gave her my note.

* * *

26 Dec. 53

My dearest Lamb,

I know I'm a wandering and clueless un-wooly lamb for not writing Christmas Eve or Christmas Day, but somehow the time never quite seemed right. I thought of you so much and wanted to say so much that I just didn't know where to begin. How can I ever tell you how much I love you, how fond and close my feeling for you is, and how over-whelming is my adoration and desire!

Christmas Eve we piled into a jeep with cameras and drove over to our adopted orphan school to participate in the distribution of clothes and candy, for which we had contributed, to the children. I got some good shots and much local color. I only wish the colorful, excited crowds of children which you'll see shortly could be accompanied by all the nois-es and the talk which they uttered. The scene is one great mass of noise and commotion.

I still have the lingerings of this stupid half-cold, which is hard-ly worth mentioning but which is just uncomfortable enough to make smoking unpleasant and make me feel tired all day. Anyway, the rest of Christmas Eve afternoon I sacked out.

After supper I took all my presents out and laid them on my cot. Not being one to open presents prematurely, I intended to wait until the next day. However, the Capt. and Weiss hadn't gotten much themselves and immediately set up a clamor for a Christmas ceremony. So for the mo-rale of all, I one-by-one opened the gifts. First, I must thank you again for the box of wonderful things that I opened early. The Lantern is still our sole source of light and is correspondingly held by all of us in high-est regard. The pocket knife is constantly in use, as is the little stove. The chess set is much fun, and the crossword puzzles are a community venture which are attacked with a great seriousness of purpose but are seldom completely conquered even by we three masterminds. The an-swers in the back often come in handy. I thank you for the writing paper and bubble gum, which I am chewing this moment. All the presents were wonderful, and I can't thank you enough for the things you sent and for managing the project at home. You are a #1 ♥♥! I'm still saving the birthday gifts.

Christmas Day dawned chilly and raining and never did acquire that bright and warm atmosphere that it always had. It was Christmas and yet it didn't seem anything like Christmas. In a way that was good, because it minimized much of the unhappiness of our being apart. But the companionship and the love and the joy of celebrating Christ's birthday were somehow not as dominant as they should have been on Christmas. Despite our mild celebration, everyone was thinking about people and places far removed from Korea and already looking forward to next Christmas.

Last night I thought of words from that old WW II song that says "Christmas Eve will find me where the love-light gleams. I'll be home for Christmas, if only in my dreams." That hit home. It seems best, however, to concentrate the mind on other things and to accentuate the positive, eliminate the negative, and latch onto the affirmative of trying to keep morale up-beat. I'm working on it.

We had a party at the "Officers Club" last night and ended up singing my favorite: "They're cutting the orders for staff school, etc" song to (bird) Col. Badger. He and Col. Moore and our Maj. Gruenther seemed to enjoy it as much as we (Reserve Officers) did singing it.

Before I forget it, your good old Uncle Sam came across with a present for the BOQ. We are now equipped with a beautiful government-issue white tent liner. It serves two wonderful purposes. First, having few openings, it cuts down drafts and acts as insulation. And second, it reflects, instead of absorbs, our minimal indoor light rays. The Coleman Lantern now brightens even the farthest corners of our tent, which before, existed in chilled murky darkness. I estimate the inside temperature has been raised at least 10 degrees.

How much do I love you!! I only wish I could tell you in person. You are my love, my idol, my wife.

I love you, Lucy. Goodnight, God bless you.

Your faithful, adoring,

Bill

* * *

29 Dec. 53

Dearest wife,

I sat down last night and wrote all of two sentences, but my morale, for no particular reason, was stuck in such a low state that after fifteen minutes of absently examining the cracks in the floor boards, I gave up and went to bed. I took a shower this afternoon, so I'm doing better, and tonight I'm a little more comfortable and communicative.

I know so well what you mean when you say you constantly want to turn to me and comment on the things you are experiencing. When the time comes to write about them, either they are too long and complicated to set down on paper or else they are insignificant in retrospect. It all comes from that feeling of closeness between us that makes us want to share each passing moment and experience.

I love you, Lucy, more completely and more fully as the days go by. I can't help feel that however miserable this experience is through which we are going, it is a great constructive and broadening time. We're both learning and loving, and because we are not together physically, I think we tend to compensate for it by drawing ourselves closer and closer to each other spiritually. Can there be a better basis for a deep and enduring love?!

Good night, Chicki. I'll keep you posted on all exit-from-Korea rumors. I love you every second of every minute of every hour of my life. Someday soon I'll be telling you all about it in person. God bless you, Lucy.

Your devoted, Bill

* * *

30 Dec. 53

Hi Lamb,

Our new Lieut., Skinner, is roughing it up on the hill this week, but the rest of us Baker officers—Capt. Sosa, Weiss, and I—still exist here in the BOQ tent, routinely earning an honest living and crossing the days off a calendar each evening.

Talking about earning our keep, tomorrow I get up at 5:15, strap on my .45 pistol, take jeep and driver and head over to Division Headquarters (where life is a bit easier). There, I pick up the monthly pay for the battery. The money is military scrip, which closely resembles Monopoly money, and is safely locked in a briefcase. However, I get that old vision of transporting a crate of gold nuggets on a stagecoach in the Old West. I'm armed and vigilant as we travel through the countryside, constantly on the lookout for desperados. What bandits might do with our military scrip, I don't know.

Good night, Lucy. You possess my heart, my love, my all.

God bless you.

Your adoring,

Bill

* * *

31 Dec. 53

Dearest Wife,

Tonight is that exciting event; that wonderful, wild, sparkling evening celebrated as New Year's Eve. In observance, Weiss and I are sitting here quietly in the BOQ with a few cans of the army's 3.2% beer. The Capt. rather reluctantly decided he needed to show up at the party at Div. Artillery Hq., and Skinner is spending a not-too-joyous night in relative solitude (with his radio operator and his wireman) on the hill in the OP.

After finishing "The Caine Mutiny" and the couple of beers, which about put me to sleep, I put my feet up on the table, lit a mild, pleasant-smelling cigar, and began to think of former New Year's Eves. One in particular is vivid in my memory. Remember two years ago at that party in Morristown, when with an arm around each other, we talked in excited, glowing tones with Tommy and Ann about our wedding plans? Getting married and going to Cambridge Beaches sounded wonderful, didn't it? We didn't know at the time half how wonderful it would turn out. We would have been even happier in our anticipation if we had understood then how satisfying, meaningful and deep our love would become.

New Year's Eve 1953 in the BOQ.

Since that evening two years ago when we talked about marriage, we have together discovered a whole new life. We found that we both have shortcomings. We had to go places and do things that we didn't like. We faced problems between us and problems arising in the world around us. But the most important thing of all is we have learned and continue to learn how to cope with these problems through faith in God.

I think we've had more problems packed into these last two years because of the life we've had to live (and are still living) than we would have experienced in many years of normal suburban married life. As a result, we have learned more and bound ourselves more closely than could otherwise ever have been possible.

Actually, we have barely made a start of our lives together, but it is such a good beginning, on such a firm foundation, that I am certain of our ability to surmount the problems that lie ahead.

We both have an unshakable faith in God and acknowledge that He will handle the rudder as long as we keep working the oars. We have a tremendously deep, unswerving love for each other. Personal pride or hurt has occasionally caused surface tension, but nothing has ever, or can ever, touch or disturb that infinitely deep, all-powerful eternal bond between us. We both understand this and it's a great, buoyant factor in our lives. It gives us firm ground on which to put our feet when the floods are raging around us.

You must know how much I live for the day when we will be united again—to talk with you and walk with you, to love you in passion and in tenderness, to laugh and cry and even quarrel with you, but most of all to be with you and live with you. The most wonderful part of life is ahead.

Tonight and the year 1953 are almost gone. Tomorrow begins the year that starts the best years of our lives.

Happy New Year, Lucy. God bless you, most darling wife. I love you.

Your devoted husband,
Bill

13
Put to the Test

LUCY!

IT HAS HAPPENED!!! AN AUTOMATIC EARLY RELEASE IS NOW OFFICIAL FOR ME AND OTHERS FULFILLING THE SAME REQUIREMENTS!!!

The regulation calls for release after 21 months active duty! I'm storming around in our tent shouting!!! I'll be home three full months ahead of schedule, for sure!!!

I'll mail this now and write more details later today. Get this!! It has happened as we have prayed for all these months!!! I'm going home! Voy para casa! Ich gehe nach hause!!!

Thank God for starting off our New Year in such a wonderful, exciting, delightful way!

Hurray for our side! We're gonna win this one!!

Yours, Bill

1 Jan. 54

Dearest Chicken Pot Pie,

I'm enclosing a clipping from Stars & Stripes which gives the official word on the 21-month Early Release. Is this 2/Lt. ever one excited and happy puppy! Do you realize that my discharge date likely will be 11 May 54?! I should leave Korea at least 30 days earlier, and you and I would be TOGETHER again by the end of April. Joy of joys, I'll be leaving for home in only fourteen weeks!! Finally I'll be a civilian, and then comes our second honeymoon. Could you think of anything more terrific! I'm so excited I can't even write a coherent letter. WOW!

Tour for Junior Officers to Be Curtailed

WASHINGTON, Dec. 30 (AP)—The Army announced today that the active duty tours of some 6,000 non-regular junior officers will be curtailed next year.

This reduction in service, the Army said, will help the Army get down to its projected strength of 1,423,000 by next June 30.

Officers affected will be largely graduates of the Reserve Officers Training Corps, the Officers Candidates Program and the National Guard. The Army said the curtailed service order will start Feb. 1 and end next Aug. 31. Thereafter the normal 24-month period of active duty for non-regular officers will be required.

Insofar as practicable those who complete 21 months service by Feb. 1 will be relieved in that month. Others junior officers will be separated between Feb. 1 and June 1 as they complete the temporarily shortened tour of 21 months service.

The curtailed tours will not apply to junior officers of the Army Medical Service (other than those in the Medical Service Corps), the Chaplains Corps, or the Women's Army Corps.

Tremendous, glorious news!

The next thought—how am I going to earn a living so I can keep (or actually, begin) you in Cadillacs, diamonds and furs? I still have in the back of my mind Harvard Business School and I'm trying to balance out the pros and cons. I'd like to start working and expect I will be successful. The G.I. Bill will give some financial assistance for school, although not enough to make us break even. The big question: Is it worth two years to a guy of my age? I'd be 27½ when I graduated. Would I learn more in two years on the job, or in school?

The other two possibilities which require more school, Law or the Ministry, I think are not to be my career: Law, because I don't think in the long run I would be satisfied in it. Ministry, we have discussed and I hesitate to completely write it off now, but I really don't feel that God wants to use me in that way. There are many ways to serve, and I think my value to Him can be better realized as a Church Layman and community and business leader than as a minister.

A job is the big question. It won't be decided tonight. Anyway, it's late now and it's sack time. In a day or two, looking toward sales and marketing, I'll write Rohm & Haas, Procter & Gamble, Vicks and perhaps General Foods, Pillsbury and Quaker Oats. I'll ask Charlie who I should contact in Investment Banking in New York. In the meantime, think about it and let me know your ideas.

Goodnight, favorite Lamb. I love you completely with all my devotion. Be sure and thank God for His wonderful care and guidance.

You anticipating, devoted,

Bill

P.S. This is #1 writing paper. Many thanks to a very smart, thoughtful Lamb!

* * *

2 Jan. 54

Dearest Lamb,

Today has been a long day. I left for Camp Casey (7th Div. Hq.) in the dark of the morning and didn't get back until supper time. I traveled well armed, with my trusty .45 automatic safely guarding the battery payroll of $600 in military scrip.

Unexpectedly, today I ran into a couple of guys I'd met earlier on my trip to the Far East. One I hadn't seen since we were in Lawrenceville together, and another, George Towner from Princeton. He's from the 47th F.A., which is opening their new Officers Club this Saturday. There'll be several Princetonians in the crowd, so I may go over.

Unhappily, our stove just ran out of oil. It's too late now to rouse boysan, the oil man, so my recourse, if I'm interested in staying warm, is to dive into the sack and continue writing tomorrow.

I love you, Lucy, today and always—Goodnight.

* * *

3 Jan. 54

Today dawned bright and crisp, warm enough for a day in early October and so clear I almost expected to hear the strains of a football march issuing from behind the nearest hill. I've been guardedly waiting for those infamous, cruel, snow-covered, 20° below, Korean winters. It may get a little cool at times, but doggone it, it won't even snow for us!

I'm so glad you liked the sterling cigarette case and the perfume. I had wonderful fun getting them for you. Knowing almost certainly that you were enough of an un-wooly lamb to open my presents before Christmas and would be left with no surprises for the 25th, the dozen roses delivered to Summit seemed the answer. I had as much pleasure sending those as any present I've ever given. Did I ever tell you, Lucy, that you are the best, the most perfect, the most lovable, divine (still without wings) angel in the whole world! Seems to me I've said something like that to you once or twice before.

However, what an un-wooly lamb you are to even be thinking of geishas. In the first place, nothing of the sort exists in Korea. The prostitutes in Korea are ugly as sin itself. The ones in Japan are almost as bad, but even if each one were attractive, what difference would it make to you or me? Besides, you know my determination to adhere to the Ten Commandments and my desire to follow God's and Jesus' teachings, so you must know that all the passion and desire that I have is channeled in one direction, that is, toward my wife, to be used as an expression of my deep love and devotion for the most wonderful person I've ever known. The only person in the world with whom I want the companionship of the ecstasy of sexual love is my wife, with whom I want to share all my life.

Thank you, Lamb, for the birthday card, which I naturally opened early. I counted the candles on the cake—fifty four! Probably on my fifty-fourth birthday you'll be accusing me of acting twenty-five, so I'm not too worried.

I seem to detect a hint or two to place a phone call. If I got on the phone in the BOQ and called Baker switchboard, asked for "Bell" (Bn.) then asked for "Boss" (Div. Arty.) and then asked for "Bayonet" (Div. Hq.), I would have gotten only the first forty miles toward New York and I would have to shout. Nobody I know has ever called past Bayonet, and like the Ancients, I have a nagging suspicion the earth is flat and probably falls off into an abyss not more than fifty miles from my

BOQ tent. As soon as I get to Japan I'll call, although I'm harboring a delusion that I could come home before I get my R&R.

Goodnight, my darling wife, my thoughts and prayers are always with you. I love you with all my heart, body and soul.

Your faithful, adoring,

Bill

* * *

5 Jan. 54

Hi Lamb,

How come you're so sweet? I opened my 25th-birthday (that's a full quarter century) presents this evening and found among many wonderful things a most beautiful and darling picture of my wife in a wonderful leather picture case. I thank you, Lucy. I cherish it.

I also thank you for the boot inserts, which arrived with record speed. I hope you realize how much I appreciate all these things you are constantly doing for me. I love you so much! As for the space heater you mentioned, I think it's very thoughtful and sweet of you, but our stoves have been working pretty well lately, and with our tent liner and hand warmers and long johns I'm feeling pretty bold in the cold.

Hmmm, those apartments in Summit sound mighty expensive, but I guess once we get out of the protective arms of the Army, things won't be so easy anymore—ha-ha!

Tired tonight, I think it's just about that time.

Goodnight, my beloved, God bless you. I LOVE LUCY!

Your devoted, idolizing,

Bill

* * *

To my parents
10 Jan. 54

Dear Mom and Pop,

Christmas and my first quarter-century mark arrived and passed with much very enjoyable fanfare highlighted by great stacks of presents from my family. Thank you for all the wonderful things you sent, from Lucy's Coleman Lantern and your apparel to Georgie's and Sonny's Christmas tree candle.

I am now wearing my two-ply long johns, which are much warmer and more comfortable than my old cotton type. We all very much enjoyed the fruitcake and the brownies and the candy. Even the flashlight caused a great sensation because prior to Christmas I had alternately been borrowing, first, Capt. Sosa's and then Lieut. Weiss's flashlight. The hand warmers are in the foot of my sleeping bag on specially cold nights and make a very reasonable substitute for an electric blanket. Pop's sweater and slippers are very comfortable and warm in the BOQ after duty hours. When I put on the slippers, it was the first time in four or five months that I had anything on my feet except for heavy combat boots. The socks and slippers make for a very pleasant change.

Every night we brew up a pot of the tea or cocoa, measure out two lumps of decorated sugar, and play Scrabble while figuring out the state of the world and how much more will have to transpire before we shoulder our duffels and return whence we came.

Ike's intention to return two divisions from the Orient was greeted with great expectation, but evidently it's to be a slow process, whichever units are to go.

In the meantime, an announcement was made from Washington which came to me as much greater a bombshell. All two-year tours of duty scheduled to terminate between May 1 and August 31 have been shortened to 21 months. That's me!!! I've just gotten three full months chopped from my term of active duty, and my discharge date is now 11

May. I should leave Korea 30 days prior to that date, or approximately thirteen weeks from tomorrow! Almost nothing could be better news!

Of local interest, the impending release of 22,000 prisoners a few miles to our north gets top attention. It won't be a haphazard movement. Plans and preparations have been made from the top levels on down. Most of these are still classified Secret, but by the end of the month I should be able to give you some interesting accounts.

I am amazed by the continued mildness of our winter. It's gotten a bit cool on occasions but never for too long, and without a wind, our average 15° to 20° is far from bitter cold, even in a tent.

After two months out of commission, our gasoline-engine-powered electric generator is finally back in service, supplying one dim light bulb in our tent in the evening and a movie in the Quonset hut some nights. Besides this source of rather doubtful recreation, a new lieutenant arrived in the battery with the New Year and promptly produced a portable radio. The Far East Network provides music without commercials, so we are now becoming somewhat civilized.

Thank you again for the wonderful Christmas and birthday presents. Also, many thanks for negotiating for Lucy's Christmas bouquet of roses. I am expecting the bill. Lucy reports a very enjoyable vacation in Summit. She is very appreciative of all the things you do for her.

My very best love to you and all the family.

Affectionately,

Bill

* * *

12 Jan. 54

Dearest Chicken Pot,

I'm struggling with new training problems, and doing much work. I've only got one class still to prepare for tomorrow. It needs to be a specially good class because the new Div. Arty. Commander, Col. Poor, will be in the area nosing around. Rumor has it that he is a real gentleman, graduated from West Point in 1920, but may not be slated to make General before retirement.

Weiss is off for a week umpiring a Shoot for another Division and Skinner is up for a couple of days on the hill with his FO party. The result is that the entire training of the battery is again on this 2/Lt.'s shoulders. Here's how it went today. I was up at 5:30, took reveille, ate and shaved and finished my lesson plans by 8:00. First class was from 8:00 to 9:00. Then I took the firing battery personnel over to the Bishop Trainer at Bn., set up and fired until noon. By this time my feet were cold to the point of insensibility, so I took the opportunity of thawing out a bit before chow and reading two wonderful letters which had arrived from you earlier in the morning.

After chow, which today was particularly awful, I sat down in the BOQ for a few minutes and soon discovered it was 1:00 PM and time to hit the Bishop Trainer again. It wasn't too cold this afternoon and it was a little more pleasant. At 3:00, we returned to the battery for my second hour class. From 4:00 to 5:00 I re-laid Baker Battery's guns. That means recalculating the aiming data and ensuring, one by one, that each of our six guns is actually parallel and correctly aimed. Then I conducted cannoneer's training on the guns. Dinner was at 5:00 and I held Guard Mount from 5:30 to 6:00. Now except for preparing for tomorrow's classes, I'm all finished for the day.

Dinner tonight featured fried chicken. It was golden brown, tender and steaming hot, and for a meal in Korea, or even at Al Shacks, or perhaps the Quicki Chicki in Lawton, it was the best fried chicken I've ever tasted!

Our lightbulb is now working, although somewhat intermittently, and both of the last two nights we have been artistically terrorized by Grade B flicks. The shows alternately run, then stop, as one or another of the several enabling mechanical devices break down.

Lucy! Your cookies were nothing short of wonderful. They arrived yesterday and are gone today—the best ever. You are the most marvelous cook and thoughtful wife. Many thanks also for the boxes of mantles and injector for our Lantern. Even now that our light often works, the Coleman Lantern is still our most prized possession.

This business of releasing the prisoners promises to become very interesting. Remembering when I taught basic training with the infantry officer (2/Lt. Jim Walker) at Ft Sill, I sketched out a simple local security and perimeter defense plan for our battery which the Capt. approved, and today found it has been adopted by all batteries in Battalion. We don't contemplate any trouble with the prisoners, but we are going to be prepared for anything. The release has gotten much attention and planning from higher levels and is expected to work smoothly. Generals Taylor and Hull will be in the area, and I hope to get some #1 movies. Did I mention earlier? The prisoners will cross nearby Freedom Bridge over the Imjin River, then down the dirt road 500-800 yards to our west.

Lucy, darling, I love you so very much! My only thought and desire is to be with you again soon. How come I have such a wonderful wife?! I appreciate and love her with all my heart, body and soul.

Goodnight, Lucy, God bless you.

Your faithful, devoted, Bill

Gen. Hull's hut at UN Base Camp. Thank goodness he wasn't in!

13 Jan. 54

Hi Chicki,

As I wrote this date, a very magnificent thought occurred to this 2/ Lt. In roughly five months I, Bill MacIlvaine, will be a very jubilant CIVILIAN!!! Moreover, you and I will probably be flying toward Bermuda five months from today. Almost seven months ago I walked into our apartment with orders for the Far East. Doesn't that seem like long ago? We're both a little older and wiser today, and still more in love. And I'm confident our future happiness will be greater than it could ever have been.

When the time begins to grow short and the end of our separation is in sight, my heart begins to get lighter. Today was a bright, almost warm day, with the air so clear that all the surrounding hills stood out sharply. On a day like this you might even think for awhile that Korea is a beautiful place. I guess standing on a hill and seeing the world around you at a distance is much like our impression as we took that sightseeing plane one day at the Westchester County Airport.

Col. Poor inspected us for an hour with Lt. Col. Moore and Maj. Gruenther. He is a distinguished-looking character with silvery hair and a gray mustache; moreover, he impresses me (favorably) as not being of the spit-and-polish school.

Capt. told me after they left that Lt. Col. Moore told his boss, Col. Poor, that I was his best Btry. Exec. The majority of my conversation with Poor covered not Gunnery or the Firing Battery, but rather Scrabble. More fun, we're playing for a penny a point now and tonight I took $1.28 from the Capt. He vows to win it back tomorrow.

I'm getting complaints in the BOQ, at the moment, for staying up so late and burning the midnight oil. (Actually, unleaded white gas obtained by trade with the good Marines of the 1st Marine Div.) Goodnight, favorite wife.

I love Lucy, Bill

* * *

14 Jan. 54

Dearest Pumpkin,

Today Battalion Personnel received the official documents autho-rizing my Early Release. They were issued by 8th Army, authorized by Dept. of Army and endorsed by 7th Division, so now I've got clearance all along the line. The discharge date on my records is being changed to 11 May 54 and 7th Division Hq. (which is usually a bottleneck) has directed that I leave my unit and start home at least 30 days prior to my discharge!!!!!

I will leave Korea sometime between the 2nd and 12th of April. April 2nd is only 11 weeks from today!!!!! I am extremely fortunate in this Early Release deal. After all the talk of Early Release that has been going on in the last three or four months in this BOQ, I'll be the first to go home. Capt. will leave about three weeks after I do, Weiss in August and Skinner in October. I've been telling them all, if they "play their cards right" (or our case, it's Scrabble tiles), I'm going to send each of them a card from Bermuda. Their responses have been somewhat less than polite. You don't suppose they'd prefer to leave Korea before me, instead of after? Do you? Ha ha.

Now I'm telling you the most important news. I love you! I love you so very much, Lamb. I respect you, admire you, need you and think you are the most wonderful, lovable creature God ever created. Goodnight. Lucy.

Your faithful, adoring,
Bill

* * *

16 Jan. 54

Dearest Wife,

I was tired last night and tonight I'm exhausted. We're going out for our Corps Test on the 25th and I spent the entire day in Bn. FDC going over and over the next Test always learning a few more fine points. Gunnery is by far the most interesting part of the army, but eight hours of it is still a big dose for any one day.

The latest, not so little, tidbit! As a matter of fact, this is an unbelievable development! I have been recommended as Aide-de-Camp to Maj. Gen. McGarr! You may remember this is the Two Star General commanding the 7th Division whom I escorted around Baker Battery for the Command Inspection, as acting Battery Commander, when Capt. Sosa was on R&R. This is a remarkable honor. I found out today that the request came down from the General to Battalion designating me by name and that Col. Moore approved it. My records have been sent over to Division Hq.

When they see how little time I have left, I'm sure I won't get the job, but at least it's an interesting turn of events. I told the Capt. that the next time the General and I come down together to perform a Command Inspection, I would recommend to the General that everyone in the Battery be promoted at least one grade! (However, the BOQ will have to continue "playing their cards right.") Ha ha.

You are the loveliest lamb, the most wonderful, darling lamb. I love you, Lucy, and need you and want your closeness and companionship. I can hardly wait for that day, not too far away, when we'll be together again always.

Your devoted, adoring,

Bill

* * *

18 Jan. 54

Dearest Lamb,

Now that we've finally gotten as many as four officers in the battery, Weiss was transferred to Hq. Btry. Also today, Skinner was placed on Special Duty for ten days at Service Btry. That again leaves me alone for all classes, reveille, and Guard Mount. There is also a possibility that a 1st Lt. Garcia may be assigned to Baker soon. Although I'd keep my job as Exec. in charge of the firing battery, Garcia outranks me and undoubtedly would be second in command. He is a Master Sergeant in the R.A. while a 1st Lt. in the Reserve and I hear is probably not the type of guy I would seek out as a good friend.

Other less than joyful news is that if the war ever starts again in Korea, it will start over the massive prisoner release issue this week. It's not that I'm worried about my own health or safety. God will take care of me, but a renewed war, besides being personal, is an awful waste of people, lives, effort and money. We are in the midst now of wild rumors and preparations. I pray that the peace lasts. By the time you get this, the answer will be known.

Observing the release of the POW's.
Video Link: http://loveslettersfromthefront.com/videos

Goodnight, my precious wife. I love you with all the devotion and affection and longing that is within me. You are the most wonderful person who has ever lived. I wish you knew how much I really love and need you.

God bless you, Lucy, my thoughts and prayers are always with you.

Your faithful, devoted, Bill

* * *

Dearest Lamb,

I finished the letter to your parents tonight, and as a result this is going to be just a line or two to keep you posted and tell you that I love you every second, with all my being.

If the shooting starts again in Korea while I'm still here, it will be within the next 48 hours. It is expected now that the Chinese may use force to try stopping the release of the prisoners. Once that happens, the war is on.

For the last two days we have been wearing steel pots and lugging our weapons everywhere we go. Two additional infantry regiments have been moved into this sector for possible reinforcement, and this afternoon we watched a column of tanks move up the nearby dirt road toward the Freedom Bridge. At present we are on eight-minute alert. I've double-checked all the guns. They are properly aligned and ready, aiming stakes are checked, including the night-aiming devices. My gun crews and I are sleeping fully clothed.

More than 22,000 POW's move through our area.
Video Link: http://lovelettersfromthefront.com/videos

I won't try to put down all my thoughts and feelings at this time because I'm not sure I can describe them well. If the shooting starts, I'll be able to tell you more about it during and after, than before. We are ready for whatever happens. If they keep the peace for the next two days, chances for resuming shooting will be practically nil. Despite the rumors and preparations, I somehow feel that the war will not restart in these next two days, but there's no value in speculation. As a Christian, I pray that it won't, as most other people in this world are probably doing.

Goodnight, adorable Lamb. I love you with all my heart and soul. God bless you and watch over and guide us both.

Your devoted husband,

Bill

P.S. Big Brass (very big) is in the area today. Gen. Hull, Gen. Taylor and tomorrow probably Secretary Stevens. I'm waiting for a chance to use the movie camera!!

* * *

20 Jan. 54

Dearest Lamb,

It looks as if the crisis has passed. As of this evening over 10,000 of the prisoners have been released across Freedom Bridge, and down the road less than half a mile west of us. It's all happened without any serious trouble or interference from the Communists. By early morning the last group of them should be on their way southward.

Groan, your 2/Lt. has had his eyes closed and his boots off a total of three and a half hours in the last two days. I am fully ready for the sack.

I took some movies, but as far as being an historical news reel they will prove a flop. We (Capt. and I) set up a BC scope on the roof of the FDC bunker and watched at a range of about 500 yards. I saw the prisoners riding in trucks, waving flags and looking happy, but I was looking too intently to take movies, and the distance was too great anyway. I did manage to take some shots of the general area from atop the FDC and also a short scene through the BC scope, which probably won't come out.

This whole episode has been a high-tension event, with a fortunately blessed ending.

Goodnight, angel. I LOVE LUCY!

Sleepily,

Bill

* * *

21 Jan. 54

Dearest Chicki,

All quiet on the (Far) "Eastern Front." To the best of my knowledge, all prisoners have cleared through the area. Now the emphasis goes back again to training. The Capt. has decided that it is time to "unstack our arms" and start following the training schedule more rigidly, exercising the troops more, and generally working more diligently. And I have the assignment of Training Officer—Groan.

Wonderful news—I am to leave for R&R on 29 January! I may not get to Japan in time to get your birthday presents to you by the ninth of February, but they should arrive shortly thereafter. Also I'm looking forward to a phone conversation with you at long last! We haven't even been able to leave the battery area recently due to the prisoner activity. Now, where should I phone you? The first chance I'll probably have will be Saturday evening, January 30th, your time. I think I'll try Summit first and if you're not there, leave word and the call can probably be transferred without any trouble. How come you are such a sweet chicken?!

But, before R&R, out into the field we go again. We leave this Sunday, the 24th, and return Thursday, the 27th. If the weather stays halfway pleasant, the five days should prove very interesting. At least it will be an energizing change in the training routine.

As the time here grows shorter, my love for you grows even stronger. I can't wait to be with you again. I can picture us together and loving, happy and free, on our second honeymoon and then working and having a home, and then a family. I love you so very much, Lucy!

Goodnight, favorite wife. God bless you.

Your adoring, faithful,

Bill

* * *

23 Jan. 54

Dearest Lamb,

I am repeatedly going through the same army routine, each day being slightly different but all falling into the same pattern. My responsibility is continuous. I am never away from my work or my job. I live, eat, sleep and breathe army artillery. Just now, as I finished that last sentence, for example, the problem arose of who should I elevate to replace the Chief of the 4th Gun Section before our Shoot coming up tomorrow. The current Chief just got the word his Rotation is imminent.

I think this R&R coming up will be just the tonic the name signifies, exactly what I need. It's going to be great to sleep late, shop for all sorts of things for you and talk with you on the phone! I am going to buy a Canon camera at the first opportunity, and if I have any money left, a good slide projector.

In advance of our field Shoot, wouldn't you know, the weather these last two days is rapidly getting colder. It actually doesn't matter much, we're all well used now to camping out.

This business of camping out, or being "in the field," is quite interesting. In Stateside, the location we're now in would be considered "in the field." From here, we go out for five days for a Shoot even more "in the field." While we are out, we will spend one night in pup tents away from the bivouac area, at the firing point. How far out "in the field" can you get? I suppose sleeping uncovered, in the open, curled up in long johns, buried in a snowbank would be the ultimate!

Lt. Garcia has turned out to be not bad a guy after all. Although he's 31 and he likes the army somewhat, he does have a bit of a sense of humor.

His orders to Baker designate him as Assistant Exec. So even though he is the senior 1st Lt. in the entire 49th Battalion, and second in command of Baker Battery, he is officially my assistant.

McAllister returns from his Korean outfit tomorrow for a few weeks before he goes home. While we are in the field, Skinner and Garcia will act as FO's while the Capt., Mac (that's me), and Mc (that's McAllister) will pilot the battery.

Talking about going home! To contemplate being with you is by far the most exciting thought! I love you so much, Lucy, and I want you and need your companionship. It's going to be wonderful to be together again!

Goodnight, darling wife. God bless you. I love you with all my heart, body and soul.

Your faithful, devoted,

Bill

* * *

25 Jan. 54

Dearest Wife,

We again bounced and jarred and jolted Baker Battery over good old Korean dirt roads at 15 mph for two and a half hours yesterday. When we arrived here in the bivouac area, late in the afternoon, it was biting cold. By the time we got the tents pitched and the stoves finally started, it began to get slightly warmer. Although the air temperature hovered around ten degrees during the night, we were reasonably comfortable in the BOQ tent. Hand warmers in the foot of my sleeping bag do wonders for a pair of icy feet.

Today we practiced firing for the Bn. Test and tomorrow the Test starts in earnest. More fun, we're staying casual. McAllister returned today for the few weeks left until his "big R" ("Rotation," meaning homeward bound) date rolls around.

I am looking forward to my change of scenery coming up Friday. I'm going to get you the best pearl ring you have ever seen! I love you with a fire, Lamb.

Your adoring,

Bill

* * *

28 Jan. 54

Dearest Wife,

We're back home again in the battery area near Munsan. It's great to return to a semi-comfortable location again. Although the time in the field flew like the wind and was a pleasant change in routine, the thermometer hovered in the fives and tens. Easy living was non-existent and the hours were long. Last night we all got a skimpy four-and-a-half hours sleep. Naturally, I'm a bit pooped tonight. However, the Shoot went like clockwork. I'm confident we performed near perfectly. We'll get the results in a few days.

McAllister is actively supportive and helpful to me in my job ever since I replaced him as Battery Exec. We're having great sport verbally entertaining each other and the BOQ inhabitants. It's nice having somebody around who is interesting company.

My R&R has been delayed two days, so now what I'll probably do is call you at Sarah Lawrence or at Scarsdale collect.

I love you with a wonderful, overwhelming longing. You are my most precious, darling, perfect wife.

All my love to the best wooly Lamb,
Bill

* * *

29 Jan. 54

Greetings and Good Evening to my favorite wife.

I've been more or less cooling it today and enjoying myself. Three of my greatest sources of local pleasure happened all in one day. That is, other than looking forward to phoning you and getting you the pearl ring: 1) had hot biscuits for dinner, 2) a shower and 3) saw a recent movie.

The biscuits were #1 with the honey that you were so sweet to send. Incidentally, the big red candle is burning right now. Thanks very much, Chicki. Skinner, Mc & I drove to U.N. Base Camp for our shower. To our immense surprise and pleasure we found a new shower unit had been built. Previously it was in a squad tent with overhead pipes with little holes in them and a timid flow of water that couldn't be adjusted. The new shower is in a little building complete with two stoves, a dressing room, individual stalls with hot and cold adjustable running water with a CHROME shower nozzle! We never had individual stalls, even at Camp Stoneman in the States. My singing in the shower, which never seemed quite right in a crowded squad tent shower, was heartily resumed and I'm happy to report that, contrary to unanimous expressed opinions, I am still in good voice.

I had the choice of seeing "Julius Caesar," "Sword and the Rose," or "From Here to Eternity." They're all at different batteries in the Bn. tonight. I chose the latter and enjoyed it mostly…because it was about the "Old Army" and familiar at that!

I forgot to tell you, one evening Mc and I went over to the 17th F.A. Bn. (which is in Corps Artillery and near our firing range). We needed to pick up some sandbags for our aiming stakes, and after we got them we stopped in at their officers club. What a great place they have! It's in one of the new-style Quonset huts with plywood paneling and a big stone fireplace. We found John Herbert had discovered this paradise and was already whooping it up. There was another Princeton lad on the scene and a friend of Bliss' from Harvard. Mc met a few of his friends from Texas A&M.

After enjoying a few beers sitting on the couch in front of the fireplace, we shifted into higher gear and the singing started. We left around 10:30 via our dependable jeep and driver as the whole crowd poured outside to send us off with a rousing chorus of "Old Nassau." The solemn and cold ancient hills of Korea must have looked down in wonderment at these riotous goings-on.

The next day the contrast was again very great. I stood alone in a desolate rice paddy in subfreezing temperature with my parka buttoned up against the wind. A few feet behind me was the makeshift FDC tent, and out in front were our six howitzers attended by their hooded gun crews.

Around me in all directions were desolate frozen hills and paddies. Patches of powdery crunchy snow dotted the landscape and nothing moved or murmured except the steady wind. Out of the FDC radio came the blaring strains of a stateside band, the kind you hear in a crowded, smoke-filled roadhouse. Hearing one atmosphere and seeing another, I once again wondered if it was really possible that I, Bill MacIlvaine recently of Princeton, could be standing in an abandoned rice paddy in the Orient. It's not often that I get that weird feeling of the unreality in the contrast between my natural former life and what I'm doing now. It's interesting to contemplate because I've gotten so accustomed to my present location and job as Executive Officer, this has now become my new natural current life.

After I've been home a day or two, I'll probably wonder if I imagined it all, and if I've ever actually been in the Orient.

The thought of being with you again soon is the most wonderfully perfect thing I can think of. I'm looking forward to four youngsters and a home and family of our own together—always together and completely in love.

Your adoring,
Bill

14
Tokyo R&R

31 Jan. 54
1:30 PM

Dearest Chicken Pot,

In about three hours we take off by jeep for Div. Arty., and from there, to the K-16 air strip outside Seoul (known as Kimpo Field) and from there, hop over to Japan!

Lt. Garcia, Lt. Aicher and I are the three officers going from the 49th. Garcia is married and Aicher is engaged. The first thing I'm going to do is get a shrimp cocktail and a tremendous sirloin, have my picture taken, and then start my shopping and sightseeing.

I'll call you from the R&R hotel (probably the Yaesu) as soon as I can get connections through. It'll probably take about 24 hours.

I'm all packed now and have my sleeping bag rolled and ready. We'll probably spend the night at K-16 and fly across to Japan early tomorrow morning.

I have your January series letters through #18, excluding #11, and I'm very embarrassed to discover that your last letter which I have actually answered is #6. I'm going to take them along on R&R and hope I get a chance to answer them. I'll probably have much to tell you about anyway, so we'll see.

I love you, Lucy. Together. That's the most beautiful word in the language. I can't wait. The time is growing short, Chicki! It will be so wonderful to be with you, in love and happy and complete again.

Your always faithful adoring husband,

Bill

P.S. Enclosed is the form showing my total taxable earnings from the army and the amount of tax already paid. We'll probably be able to get a refund on our tax.

* * *

1 Feb. 54
Tokyo, 7:20 PM
Sack Time!

Dearest Lucy,

This wonderful civilization! I never realized it earlier, but Tokyo is a magnificent town. We are having a wonderful time and it's ninety percent because of you. In my mind's eye I've already bought you $400 worth of presents.

Since my letter yesterday here's a quick rundown of my travel log.

We left Baker at four PM and set off in convoy for Div. Arty., where we were paid. Then we rolled down to K-16 outside of Seoul, and after getting lost twice in the metropolis, arrived at the airfield at nine. From nine until four in the morning we sat in the waiting room and at four-thirty we took off in the biggest four-engine, cavernous ship you have ever seen. We were carrying about 180 men, or three times the load for a normal-sized civilian four-engine (like our Bermuda flight) plane can carry.

Arriving in Tokyo for R&R.
Video Link: http://lovelettersfromthefront.com/videos

After three and a half hours of flying time, during which I slept not too soundly, sitting up in a straight-back bucket seat, we landed at Tachikawa A.F.B., an hour's drive from Camp Drake, somewhere near Tokyo.

True to the best army traditions, at Drake we processed for several hours and by two this afternoon, complete with shower and shave and O.D. uniform with ribbons, Garcia, Aicher and I set out for Tokyo. After many taxi rides and more signing of papers we got ourselves situated at the Yaesu Hotel. We are sharing a dormitory-type room with three Turkish regulars also on R&R. They look like the harsh characters of whose alarming reputation we've heard plenty. We've never figured out how to communicate.

I can't begin to tell you what a wonder it was to see electric lights and American cars and paved streets and big buildings. It is almost like visiting Dallas from Lawton.

Tokyo R&R.

Travel log continued: Once we got situated we decided the sportiest move would be cocktails at the Imperial Hotel Lounge. What a place! Swankier by far than any place I know in New York. It is frequented by the International Set. The hotel was designed many years ago by none other than Frank Lloyd Wright and is a masterpiece combination of Oriental and Modern Architecture. It is also highly touted to be earthquake proof.

Having had no sleep the previous night and nothing but breakfast during the day, we lingered over two Gibsons from three until four and then chanced a peek at the shops in the Imperial Arcade. That's when I almost lost my head. There is a Japanese mink cape that is beautiful for $180. I wonder, would you like it? Your Mandarin jacket for $20 is absolutely perfect. Lacquered music boxes and cordial glasses look awfully tempting. Your pearl pendant is just what I imagined. The ring will require a little more consideration. The black pearls at their darkest are a light blue and not included in Mikomoto's standard jewelry production. I can get the black-and-pink pearl ring, but it will cost twice what twin pink pearls cost, since it has to be custom made. The salesman tried to dissuade me from the idea on artistic grounds. I'll withhold my decision until I talk with you about it tomorrow.

Now the question is how in the world can I get you all these things and still not go into hock? And what about the Christmas presents I was going to get for our families?

Here's my solution. First, I'm going to sit for a formal photograph and send a copy to all concerned, then I'll put aside a little steak and shrimp cocktail money for the next six days. Finally, I'm going to buy you birthday presents until I'm broke.

Did I ever tell you that I love you?

From the Arcade we went to Irene's Hungaria, a sort of half-Japanese, half-Hungarian basement restaurant. It was small, with checkered tablecloths, low music and the best food this side of San Francisco. Oh, how I wished you were with me!! The entire meal was spent talking about our wives and fiancées, respectively. I had shrimp cocktail first, then oysters on the half shell, and then a filet mignon complete with boiled onions in sauce, French fries, and baby limas in the pods! Hot rolls included.

Fresh strawberries finished us off and we hailed a cab for home. I'll have no trouble sleeping tonight.

As I sit here writing in our hotel room, my thoughts and love are with you, as they always are, but especially today. I told Garcia and Aicher that when I opened my first branch office, I plan to locate it in Tokyo, you and I were going to spend one week of every year in the Imperial Hotel. You would love it as I loved experiencing the fun of today and sharing with you everything I did and saw.

I love you, my darling wife, with all my devotion and yearning. I need your companionship and love and long to be with you close in the love of heart, body, and soul.

Goodnight, Lucy, God bless you and help the remaining weeks to pass swiftly.

Your adoring, faithful husband,

Bill

* * *

3 Feb. 54

Hi Lamb:

Happy Birthday to the sweetest white woolly one of all.

Your birthday present goes off tomorrow, to be followed shortly by your Valentine card and present. The pearl ring is your birthday present. I tried to call you this morning (Monday night your time) but you were out, so I went ahead on my own, and I do hope you approve. I went to Mikomoto's main store on the Ginza and tried again without avail to get the black pearl. After much discussion and phone calls to the factory, I found they could match a black-and-pink but they wouldn't be of top quality and it would take ten days. I'd be gone from Tokyo then, and they couldn't mail the ring out of Japan.

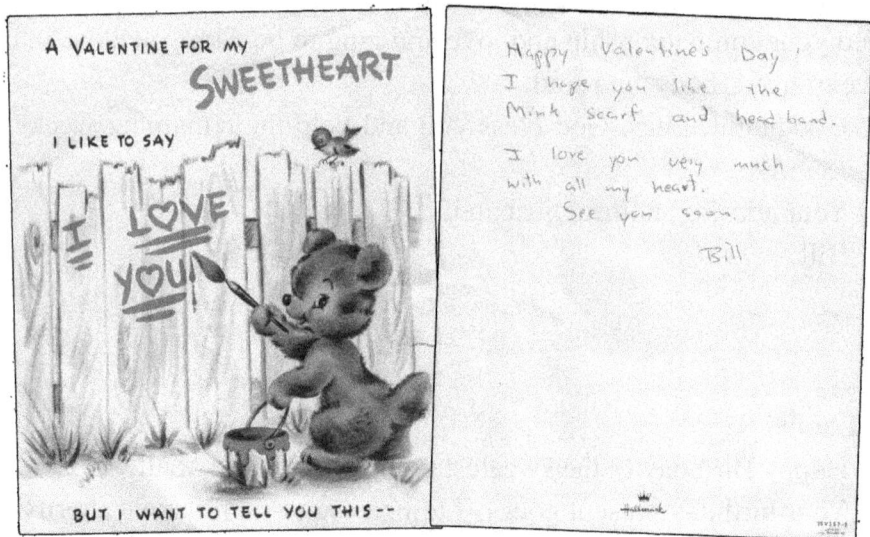

Valentine's Day 1953.

Valentine presents for Lucy.

What I got you was a perfectly matched pair of the best pink pearls mounted in a 14 karat gold setting. I think it is really a beautiful ring.

Your Valentine's present I'll get in a day or two, when I've shopped around a little more. You'll be amazed and astounded when you see it. Its Stateside price runs about $150 and is luxury, plus! Curious?

Tomorrow I'll try calling again and I hope I won't let the cat out of the bag.

Aicher and I spent the entire day shopping and comparing. Dinner was at Suehiro's and afterwards we met Garcia and another lieutenant he knew, and went to the show at the Music Hall. It was racy—probably would be banned in Boston—but nevertheless quite a glitzy production.

Incidentally, we ran into Jim Walby, ex-Lawrentian, and now Navy pilot, in the Imperial Hotel cocktail lounge. It was great sport talking over the old school days.

I can't wait to talk to you in the morning. I have so much to say, I probably won't say anything except I love you—that's the most important thing I can say anyway. I mean it with all the devotion and adoration of your favorite lieutenant.

God bless you, Lucy. I love you.

Lovingly and faithfully,

Bill

* * *

4 Feb. 54

Dearest Pooh,

It was by far the most wonderful experience of the past five months— talking with you—and twice in one day!! I'm sorry I sounded so formal and stilted the first time, but with an audience of five roommates (three of whom were the previously mentioned Turks), I found privacy wanting. As soon as we said goodbye I knew I'd have to call back. I'm glad I did. You are such a pumpkin and I love you so much! It was just like being with you again for a few minutes.

I was so inspired by our conversation that I went out and made some more purchases. Your Valentine present will go off tomorrow: Japanese mink of the northern variety. I hope you approve.

I think the time has come to be a little more mysterious about my gifts. From now on I'm not talking. Some things you may get in a few days, others you may not see until Christmas. Ain't I a stinker!

Aicher got a bug or two in his stomach and has been feeling very low since the middle of the morning. I've been feeling a little on the queasy side myself, so today was a relatively quiet day. Aside from three shopping excursions, I've been spending the day in the supreme luxury of reading, stretched out comfortably on a real bed. Remember me with Life magazine! The only trouble is the more you read and have rest time, the more tired you get. It's almost 10:30 now and I'm at the point where I can hardly keep my eyes open.

Talking to you today only intensified my desire to be with you again. I miss you, Lucy, and need your companionship. With every day the time apart grows shorter and the future seems more wonderful and my love for you grows.

Goodnight, my perfect wife. My thoughts and prayers are always with you.

Longingly, faithfully,
Bill

* * *

5 Feb. 54

Dearest Lamb,

I'm sure of today's date, although without a calendar I have a feeling some of my recent letters might have been in error.

Much traveling today. Aicher and I went down to Yokosuka, about two hours on the train. The PX there was not all it was cracked up to be, but on the way back we heard the Yokahoma PX was actually the best. It was. I bought a Canon camera for $112. It's Japanese made and identical to the Leica. The lens is f 1.8, which is about the largest you can get. It is a #1 piece of equipment.

I sent off a roll of movie film which is largely the sightseeing tour we took of Tokyo. It has short, unconnected scenes and probably won't be of great artistic value but I hope it will give a little idea of what this town is like.

Tonight Aicher and I went back to Suehiro's, this time for sukiyaki, the traditional Japanese meal complete with chopsticks. We took off our shoes at the entrance to the dining room and sat on the thin pillows cross-legged. The table was about twelve inches high, with a little burner in the center. All the food was brought in raw and cooked on the table. We ate sukiyaki (pronounced skee yock e) and rice (gohung) and had a little urn of hot sake served in half-ounce cups. It was a very tasty meal and an experience of a lifetime. I wish I had taken a picture, or better, a movie of your 2/Lt. manipulating chopsticks—what sport!

Goodnight, precious wife. Your Love has had a long day. I love you with all my heart and I can't wait to be with you again. Day after tomorrow I'll call you again.

God bless you, Lucy.

Adoringly, affectionately, faithfully,

Bill

* * *

6 Feb. 54

Dearest Wife,

I've spent all afternoon and evening thinking and talking about you—how can I ever tell you how very much you mean to me?!!

I bought a few extras for the camera this morning, then met Aicher at the Imperial. He talked about Ann and I talked about Lucy and so it went for eight hours. We're to be invited to their wedding in the latter part of June and we've planned a get-together in New York sometime before then. We'll meet under the clock at the Biltmore, have dinner at some little place on Lexington Avenue and then to the Champagne Room. Sound like fun?

We had dinner and Cointreau at George's and afterwards a long chat with George.

I'll call you in the morning. Until then, goodnight, angel.

I love you.

Your loving, faithful,

Bill

P.S. Enclosed are the proofs of the photos I had taken. Six copies will arrive soon. Please give one to each member of the families with my love and regards.

* * *

8 Feb. 54
Camp Drake

Dearest Lamb,

The R&R is just about over now. We reported into Drake at 2:00 PM and changed back into long johns, O.G.'s (Olive Greens) and pile Siberian caps. It is now 4:15 and we have been assigned to a shabby but super plushy furnished BOQ to await our departure time. It will probably occur sometime after midnight. In the meantime, we are sleeping in this very tumble-down room under bare electric light bulbs, but on Hollywood-style beds complete with matching white bureaus and wardrobe closets and brand new chrome and leather couches. Do you suppose some general ordered this garish furniture from a catalog, then when it arrived, seeing it up close, refused it and consigned it to our transient BOQ?

The atmosphere is very pleasant and the waiting should be quite painless—later, maybe with dinner at the Officers Club and a movie.

The thought of going back to squad tents and frigid out-houses is not all that pleasant, but actually, with only seven weeks and a few days, who is complaining! Right now it seems like an eternity, but it will pass.

R&R was wonderful compared to our life in Korea but it couldn't begin to compare with Rotation. The thought of being with you once again, this time for always, makes me almost tremble with anticipation. I love you so much, my wonderful wife—I miss you so, and need your companionship. You are everything in the world to me, Lucy. You are a symbol to me of everything that is good and honest and beautiful. You are a part of my life, of my love and of me. I love you more than I can ever hope to tell you. There is too much love and emotion and feeling to put into words on a page or to try to tell over a telephone. Perhaps the best way I can tell you is when, in love together, we enjoy the daily companionship of our future lives.

I can see out the window of our BOQ the telegraph office where I sent you that cable in September saying I'd just arrived in Japan. That seems like a long, long time ago, and when I look forward to the limited weeks remaining I am encouraged.

It was so wonderful to talk with you on the phone. I'm sorry about the wee hour of the night and about the bad connection. For my part, hearing your voice would be worth having to shout across the ocean.

I got your Mandarin jacket and am now reduced to three dollars for the rest of the month in addition to owing Aicher $115. I think the jacket would make a good maternity outfit. I'll give it to you when you're ready for it!! I hope that will be before our third anniversary.

I'm delighted with my new camera. So far I've taken ten pictures in Tokyo and still have ten left on the roll. My next purchase will be a light meter from the PX at about 40% off, and if I ever get any money in my pocket again before I'm discharged, I can get a TCD slide projector at about 25% off!

R&R was fun and a pleasant change. Aicher and I enjoyed ourselves primarily with shopping and sightseeing. The weather was bright and warm enough. Most of the days did not require an overcoat. I got plenty of sleep, ate steaks every day, and sat over several beers listening to "Lili" and talking to Aicher about the States and the wonderful love of my life.

You know perfectly without my even mentioning it that I have been, am, and always will be completely faithful to you in every way. I love you too much for anything else. Always remember and know that I cherish you above all else in life. You are my wife, a part of me.

God bless you, Lucy. I love you.

Devotedly,

Bill

15
Baker–Bell's–Best

11 Feb. 54

Dearest Wife,

Back again—groan.

We spent all of 9 February in transit, arriving in the battery late that evening. I thought about you all that day and wished you a HAPPY BIRTHDAY! I hope the pearl ring didn't arrive too late.

Yesterday I was in the depths of trying to get readjusted to this existence.

Things were beginning to progress nicely until just about an hour ago. Then a phone call from Bn. changed the situation. We have our big Corps Test coming up in a week. This is to be the culmination of all our previous Tests. The Colonel is in a big stew and is leaving no stones unturned to insure that the 49th Bn. makes a commendable showing.

He thinks that Baker and Charlie Batteries are going very well but that Able's shooting is not what it should be. I am now appointed as trouble-shooter and will take over as Exec. of Able Btry. from tomorrow until the Corps Tests are over. Who is the Btry. CO of Able? None other than First Lt. Anderson. He's the R.A. plus who, until a month ago, was Bn. Asst. Operations Officer and whom I wrote used to harass the Batteries. He doesn't know what he's doing but he does it with gusto anyway. Isn't it interesting—actually ironic—how our working situations change and evolve over time. A couple of months ago this fellow was bothering me. Now I'm his ticket to improving his battery's performance and his reputation.

I love you, Lucy. Your loving, harassed, Bill

* * *

12 Feb. 54

Dearest Wife,

Received three very sweet, very wonderful letters from you today which cheered me considerably. They were the one written just before, and the two written just after, my first two phone calls to you. How come you're such a Lamb?

I moved over here to Able late this afternoon and it looks now as if I'll have to be here only one week instead of the month originally planned. I surely hope so. I'll be glad to go back to Baker—but not half as glad as I'll be that day when I leave Baker for good, when I can "speak sayonara" to the Land of the Morning Calm!

Tomorrow is preparation for our field test jaunt. Then we'll have three days out, three days back. Then we turn around and go out again. In the next three weeks we'll probably spend over half the time in the field. With that and switching between batteries, I am not feeling at all like a comfortable, garrison soldier. Here, you never get a chance to get settled. Anyway, on the plus side, it will help make the time pass faster.

No good news when I arrived back from R&R. Our friendly, trusted houseboy took off with everything in the BOQ he could get his hands on, including McAllister's and Skinner's cameras. I was relatively lucky, losing only a field jacket, a set of O.G.'s and my coveted, treasured two-ply long johns. (He got two of my four pairs.) The more I interact with most Koreans, the less I trust them. Also, I see more clearly the difference in people and important impact made by Christianity. I hear that the Christian Koreans are reliable and honest, from the biggest to the smallest.

The thought of seeing you again, of being with you, talking to you, kissing you! It all seems so wonderfully magnificent I can hardly believe it's only a matter of weeks. I only hope I can be half the sweet and wonderful person you deserve. I love you so very much, Lucy.

Goodnight, my favorite wife. God bless you and lead us together with all possible speed.

I love Lucy, Bill

* * *

13 Feb. 54

Dearest Wife,

Thanks for the two very adorable Valentine cards. I especially liked the one that had the rhyme about "complex" and you on a green velvet couch!

Today, Saturday, was a full working day in which I spent most of my time planning the coming operation with Able Battery's FDC and Chiefs of Section. I think things are going to begin running pretty smoothly.

Life over here is not as comfortable or as well-oiled as in Baker. The two lieutenants here are young, pleasant, but seem to be personalities without extensive weight or message. The BC, Anderson, is hard working and although he loves the army and personally we are very different, we do manage to get along pretty well.

The Able BOQ has only recently been pitched in its present location and leaves much to be desired. The tent has no liner, no wooden doors and no plastic screen window, as we do now in Baker. The BOQ as well as the battery area doesn't seem as neat or as well organized as BAKER—BELL'S—BEST—BY TEST.

I am out of words tonight after laboriously composing a letter to Harvard Business School. I think it's an acceptable letter. I told them what I'd learned in Korea and why I want to go to Harvard. I'm a married vet—that's also in my favor. We'll see. I wish I was sure I wanted to study two more years before I start on an earning career.

I love you, my darling Lamb, with a great, overwhelming, yearning desire. You are the most wonderful wife a guy could ever have. I need you, Lucy.

Adoringly, faithfully,
Bill

Dearest Chicki,

Here we are in the great Korean outdoors again, this time with Able Battery. The location is the same as our Shoot back in October, on my first exercise testing my gunnery as Battery Exec. I feel like an old-timer this trip.

Enclosed are two very posed pictures—one of your Lt. climbing a very steep (but not too high) cliff. In the other shot, we were horsing around and the Capt. called attention, and somebody took a picture during the two seconds I held the pose. I don't like either picture but I'll send them along for your chuckles.

Steep, frozen terrain.

* * *

Distractions proved too much competition last night for any extensive letter writing. Hurrah! I'm now back, living in Baker's BOQ, where radio and a loud bull session pervade the atmosphere.

Tomorrow we're up at 0500 for the Grand Bn. Test, and afterwards happily on the trip back to our Korean home away (far away) from home.

Maj. Gen. McGarr (you know him by now, our 7th Div. Commanding General) came by to observe our Baker Battery firing operations (and others) today and reportedly was very happy. It seems years ago when he landed in his chopper in Baker Battery and I escorted him around on his Command Inspection. That was when the bulldozer got stuck in the deep mud and I borrowed a tank from the Marines to haul it out, seemingly only minutes before McGarr landed. Some fun! It was interesting to talk with him again. By the way, as I may have mentioned earlier, the proposed Aide-de-Camp position would have required extending my tour in Korea. No way, no how. Not a chance! Thanks just the same, sir.

I love you, darling wife, with all my devotion.

See you soon, Lamb.

Adoringly,

Your sleepy Lieutenant

P.S. The check is on its way by mail from Tokyo. I got your letter saying you'd sent me the money by cable. That was two days ago. It's good there's no hurry because that darn cable is going to take two weeks before it finally arrives. C'est la guerre (or something).

* * *

18 Feb. 54

Dearest Lamb,

We pulled in from the field and the Test late last night with this Lt. exhausted from slogging around in ankle-deep mud all day. From a personal standpoint my gunnery work as temporary Exec. at Able Battery went very well, and the overall results for the Battalion were commendable. The Colonel is highly pleased. After we arrived last night, I came back to Baker, and here I think I'll get to stay until I go home.

McAllister is scheduled to ship home (from Inchon) in five days and spends his waking hours intermittently shouting, "I'm going home!" to anyone nearby, or to nobody. I've spent most of the day smiling over a homemade calendar. Forty-two days, or six weeks from tomorrow, is my bug-out date, about five weeks from the time you get this. Also by the time you get this, I will have received my silver bars as First Lieutenant. My promotion is retroactive to 12 February. It's been approved and is on the way down through channels. You may now begin addressing me as 1/Lt.

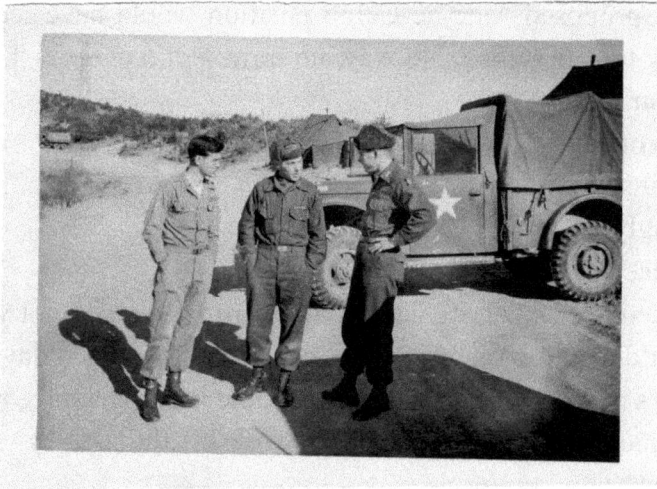

Lt. McAllister and I "instruct" the newly arrived Lt. Skinner.

Besides my calendar, the Capt. has one hanging over his bunk. Every night after chow, Mc, Skin, Garcia and I stand at attention, salute and hum taps while the Capt. crosses off one more day. At month-end, he tears off the month, balling it and burning it as we stand at attention. This is just the kind of craziness that continues to keep us sane and smiling.

Just had a half-hour time-out while I explained to the Capt. and McAllister the wonders of Bermuda and Cambridge Beaches. Mc says he's sold and is all set to go on his honeymoon, if and when.

News flash! We just got a phone call from the Colonel. The 49th Bn. unofficially scored 92 on the Test. The Colonel is jubilant. We are all now the Colonel's fair-haired stepchildren. The results of the Test go to Dept. of the Army, and (West Pointer) Lt. Col. Moore's career is undoubtedly looking very bright—increasingly so. He is one outstanding leader and knows how to make it rub off on his officers.

I'm taking reveille tomorrow morning and it's already eleven. I've been having great trouble tonight keeping out of the bull session. At best, it's very distracting for this letter-writing 1/Lt.

Goodnight, precious wife. I love you with all my heart, body and soul. God bless you and hasten the remaining days.

Your adoring, devoted,

Bill

* * *

19 Feb. 54

Dearest Pumpkin,

The BOQ held taps again tonight honoring the dying day; however, we decided that it's much more dramatic to mark off several days at a time. Accordingly, we are going to suspend the ceremony until we return from the field. We'll have a long weekend coming up with Monday, Washington's Birthday, as a day off.

Tuesday we exit home base, and Thursday we return from our Night Shooting phase of the Bn. Test. To all intents and purposes Friday is a day off for the officers because the Battery is engaged in maintenance and cleaning of equipment. The following Monday we go out for four days of maneuvers.

Mc leaves Monday, and tomorrow he and two other Sayonara Lieutenants are throwing a last blast at the club. Champagne is "Hav-a-yes" (as Papasan always says), so it should be a very colorful affair.

This afternoon all officers attended a very boring four-hour class at Bn. on how to inspect vehicles. Two interesting topics, however, came up during the afternoon. One was again hearing the report that the Bn. made 92% on the Bn. Test. I'm still amazed—things seemed to go smoothly but I didn't realize we were that proficient. This is way above a "very good" performance. The other juicy item: after the maneuvers are over on March 4th, there are no more tests or problems scheduled until after my, and several other officers', departure date.

Enclosed are two snaps which I don't like in the least and hope you won't show around. The first was taken in October before the practice for a parade (which you have movies of) and the other is of Mc and me giving Skinner the straight poop on what it takes to be a soldier. He seems to be taking it very lightly.

I love you so very much, Lucy! I've been thinking about our second honeymoon all day. You're my favorite Pooh Bear.

Hugs and kisses,

Bill

* * *

To My Parents
20 Feb. 54

Dear Mom and Pop,

Thank you both for your recent letters. During the past few months we have been spending five days out of every week out on the artillery range in bivouac-style camping sprees, so my letter writing has been below the usual bare minimum.

As for this business of being selected as the General's Aide-de-Camp: it is a relatively exacting job and decidedly an honor, but very different from being the Exec. (field leader and gunnery officer) of a firing battery. Accepting the job of Maj. Gen. McGarr's Aide would not have been a matter of extending here a few months, but rather of signing for three years in the Army and spending an extra year in Korea beyond time I already have here. I didn't have to make a big decision. I didn't even consider the job on those terms. Besides, I already knew that my promotion was coming up shortly. Even if they bumped me to Captain for the General's Aide job, it would still out of the question.

My promotion to First Lieutenant was approved, effective 12 February, and I'll get official confirmation and pin on my new silver bars in the next few days

I wrote to Harvard Business School last week indicating my desire to apply for admission. It is possible that I could profit more, in the long run, from two years at business school than from two years' experience on my first civilian job. Besides, I've been told the average starting salary after business school is about $100 a month higher. On the other hand, I'm impatient to settle down to a career, get to work and start making progress in business.

The grand date for my Korean departure is scheduled for about the first day of April. I hope they won't say "April Fool" when the day arrives. I'd expect to reach the States by Easter, although it is too early yet to make any solid predictions.

Our field excursions and the constant shooting make time go fast, since there is so much work to get done. This is giving me increasing satisfaction, as it's going extremely well and has a purpose which needs to be accomplished.

I hope by now you are both in good health. I'll see you soon.

Love,

Bill

* * *

21 Feb. 54

Dearest wife,

Barbados—isn't that the place friends told us they liked so much? It may be a trifle far, but why don't you check the plane fare, etc. Also, I reread your letter mentioning Acapulco. That doesn't sound too bad either. I still have an open mind about the whole excursion. What do you think? Hmm—Bermuda is a lovely place. Let's go to all three! I'm ready to leave tomorrow.

Mc leaves at 0600 tomorrow and is as keyed up as a kitten on catnip with a ball of yarn. He can't carry on an intelligible conversation and can't even sit still. I'll surely be the same when my time comes. He retired to his cot this evening exclaiming that his expectation and anticipation was that of a wide-eyed kid on Christmas Eve seeing piles of glittering presents awaiting him under a colorful, sparkling, brightly lighted Christmas Tree.

I forgot to mention while we were out in the field, we went down to Camp Casey to see a USO Show. Marilyn Monroe sang two numbers from "Gentlemen Prefer Blondes" as the featured attraction. Everyone agreed afterwards, except John Herbert, that she's not half of what publicity makes her out to be. She's on the fat side, and regarding stage personality—Hav-a-no (again quoting Papasan). I heard she even forgot the lines to one of the songs when she sang for the 3rd Division. Nice of her to come anyway.

Goodnight, favorite Wife. I love you as always with a great longing and fire. You are the sweetest Pooh Bear I have ever known.

I love Lucy,

Your First Lieutenant

* * *

22 Feb. 54, Monday

Dearest Wife,

Today was a very pleasant, quiet, cool Washington's Birthday. The only activity of the day consisted of a few last-minute preparations for tomorrow's March Order. We now discover that upon orders of Gen. Pyle we are to be out for four days instead of the planned three. This time it's fairly certain that at least one night will be spent on the (frozen) ground in a pup tent.

The maneuvers on March 1 to 4 are expected to be more of the same—pup tents. If it's cold and/or muddy and we have to move every day, your Lieutenant is going to be one grumpy puppy. The consolation prize is that it will be my last field problem in Korea and the last of my entire military career! Am I tempting fate with talk like this?

I'm glad you liked my birthday and Valentine presents. I think they are both things you will always like. How does the ring fit? According to the best calculations, it is exactly 6¼ and should be perfect.

On credit, I managed to pick up a G.E. Light Meter and a Flash Attachment for the Canon. Now all we need is a slide projector and we're in business. The more I think of it, my Canon was a #1 buy.

I love you, my wonderful wife, with all my being. You are the most precious and perfect wife in the world. God bless you and guide us both and hasten our wonderful reunion.

Goodnight, Lucy. I love you.

Devoted and faithfully,

Bill

* * *

25 Feb. 54

Dearest Wife,

How I'm [not] going to miss the army and camping out in all weather! It has been raining steadily since late last night and at present the entire area inside our temporary tent is divided into roughly 40% slime and ooze, and 60% open water. Rubber boots are a must. With every step your foot sinks two inches into Korea, accompanied by slurping, gurgling slosh. The suction effect is enormous, so that walking today has literally meant stretching your legs.

Our two oil-burning pot bellies (sitting on stilts) are putting forth at full blast so my parka, fatigues, long johns and leather boots which I've been wearing for the last 36 hours are starting to dry.

We left our bivouac area early yesterday morning to begin the Corps Test, and spent the day preparing our firing position for a deliberate night occupation. We moved out of an assembly area at eight in pitch blackness, and carefully threaded our way along high-crowned dirt roads and over high wooden bridges. At the firing point, still under blackout conditions, we emplaced the howitzers, set up FDC, and I laid the battery. All four howitzer battalions of the 7th Div. Arty. participated in the test, so our fire missions were pretty well spread out through the night. I slept several times, for thirty minutes each, while sitting on a instrument-storage crate under a tarpaulin at FDC [Fire Direction Center]. Actually I was enjoying myself until the rain started. Being Exec. of a well-practiced firing battery that is efficient and crisp, confident and shoots well is probably the best job in the army.

Results of the first part of this major Corps Test (last week) are unofficial as yet, but the 49th Bn. was highest in Division, highest in Corps, and of the three Corps in Korea, "I" Corps (that's ours) scored as the highest. That makes the 49th Bn. the best shooting artillery in 8th Army. Baker Battery had been previously designated to be Bell's Best, i.e., the top in our 49th Battalion. What I am attempting to say, while trying not to overstate too much, is that my Baker firing battery has excelled in a series of competitive field Shoots and could reasonably be ranked the best, the most effective firing battery in Korea! No small honor for a bunch of reservists! (Or their Capt. and Exec.)

Incident: The Guard just came in with four ROK's he caught in our Motor Pool. We handed them over to the MPs for questioning. All the Christian Koreans that I've met are good men. The rest of their countrymen (but not all) that I've had contact with are suspect. Being a Christian makes all the difference in the world!

Tomorrow we rise at five, break camp and head "home" for Munsan. After last night and all morning of firing, I'm getting a little on the sleepy side.

Goodnight, precious wife. I love you with all my heart, body and soul. You are always in my thoughts and prayers.

See you soon, Lamb.

Lovingly, adoringly,

One Happy 1/Lt.

No enemy in view.

16
A Silver Bar

26 Feb. 54

Dearest Lamb,

Back home now in the vicinity of Munsan.

We hit the slippery, muddy homeward-bound trail at 0700 and arrived mid-morning. The rest of the day has been devoted to maintenance and cleaning—an especially big job this time. Tomorrow, Saturday, will be more of the same with not much work involved for officers. Tomorrow evening will be a command performance party at Div. Arty. Hq. in honor of Gen. Pyle's promotion. I'm not much enthused because it's a half-hour bouncing jeep ride each way and I'll have to press my O.G.s with our antique flatiron.

My exit news is still cheerful although the Capt. and I had a bad scare today. Rumor was that everyone with less than three months to go in Korea would be extended one month. We sputtered and fumed and took off for Personnel. There we quickly found it did not concern us, although people who have several months still to serve after returning to the States are affected. The Capt. and I are going home on expiration of term of service (ETS) and are certain not to be delayed.

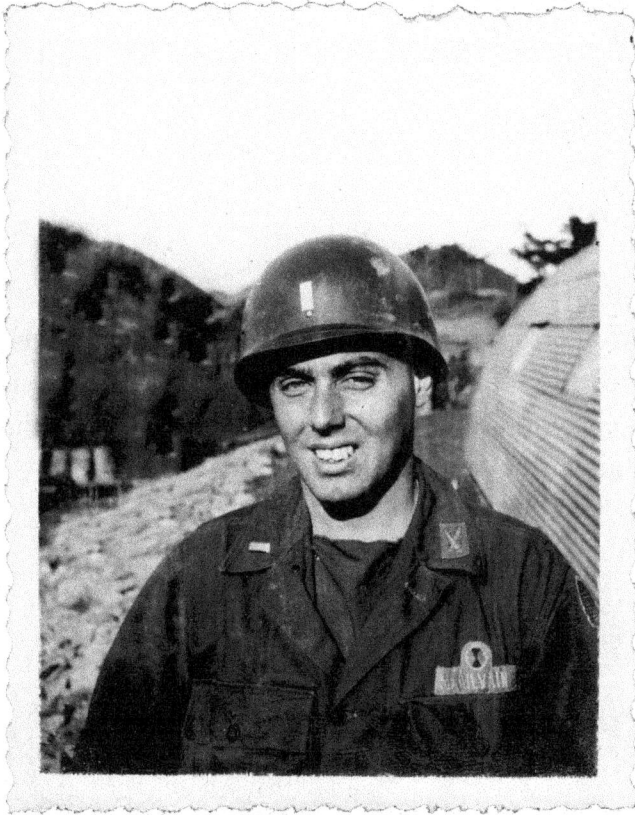

That new bar on my helmet is white adhesive tape.

You've convinced me on Cambridge Beaches. As a matter of fact you put it so well it seemed like what's been in my mind all along. The Barbados and Acapulco will be fun later, but Bermuda is our old stomping grounds and will be comfortable and familiar. I agree that we shouldn't stay at Sunset Cottage this time. It's not the $40 per day I'm thinking of [I may be Scottish, but [ha] rarely cheap]. It's because this is another honeymoon, not the first one relived, and we have to make new tracks. Motorbikes, here we come!!

Did I ever tell you how much I love you? With all my heart, body, and soul and then some!

Goodnight, precious wife. You are always in my heart.
Your devoted, desiring,
Bill
P.S. I love you!!!!!

* * *

27 Feb. 54

Dearest Pooh,

Groan—tomorrow is Sunday and my arising hour is to be 0345. Purpose: to go over to Camp Casey to pick up the battery payroll at 0530. Why it's so early tomorrow I can't imagine, but that is the plan from above, and mine is not to wonder why.

Delivering the payroll.
Video Link: http://lovelettersfromthefront.com/videos

We are building an Ark to navigate the tide when the floods come. Thirty-seven more days of rain will make an even forty. Noah had his animals to look after; I have the payroll. He landed safely on Mount

Ararat. I hope my jeep doesn't sink in the mud before I make it back to Baker.

You are my favorite Pumpkin.

Your loving Fireside husband,

Bill

* * *

Hi Lucy hi lo,

I'm sorry I can't write the "Lili" music to go along with the salutation. Bet you recognize it!

Tonight, being the month-end, we had an extra special ceremony at the calendar. Capt. called us to attention, marked off the day, then tore off February, ripped it into three strips, as he, Garcia and I each burned our pieces amid great glee and howling. Now we're in March. I would be very pleased to say sayonara before the end of the month—who knows?

It's interesting to see on our "Rexall Weather Chart Calendar" (size about 12" x 24") that the March illustration is a man with a suitcase in each hand running like the wind with a big grin on his face. Capt. says that symbolizes our departure. The next page, for April, is a girl in a bathing suit with one hand shading her eyes. That's supposed to symbolize our wives waiting for us on the beach. If you can find one of these Rexall Calendars you'll get a big kick out of the pictures.

It was an awful ride to Camp Casey Finance before four this morning, and then back. The rain has stopped, but in some places the ruts were 10 inches deep. Our wet microcosm is a slippery sea of slime, but we finally made it back to Baker without sinking. Happily, nobody tried to hijack our stagecoach-ark carrying that precious scrip. Another safe voyage by Noah.

I paid the troops, and tomorrow I'm off again, back to Casey to return the pay signature sheet, stopping at "I" Corps Hq. to pay Skinner.

He's in his second week of a two-week course on how to be an Exec., so you see my replacement is already here and preparing!

This afternoon was shower day for this muddy puppy and wonderfully well appreciated. With clean socks and a little foot powder, this 1st Lt. cavorts, and barks, like a new dog again.

It's been a long day, so I'm going to kiss you goodnight. Remember and know how very much I love you. We have so much to do together, so many places to see and so many walks to take hand in hand.

God bless you, Lamb.

I love Lucy,

Bill

* * *

1 March 54
Monday

Dearest Lamb,

I spent the entire day on the road banging, bouncing, jolting and hanging onto my hat. Some parts of the roads are drying out and the result is a giant washboard. Tomorrow we go out on a reconnaissance for the coming maneuvers. Our excursion will be about four hours of jolting in each direction—sound like fun? The following afternoon the Bn. moves out into the Chorwon Valley to occupy (after dark) the area we'll be looking over tomorrow. The next day we drive back home again.

For the next couple of days my plan of action will be to grin-and-bear it. I will do my best to write you a line or two every day but please forgive me if the next few letters aren't very long. I'll try to make up for it by taking some good pictures.

I love you terrifically, Lucy. Tonight I feel more than anything like sitting with my arm around you relaxing in front of a blazing fireplace and sort of cuddling to sleep.

God bless you, Lucy, goodnight. You are my favorite angel.

Your loving, Bill

* * *

2 March 54
Tuesday

Dearest Lamb,

We took the interesting trip over to Central Korea today, but much too far for this already well-traveled short-timer. From our 1st Marine Division sector, we went through the 1st Commonwealth Div., 1st ROK, 25th, 3rd, and 40th Divisions, then stopped just this side of the 2nd Division. From our temporary position in the southwest corner of the expansive Chorwon Valley we were in easy sight of the Chinese-held hill, "Papasan." You may have heard of it. One of the highest hills in the area, it became infamous before the shooting stopped. The country over here in Central Korea is more mountainous and rugged than our home area, but with occasional broad flat plains. I took several landscape scenes, then pictures of several Navy planes doing practice bombing runs on our column. It was probably a lot more fun for them than for us.

We spent an hour in our future position marking out proposed locations for the various elements of Baker Battery. Then we turned and headed home, arriving at 6:30 in the evening.

With McAllister. Tire chains were essential in mud.

Tomorrow when we take the Battery over we'll have to take a longer route and probably won't arrive until ten or eleven at night. We stay one full day and return Friday.

Goodnight, precious lamb.

Your exhausted, everloving,

Bill

* * *

4 March 54

D Day + 28

Dearest Lucy,

Much news of interest to relate today. First, if you will pick up the envelope and carefully check my return address you will notice something changed. You can now openly refer to me grandly as First Lieutenant, newly elevated and highly deserving! No more of that low-life second lieutenant "shave-tail" designation! The promotion raised me to the majestic heights of 1/Lt. as of 12 Feb. 54.

What a sticky, messy time we had yesterday! The Battery left our area at two PM, but I went out early with the advance party to set up our bivouac. The Battery arrived at our assigned area at ten that evening and it took us four hours to travel the last 400 yards. Mud. Every single vehicle in the Battery, all eighteen, had to be towed out after each got stuck, and then the tow truck got stuck.

It was all under blackout conditions and I stumbled into the slime almost up to my knees at one point. Actually it was a mixture of quicksand and mud with a thin frozen surface that was very deceiving until the first heavily laden truck crashed in. We went to bed at 0330 and arose at seven this morning. No cots used on this trip, so we're settling down to earth, with an air mattress cushioning us from the ground. If it rains hard without freezing, we'll all float away on our inflated surfboards.

As a result of the short sleeping hours I was in the supine position trying to catch forty winks when Bill Bliss walked into our tattered tent! We chewed the fat for two hours. I told him we were headed for Cambridge Beaches on the 14th of May and issued a cordial invitation for them to join us. He showed me some pictures of their daughter Carolyn—very pretty. He is Survey Officer with the 40th Div. Arty. and heads Stateside within two weeks—about two weeks ahead of me. He has no idea what he wants to do when he gets out, but he mentioned living in Connecticut and working in a small company in the area. Now, that is a capital idea!

As for Cambridge Beaches, I am 100% in approval. I get $300 mustering-out pay. The other $300 we can easily afford when you consider the value. I wouldn't miss the trip for anything! After I've been home one month, we'll start being frugal, O.K.?

Am I ever tired! I started this letter this afternoon so it's not too late now, but even so it's sack time. Goodnight, my darling wife. I love you passionately with all my heart, body and soul. You are a wonderful wife, Lucy. I need you and long for your companionship.

God bless you.

Your devoted, loving,

Bill

* * *

5 March 54
D Day + 27

Dearest wife,

We arrived back at "home" in Munsan after an all-day holiday-like traffic jam. The whole 7th Division was on the move, and we'd go and stop, stop and go. After an early snack for breakfast we missed dinner completely and thoroughly enjoyed our steaks (thin) which were awaiting our arrival in the home battery area at five this evening.

I love you so very much, precious lamb! Goodnight, God bless you.

Your devoted, faithful, loving, adoring,

Bill

* * *

6 March 54

Dearest Lamb,

They threw a great blast for me tonight in celebration of my silver bars. The transition is now complete as I've given to Skinner all my gold bars except the original pair which you and Mom pinned on me after graduation ceremonies, at Cannon Green, behind Nassau Hall. Was that ever long ago and far away!

Our newest officer in the Bn. was an enlisted trainee at Easy Btry. in the old Ft. Sill FARTC where I taught artillery basic. I didn't recognize the face but when we were introduced I remembered the name. Now your First Lieutenant is really starting to feel like an old-timer. Don't you think it's about time I came home?!

So do I!

First Lieutenant.

I'm getting to the stage where my eyes are starting to close, so good-night, sweet peach.

I love Lucy,

Bill

* * *

7 March 54
D Day + 25

Dearest Chicki,

Sorry about the shortness of my recent letters. I think it's a form of chafing at the bit. I wish we had some field problems during these next few weeks to break up the home stretch! Can you believe I said that? I have to admit, at times I find gunnery and the challenges of a Battery Executive Officer highly satisfying and very rewarding.

Perhaps I'm turning into the outdoor sportsman type. Let's buy a house in rural Connecticut and go camping in the hills on the weekends. There can't be any sticky mud there. Could there?

I'll be so glad, happy and excited to get home and be with you, I can think of nothing else. I love you, Lucy, with all my heart, body and soul. I need you; I need your love and companionship. God bless you, precious wife.

Your adoring husband,

Bill

* * *

8 March 54

Dearest Lamb,

The Capt. is having the same trouble McAllister had, and I'm also having. He departs twenty days after I do and he just complained about having an awful time trying to concentrate long enough to write a letter.

Today was a big change in the routine. Skinner and I were sent over to a nearby battalion to hear an eight-hour lecture on Military Justice. It was very interesting in places, but was too long to sit still in one spot.

As our luck would have it, a USO show was held in a tent-auditorium during the hour after lunch, so we took a pleasant interlude from Courts Martial. This show was better than Marilyn Monroe on a distant stage a hundred yards away. This one featured a juggler, banjo player, singer, two dancers, comic and three-piece combo. The event was similar to a TV variety show—fair to middling quality, but happily, very diverting.

New officers are streaming into the battalion like ants to a picnic. Most are fresh out of BOC (Battery Officers Course) and are taking their first troop duty. I met one this morning who addressed me as "Sir." I almost looked behind me to see who he was talking to!

See you soon, best wife!

I love you, Lucy.

Your devoted, faithful,

Bill

* * *

11 March 54

Dearest Lamb,

For the last two or three days we've been enjoying our first spring-like weather, but late tonight the sky clouded over and a west wind is driving frigid droplets of rain against our tent.

The afternoon was so pleasant that Capt. and I dropped our routine of duties, procured two shotguns and took off along a back trail in search of the always elusive pheasant. Not one was sighted but we had a great hike, investigated some tiny bits of new greenery along the path and watched an abandoned rice paddy full of playful frogs, newly grown from tadpoles.

Without targets, we were reduced to shooting at tin cans and old bottles. One time, we thought we'd be bagging supper for the whole battery when a flock of ducks winged by in formation. They were too high, and although we both fired away enthusiastically the ducks remained aloft, totally unperturbed and quite aloof. No pheasant under glass. No duck soup. Just army chow, after a nice walk in the country. Besides the hunting and the physical training I've been featuring recently, I've been knocking myself out via softball. I'm so stiff, I creak when I walk.

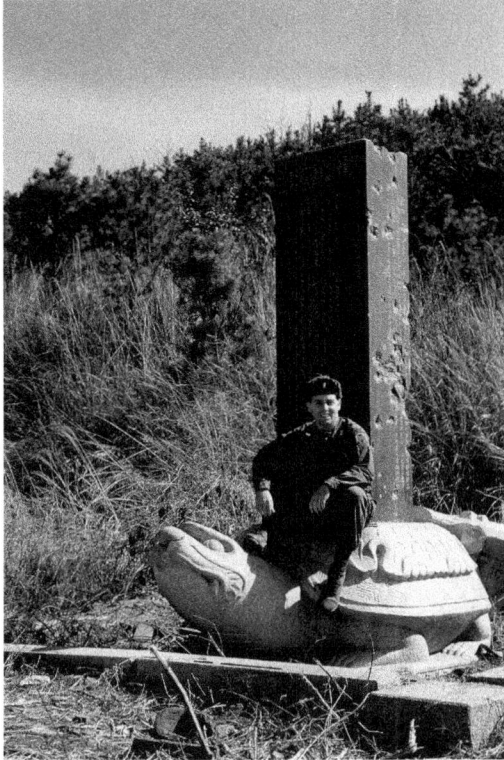

Taking a break.

News flash: Rumors are rapidly growing and now being confirmed. We are going to move to a new battery location, and probably before I sayonara. The latest poop is that we'll take the 25th Division's place just west of the Chorwon Valley. That's where the 7th Div. was in the closing days before shooting stopped, near the infamous hills: "Pork Chop," "T-Bone," and "Old Baldy."

Let's hope we'll move into a position already well prepared by the 25th. In any event we'll probably be living like gypsies for the first few days until we can get settled again. The move nevertheless promises an interesting event ahead and perhaps, a challenge.

I got my formal application blank from Harvard Business School and I can see that it'll take several days to think up good answers. Although letters of recommendation aren't necessary, they can't do any harm. When Lt. Col. Moore returns from school in Japan let's see if he'll write me a good recommendation.

Do I ever love my favorite Chicki!! Lucy, you are the sweetest, most wonderful, lovable person in the world. I love you with a desire—with all my heart, body and soul.

God bless you, my darling wife.

Your adoring, faithful,

Bill

P. S. Thanks for the pamphlet on Cambridge Beaches.

* * *

To My Sister
12 March 54

Dear Sis,

Thank you for your letter thanking me for my picture. Also many thanks for your birthday card and present. It will be put to the best use after I return.

The way the cloudy and uncertain Rotation scene looks at present, I should arrive in the homeland, in fact New York, somewhere around 25 April. It certainly sounds exciting, but very remote. I've almost forgotten what it feels like to exist in a civilized condition.

I just took time out from letter writing for a small "Red Alert." Four Russian jets, north of the truce line headed south, and were picked up by radar. These incidents have been happening less frequently lately. Remember when we shot down that MIG about a month ago? There was much hustling then. All units along the front were alerted and put on eight-minute notice. Small-arms ammunition was passed out and we donned our steel pots and waited. This time, as usual, after an hour or so, we got the all-clear flash. But not until four U.S. jets buzzed our battery and succeeded in scaring us out of our boots.

Less than a month now to go! I'm anxious to see you all. Best love to you, and family.

Cheers,

Bill

17
Back to the Front

14 March 54

Hi Chicki,

After church the BC and Exec. of Baker Btry. 69th F.A. Bn. (25th Div.) arrived in our battery area to look it over. On the 20th and 21st of this month we'll switch positions. They expressed amazement at the beauty and organization of our battery area. From what they explained of their inhospitable location, we have had it! Our future area is built into the side of a steep hill, with the guns below in a rice paddy. With each rain the battery washes downhill about six inches. The mud is 18 inches deep. It sounds a total #10. Evidently the area is not at all suited for a firing-battery position.

Tomorrow the Capt. and I, with four of our Section Chief sergeants, go to look over the site of our next challenge. We'll be in more beautiful country, but in infamous territory near Pork Chop and other well-known places.

We have another new Lieutenant in the battery, a West Pointer. He graduated in '52 and spent thirteen months near Detroit with Anti-Aircraft Artillery. He reports that Stateside duty is not the great deal that we think. He is a likable sort, doesn't seem too R.A., and I think will get along here very well

I LOVE LUCY, my wife, with all my heart, body and soul!! How can I ever tell you how much you mean to me? I look forward with such wild anticipation to being with you again. How wonderful can life be! I felt very close to you in church today.

You are a darling, sweet, adorable, lovable wife. See you soon, Lamb.

Your loving

Bill

P.S. Hmmm.... it's kind of late. Maybe I'll write the parents tomorrow.

* * *

Overlooking T-Bone and Pork Chop, the site of recent horrific battles.

* * *

18 March 54

Hi Lamb,

In preparation for our move the day after tomorrow we sent out our FO and Liaison parties to our infantry (17th Regiment) today. Included in the parties were Garcia, Skinner, Toepel (the new West Pointer), and Hallowell. That leaves the BC and Exec. in the battery. Just when we were getting wealthy in officer strength, and Guard Mount and Reveille was a duty once in six days, we go back to the old business of this puppy having both duties every day. I had just about given up all work and turned over my job to Skinner, and now I've got <u>all</u> the battery duties except BC. Groan!

True and also encouraging, this deal can't last much longer, as my time gets shorter and shorter. However it is discouraging to have to un-stack arms. I'll probably be working full blast up until the day I sayonara.

Tomorrow I'll move out to the new area to check property and make preparations for receiving the battery.

I love you, Lucy,

Bill

* * *

22 March 54

Dearest Lamb,

Sorry again for not writing. I have been thinking about you constant-ly in everything I do. Tonight is the first time that I've gotten a chance to sit down in a settled sort of way and tell you what we've been doing.

I drove over here Friday with two truckloads of equipment including my gear. I dumped my stuff in the 69th Bn. supply room (Quonset). Un-til our battery arrived in the new area late Saturday night I inventoried property and surveyed the area with the BC of the departed battery.

After Baker's arrival the Capt. and I have been industriously direct-ing a rebuilding and improvement of the area as well as getting person-nel housed and located. Up until tonight we've been sleeping with gear still packed in Supply. In addition to regular organizing tasks, I have been exploring the surrounding terrain and visiting the OP's.

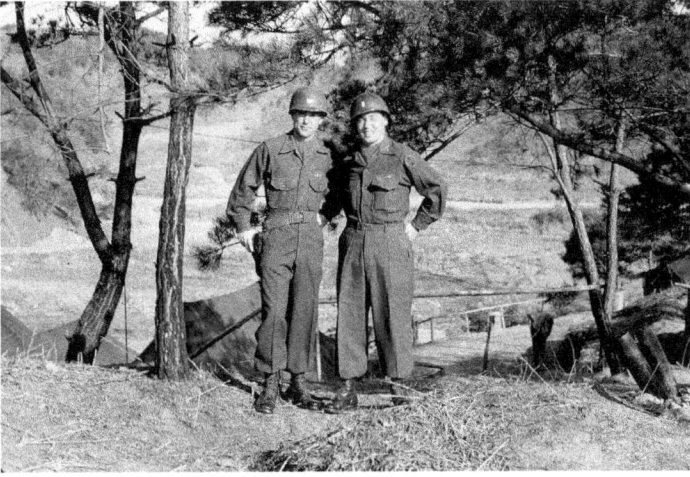

Capt. Sosa was a great C.O. and friend.

Do you remember "Operation Smack," which was the scandal many months ago? Printed programs were made up for a group of Stateside generals who watched a patrol go out and get shot-up pretty badly. There was a congressional investigation which tried to decide whether we were sacrificing lives to put on a show for some brass. The report's opinion was negative, but the affair got much publicity. The OP from which the generals watched is now interesting stomping grounds for me. It's very tidy and well located on a vertical hill 1200 feet high directly on the DMZ. Someone even installed a jeep windshield in one opening, for the brass. It is the best view in Korea, looking straight down the "T" in T-Bone. I had a field day with movie camera and Canon. If my pictures aren't great photography, at least they are documentary.

Goodnight, wonderful wife, I love you with all my heart and body and soul. God bless you, Lucy, you are ever in my prayers.

Love you,

Bill

* * *

23 March 54

Dearest Lamb,

Today, inconvenience dominates. The Coleman Lantern is on the blink. The problem is the gas injector, so unless I can find a very fine piece of wire, we've had it. The electricity is also on the blink, so at present I'm back to the old OP days of candlelight. Don't ever dare suggest a candlelight dinner!

That reminds me, Cambridge Beaches has Hurricane Lamps with candles. Well, I guess under the circumstances and considering the person I'll be with, candlelight might not be too bad after all. For some reason I've gotten quite attached to you and your companionship over the last few years. You are the world's sweetest wife, Lucy, and I love you very completely.

Goodnight, my love, God bless you.

You devoted husband,

Bill

* * *

25 March 54

Dearest Lamb,

This business of Reveille every morning and Guard every night is at best tiring. Now that the rest of the 7th Div. is firmly established on the line, the brass thinks it's a big deal and although other divisions don't do it as we have been all along, we are ordered to wear steel pots and carry weapons even in the battery area! Besides that, we are blackout at night. These are little things which become a burden because I can't see any earthly use for them. Even during the active shooting Baker never blacked out.

My consolation is that I've only got about a week to go. Happy day!

I talked to Col. Moore today and he will be happy to write a letter of recommendation. I've a feeling it will be very favorable. I also found a picture to enclose with my application and have the medical report finished. Now all that's left is to finish the application. My spare time is rather limited, so it may take a couple more days.

I love you, precious Chicki, and I'm looking forward longingly and lovingly to having you in my arms again.

Goodnight love, God bless you.

Your tired, loving,

Bill

* * *

27 March 54

Dearest Lamb,

After last night's heavy rain the air smells of spring. The sun has been ducking in and out most of the day. There's a gentle breeze blowing but even so, in the sun it's very warm. Signs of spring are all over. This is really beautiful, hilly territory with many lush evergreens. The foliage in the summer is beautiful. Isn't it too bad I can't stay to see it!

Our work continues toward conquering the mud. The bulldozer has been going most of the week working the road and grading the landscape. We're digging drainage ditches and culverts and hauling gravel and rock.

I've taken special interest in building a good PX and progress is amazing. It's set up in one end of a Quonset, with a waist-high counter, and looks much like a bank with one large teller's window. The remaining section is fenced off with vertical steel rods which come to us as part of the packing for our howitzer ammo. The design of the PX was conceived and then constructed to utilize available excess material, and all who have inspected it so far agrees it's first rate. I'll get a picture before I leave.

By the way, I love you very, very greatly with all my heart, body and soul. There's no use of my trying to write about my love for you. When I think about you now with the time drawing close, the thoughts and feelings tumble over each other in a headlong rush and I become inarticulate. Just to imagine us together again!

God bless you, darling.
I LOVE LUCY.
Passionately, Tenderly, Completely,
Bill

* * *

29 March 54

Dearest wife,

Two items of interest today. First, a new officer in the battery to share reveille with. He's from Savannah, young, fairly quiet, but a likable sort and has thirteen months to do in Korea. Now there are three of us in the BOQ. Skinner and Garcia are still working as Liaison Officers with the infantry, and Hallowell and the West Pointer, Toepel, are at Exec. school at "I" Corps.

I saw a draft of the letter the colonel wrote to Harvard. I hoped it would be good, but I was flabbergasted! He said I was one of the most outstanding officers he'd ever met and that I was superior in every respect. It was a surprising letter and probably the most complimentary bit of praise I've ever seen in writing. I will have a copy to send to you in a day or so.

Nine days and I'll be on my way!!!

How I love you and how I am looking forward to being in your arms.

Goodnight, Lamb—Reveille tomorrow again so it's to the sack now. Care to join me?

Your devoted, faithful, adoring,
Bill

18
Heading Home

Chicki!!

This is the Departure Letter you've been waiting for!

Battalion informed me this morning that I depart Baker, bag and baggage, Friday 9 April for shipment to the United States and separation from active duty with the U.S. Army.

I'm taking the Battery Commander's jeep.

The ship is scheduled out of Inchon on the 15th and, depending on weather, arrives on the West Coast the 30th of April.

Upon arrival, I believe I'll quickly be assigned to Camp Kilmer, New Jersey (about 15 miles from Summit). I immediately fly home to you, report to Kilmer 10 days later when my travel time is up, and then be discharged right away, about the 10th of May!

What do you think of all these happenings? Not too bad?!

I love you, Lucy!!!

Tonight I'll write again.

Your excited, loving, almost erstwhile,

1/Lt.

* * *

1 April 54

Hi Lamb,

I have been re-reading the Colonel's recommendation letter. It's mighty flattering to hear all those wonderful things. I'm planning to hang on to the letter and send it along to you with my last letter from Korea. Who knows, if I mailed it now, before I'd left for home, maybe you'd encourage me to stay put and make the army a career. Or, maybe not!!! We both know the separations are much too painful.

As for Harvard, I am applying, but as you mentioned, there are points pro and con. A final settling down is something I'm looking forward to equally as much as you. Another point is cost. The GI Bill will pay me $135 per month ($160 with children). Tuition at Business School is $1,000 plus apartment plus food plus books, etc., and probably total $3,000 for nine months. We'll be about $1,500 short, so I'll need some earnings.

Surely we can find a way to afford it. So whether or not I go to school depends on: if I'm accepted, what kind of a job I can find, and most telling, how you and I, once we talk together, feel about two more years of waiting for my career to begin.

I've spent most of today packing a small crate to ship home by slow boat from China. It will probably arrive after I do, but who cares? It is mostly uniforms, etc., for which I won't have much need, except when I wash the car!

I just talked to George Towner in the 47th Bn. He's a Princetonian who is to leave on the same ship with me on the 15th.

Incidentally, when I find out the name of the ship I'll let you know right away. Here's why: I noticed a paragraph in the N.Y. Herald Tribune Ship Arrival and Departure section which stated that "For information about military personnel and dependents arriving on the West Coast (from Korea only), call Whitehall 4-7700 extension 8239." When you get the name of my ship, you'll be able to find my exact time of hitting the good old Stateside. I'll call you right away, and then (from Seattle) it's Northwest Airlines and seven hours to Idlewild!!

Troop Ships From Far East

For information about military personnel and dependents arriving on the west coast (from Korea only), call WHitehall 4-7700. Ext. 8239; for east coast arrivals, call the New York Port of Embarkation—GEdney 9-5400, Ext. 422.

SATURDAY, APRIL 24
Mann (April 11)............San Francisco
Black (April 9)............San Francisco
TUESDAY, APRIL 27
Breckenridge (April 14)......San Francisco
Buckner (April 17)...........San Francisco
WEDNESDAY, APRIL 28
Sultan (April 18)............San Francisco
FRIDAY, APRIL 30
Marine Serpent (April 15)...........Seattle

Lucy found this notice in the Times. Later, I wrote her with my ship's name.

I hear some Military Sea Transport ships are almost comfortable. We'll see. I'll take the Scrabble along. We're never tired of playing. It's a wonderful time-passer.

A week from tomorrow I hit the road. I love you so very much, darling Lamb, I am about to burst. I can't wait to be with you again. Why are you so wonderful?!

Your adoring,

Bill

* * *

3 April 54

Dearest Lamb,

The weather has been sunny and spring-like for the last week. As a result I've discarded long johns in favor of T-shirt and shorts. Tonight we even moved our home-made chairs out of the BOQ to our little hilltop patio overlooking the battery on one side, and the valley on the other. By the time the sun went down it got a little cool and we adjourned back indoors and lit the stove.

We had a parade this morning with the entire 49th Battalion participating in honor of those going out on the ninth. The band played "Auld Lang Syne" and the Batteries marched by, with salutes and flags waving, and I was very impressed. It was the first time I'd ever been on the receiving end of the ceremony.

The rest of the day I've been taking it pretty easy, snapped many pictures and thought about you and coming home. Five more days of duty in the army!

How I love my wife!!! And how I look forward to being with you once again. I'll probably kiss you for a full ten minutes when you meet me at the airport!

Goodnight, Lamb. Thank God tonight for watching over and taking such wonderful care of us.

I love you, Bill

* * *

4 April 54

Hi Lamb,

A very fast note to tell you that I love you immensely.

I've taken my last Guard Mount and Reveille of my army career! Tomorrow, first thing in the morning I turn over my FDC, guns, ammo, and eighty men, to Skinner. Then in the afternoon I start my preliminary clearance with Personnel. From then on I'll have no duties, only packing and photography—sounds good! Better than that, it's fantastic!

Two new officers moved into the battery, a 2/Lt. Youngblood from Georgia and a 2/Lt. Annala from Oregon. Hollowell and Garcia are being transferred to Bn., so after the Capt. turns over the battery to Toepel this week, all the old-timers will be gone. Most of these officers now coming in are getting their first troop duty, and have a long time to go in the army including as much as sixteen months in Korea. Ugh.

Annala was married two weeks before he left California and Youngblood about two months before he sailed. I hope they can get some kind of Early Release some day.

I love you with all my being, Lucy, you are a wonderful person and a darling wife. Let's thank God together always for His generosity and watch over us.

I love my Chicki.
Your homecoming
husband,
Bill
P.S. See you soon!!!!!

* * *

6 April 1954

Hi Lamb,

Today I finally bought that TCD slide projector. Only by a stroke of luck was I was able to find it. Skinner had befriended the PX officer in the 17th Regiment and today we went over to visit him. A large shipment of critical items had just arrived including my projector and a camera, just like mine, for Skinner. The price of the Canon has gone up to $127—looks like I bought mine in the nick of time!

The projector will be crated and off tomorrow.

The day after the day after tomorrow I start home!!

Never before has anyone been so anxious to sail. It's getting more difficult to write as these last days move by. Once I get under way! Wow, I can't wait!

I love you, adore you, idolize you more than you can imagine. How can one wife be so sweet and so wonderful?

Lucy, I love you!

See you soon, Lamb.

Your happy

homecoming

Bill

* * *

9 April 54
Inchon Replacement Co.

Dearest Chicki,

I'm on the way!! The first and shortest leg of my homeward journey has been successfully accomplished and here I sit at the Port of Inchon Replacement Company, cooling my heels.

I left the Battery early this morning as the first rays of the sun were cutting the frost from last year's withered grass and the green budding trees of the coming spring.

Leaving the Battery we turned south, and as the curving road circled past the FDC and the six gun emplacements, I took my last look at Baker. The big sign still reads BAKER—BELL'S—BEST—BY TEST.

Headed home aboard the Marine Serpent.
Video Link: http://lovelettersfromthefront.com/videos

An hour later I checked in at the 7th Div. Replacement Company, picked up George Towner of the 47th F.A. and hit the road again. Eighty-five miles later, coated with the fine, gray dust that covers the roads, we arrived here. We snapped pictures along the way, stopped at Kimpo Field (remembered from R&R) for lunch, got lost once again in the maze of Seoul and had a lovely scenic trip.

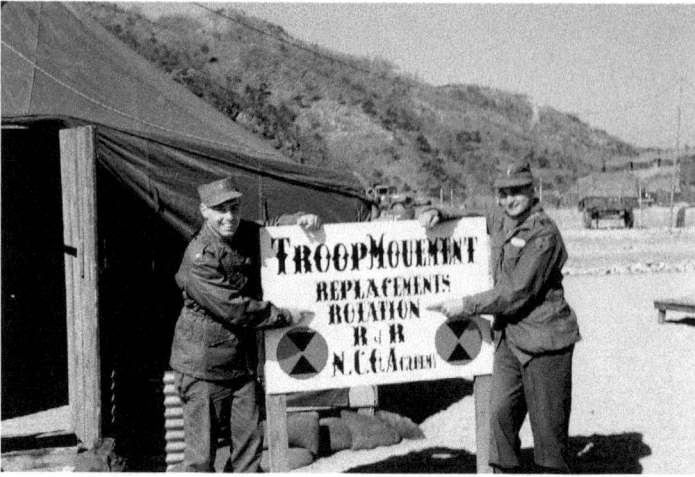

Homeward Bound!

We are billeted in a Quonset complete with iron cots with sheets, heat, and #1 electric lights. The shower is near and hot, chow is reasonably good; now all we've got to do is wait.

Cleaning mops at sea.
Video Link: http://lovelettersfromthefront.com/videos

The next ship leaving will be the Marine Serpent, sailing for Seattle, as I had guessed earlier, on or about the 14th of April. She should arrive the 30th. You know I'll do everything in my power to speed my journey. If I can avoid taking a troop train east, I'll fly immediately. I'll call you as soon as I land in the States. Don't try to come west to meet me because if I have enough time to see you in Seattle it will mean that I didn't take the train and am already flying east to you.

Never forget that we have been wonderfully fortunate to have God's close guidance and support. I know these months apart have been tough for you. I have been, and always am, very proud of you. You're a wonderful person, Lucy, and a wonderful wife. Don't worry about not being perfect—to me you're the most perfect person I've ever known. I love you, Lucy, with all my heart, body and soul.

Before I left Baker this morning I gave Papasan, that priceless old character who waits on our table, five dollars in Korean hwan to buy something for his twin youngsters. He bowed and smiled and thanked me in his hoarse voice for about five minutes. I only wish I had remembered to get a picture of him before I left. He is one Korean of whom I think very highly. In case I forget, for the record his name is Lee Sang Oo. I'll tell you all about him when I get home.

Goodnight, precious wife, you are always in my thoughts and prayers. God bless you.

I love Lucy,
Bill

* * *

10 April 54

Hi Lamb,

If the Inchon tide is high enough on the evening of the 14th, we'll leave as soon as the ship is loaded. She will come in on the 14th, unload and reload, and leave immediately for Seattle. It will be the Marine Serpent and she'll probably be very crowded. It's not supposed to be the greatest ship afloat, but who cares, if she carries us quickly to Seattle.

We're to take the shorter, rough, northern route, possibly refueling in the Aleutians (Alaska) rather than Hawaii. So-long to any ideas of a warm sun-tan cruise. The voyage should take about fifteen days. Also I'm told it's mighty bumpy sailing in the north Pacific this time of year. That's OK with me as long as we keep moving.

Well, Lamb, here I sit and here I wait. Thank goodness we have reasonably pleasant accommodations.

I love you, my darling, precious wife, with all my heart and body and soul. Keep your chin up, Lucy, and remember that I love you, I'm proud of you and I'll be home soon.

Goodnight, my love, God bless you and guide you.

Your adoring, devoted, faithful,

Bill

* * *

14 April 54

Inchon

Dearest Wife,

For the last couple of days I've been living in a sort of suspended animation, passing time sacked out most of the day. Tonight is my last night in Korea, all processing is completed and tomorrow at 0530 we get up and move down to load on the ship. I imagine we'll sail with the high tide tomorrow afternoon. Next stop: Seattle!! No refueling is necessary. Arrival expected on the 1st or 2nd of May depending on the weather.

I am tremendously anxious to get started. When I first arrived here and found there was to be a five-day wait for the boat, I settled down to while away the time; now I'm increasingly restless reading and sacking. And to think I've got another two weeks of the same aboard the ship. Groan. At least we'll be moving forward (as well as pitching and rolling). Doesn't the moving forward part sound good!

I can't wait to be with you, Lucy. I've been looking forward to being together for so long that it seems wonderful that it's actually in progress now. There are so many exciting and companionable things we have to do together. I'm going to make you happier than you've ever been in your life and we will act as each other's constant shadow. How come you're such a darling Lamb?

Glorious arrival at the Seattle docks.
Video Link: http://lovelettersfromthefront.com/videos

Well, Lamb, this is to be my next-to-last letter. I have one chance left to mail one as we get on the ship. I promise to enclose the Colonel's letter of recommendation with that final letter.

It won't be long now, Chicki. Remember to thank God tonight for taking such good care of us and for sending me home to you three months earlier than scheduled. I love you, beautiful wife, with all my heart, body and soul.

Goodnight, God bless you, I'll be in your arms soon.

Your faithful adoring husband,

Bill

Inchon Boarding

* * *

Thursday 15 April 54

Hi Lamb,

I just have time to scribble a line before we shove off, and to show you the enclosed recommendation letter.

I'm also sending my old driver's license—how about doing me a favor? Have someone pick up an application blank from the NJ Motor Vehicle Agency, then fill it out, ready for my signature. I'll turn it in with my old license and three dollars and can drive soon after I get home. I forgot all about this.

Enclosed is that letter from the 49th Field Artillery Battalion Commander, Col. Moore.

I love you, my most precious, darling wife!

I'll call you as soon as we dock at Seattle.

All my love and devotion,

Bill
P.S. Voy para casa!
P.P.S. Ich gehe nach hause!!
P.P.P.S. I'm going home!!!

Enclosure to my April 15th letter.

* * *

Docking at Seattle.

My wire from Seattle.

19
Epilogue

Northwest Flight 10 landed smoothly and taxied toward the gate. As it slowed and swung around, the engines idled, sputtered, and coughed to a stop. A ground crew wheeled movable stairs into place, and the door swung open.

In the 1950s at Idlewild Airport (now JFK), the boarding gate was simply an opening in a wire fence between terminal and tarmac. My explosive excitement was tempered with anxiety. This was the culmination of all those months of waiting and yearning. It was both disorienting and such an overwhelming thrill to once again experience the vivid colors and sounds, the free-flowing sights and tempo of civilization. It was even more overpowering to contemplate the wild joy of seeing Lucy again.

I was among the first passengers jogging down the steps and striding toward the terminal. Lucy had been waiting unnoticed behind the fence. When the gate opened, she slipped through, sprinted across the pavement, threw her arms around me, and nearly bowled me over. We were ecstatic. We kissed and hugged and laughed and cried until the last of the smiling passengers carefully edged around us and through the gate. It was truly the most wonderful homecoming. It was everything we had imagined and had joyfully anticipated all those long, lonely months apart.

We checked in at the Biltmore Hotel for several delightful days in New York before visiting both families, then took that wonderful second honeymoon to Cambridge Beaches in Bermuda that we'd promised each other.

Our eagerness and determination to start a career and find a place to live consumed the next few months. The effort required to achieve these seemingly basic goals took more time and much greater patience than we had ever anticipated. It was fully several months, rather than weeks later, that I found a promising position. It was at a fledgling company which had developed a commercial process for vacuum-packaging perishable food products in flexible plastic materials.

My first job as sales trainee promised potential, both for me and the new company's unique product line. The pay was $80 per week. We lived in very modest comfort in a borrowed apartment in Manhattan for most of my training period. After ten months of commuting from New York out to Jersey City, I was pronounced ready to take over a newly designated upstate New York sales territory.

Along with the territory came a move to Syracuse, a company car, and the salesman's elevated salary of $100 a month plus commissions. A quarter-century and five moves later, in Milwaukee, I became president of another manufacturing company in the same industry.

Our firstborn was a wonderful boy, followed over the next dozen years by three lovely girls. All married, they have presented us over the years with ten grandchildren and six great-grandchildren, so far. My career eventually evolved into banking and trust, where I held senior management positions during the next twenty years. In 1990 I had the unique and exciting business opportunity of a move to Florida. Lucy and I relocated to Naples. Years later, following my retirement and a number of volunteer jobs, I was elected to the Naples City Council, serving eight years, until I again retired, this time by term limits.

I never did get to business school, and it was decades before I would finally earn a graduate degree. We never lived in Connecticut. That idle dream became less enchanting as we spent our first ten years in several great locations in the East. My third promotion took us to the upper Midwest, and we never looked back.

When it came to the camping I had suggested in my Korea letters, we did enjoy some roughing it, but only while the children were young.

Instead, through the years, we have most loved sailing together. In upstate New York, our first sailboat was a Lightning, the same type we had sailed during my leave before Korea. Two decades later we ventured a tropical bareboat sailing charter and were hooked. We still regularly sail with our children, now including our grandchildren, both in the Caribbean and more distant locales. Tonga is one of our favorites. And finally, we never bought that Jaguar, nor did we name another dog Jag. We discovered other cars, and the kids always came up with a name for our dogs.

Through all these years, through many travails—the challenges of raising four children, the challenges of developing a successful career, and the challenges which distinct personalities bring to a marriage—Lucy has been the best thing that ever happened to me. The love and joy of being together, of which we wrote in our letters to and from Korea, continues to fill our lives over sixty years later. Our early, distressful Korean separation nurtured an appreciation of each other, our faith in God, and our Christian marriage, which enabled us to grow and mature into a lifetime of love and commitment.

It's still honest-to-goodness true: I love Lucy!

Overjoyed to be home!

More About the Author

Bill MacIlvaine (BA Princeton University; Certified Financial Planner [Ret.]) was born on Manhattan and grew up in Summit, N.J. After his service to the U.S. Army, Bill held various leadership positions in industry, both on the East Coast and in the Midwest, and ultimately assumed the presidency of a Wisconsin-based manufacturing firm.

He completed his career in southern Florida in banking and financial planning, and in retirement served two-terms as a city councilman in Naples, Florida. A strong proponent of active civic engagement, he has served as a Florida Supreme Court Certified Mediator and has led many local boards in southwest Florida.

Bill and his wife, Lucy, were married in 1952 and have four children, ten grandchildren, and six great-grandchildren. An adventurer at heart, his lifelong avocation has been ocean sailing, and he has captained multiple bareboat charters in the Great Lakes, Caribbean, Atlantic, and Pacific.

He is an ordained elder in the Presbyterian Church and has served in humanitarian-based missions ventures in both Somalia and Cuba.

If you would like Bill to speak at your next event, please contact the publisher at rod.macilvaine@gmail.com.

Visit us on FaceBook and Our Web Site

www.lovelettersfromthefront.com

www.facebook.com/LoveLettersfromtheFront